The Aesthetic Understanding

By the same author

Art and Imagination
    (London, 1974; New York, 1979)

The Aesthetics of Architecture
    (London, 1979; Princeton, 1980)

The Meaning of Conservatism
    (London and New York, 1980)

From Descartes to Wittgenstein
    (London and Boston, 1981)

Fortnight's Anger (a novel)
    (Manchester, 1981)

The Politics of Culture
    (Manchester, 1981)

Kant
    (Past Masters, Oxford, 1982)

A Dictionary of Political Thought
    (London, 1983)

ROGER SCRUTON

The Aesthetic Understanding

Essays in the Philosophy
of Art and Culture

METHUEN
LONDON AND NEW YORK

First published in Great Britain in 1983 by
Carcanet New Press Ltd

First published as a University Paperback in 1983 by
Methuen & Co. Ltd
11 New Fetter Lane, London EC4P 4EE
Published in the USA by
Methuen & Co.
in association with Methuen, Inc.
733 Third Avenue, New York, NY 10017

Photoset by Anneset, Weston-super-Mare, Avon
Printed in Great Britain by SRP Ltd, Exeter

British Library Cataloguing in Publication Data
Scruton, Roger
The aesthetic understanding. (University paperback 825).
1. Aesthetics
I. Title
111'.85   BH39
ISBN 0-416-36160-9

Library of Congress Cataloging in Publication Data
Scruton, Roger.
The aesthetic understanding.

(University paperbacks)
Bibliography: p.
Includes index.
1. Aesthetics—Addresses, essays, lectures. I. Title.
BH39.S38   1983   111'.85   83-8341
ISBN 0-416-36160-9 (pbk.)

Contents

Preface

These essays were written over a period of seven years, and cover a variety of subjects in pure and applied aesthetics, reflecting both my own interests, and also a wider interest among Anglo-Saxon philosophers in the problems posed by the experience of art. For the most part they employ forms of argument and intellectual devices culled from the methods of analytical philosophy. It is now fairly evident that these methods are as applicable in aesthetics as in other areas of philosophical enquiry. If that were not so, then I believe that analytical philosophy would have failed to establish itself as a coherent intellectual discipline. For aesthetics is a central area of philosophy, as central as metaphysics, and as basic to our understanding of the human condition. But, like all works of analysis, the following essays do not presuppose the truth of that generalization. I hope only that they give some grounds for it. As explorations and reports, they must speak for themselves.

I have divided the collection into four sections. The first contains a brief résumé of modern analytical aesthetics, which I hope may serve as an introduction to some of the assumptions made in subsequent chapters; it also contains an essay reflecting on current problems in literary theory. The second section is devoted to the problems of musical aesthetics, and attempts to give both a summary of the main questions, and also a sketch of a theory which might answer some of them. The third section contains two essays on photography and the cinema: the first concerned with the concept of representation, the second with certain issues in the philosophy of mind to which I also return in subsequent chapters. The final section is the most diverse, containing various essays devoted to the 'aesthetic understanding'. It is my hope that these essays hang together sufficiently well to justify publication in a single section. From its own special field of study, each chapter approaches the main problems, as I see them, of aesthetics; what is aesthetic experience, and what is its importance for human conduct?

Three of the essays — chapters 10, 13 and 14 — appear here for the first time. The remainder reproduce or adapt material already published.

London, December 1982   ROGER SCRUTON

Aesthetics and Criticism

1 Recent Aesthetics in England and America

Aesthetics owes more than its name to Greek philosophy. Nevertheless it is a peculiarly modern discipline. Its rise and fall (as we presently perceive them) have been contemporaneous with the rise and fall of Romanticism. Now that art looks back to the upheavals which created the 'modern' consciousness, philosophy stands at its shoulder, discoursing on their common loss of faith. To understand the state of contemporary aesthetics, we must therefore reflect on its romantic origin. We then find a peculiar synthesis of British empiricism and Leibnizian idealism, achieving systematic statement in Kant's *Critique of Judgement*. It was Kant who gave form and status to aesthetics. And it was Hegel who endowed it with content. In the light of those facts, we should not be surprised at the difficulties which analytical aesthetics has experienced in attempting to make sense of its inherited subject-matter.

Kant put forward a threefold division of rationality: aesthetic judgement was distinguished from morality (practical reason) and from science (understanding), to be united with them only through a general theory of agency the details of which Kant did not disclose. Hegel offered to reveal the details of this as of everything. He found that it was not possible to discuss aesthetics without advancing a theory of art. Kant who had preferred real flowers to painted flowers, thereby suffered a radical transformation. Both philosophers were convinced, however, that aesthetic judgement is no arbitrary addendum to human capacities, but a consequence of rationality, a bridge between the sensuous and the intellectual, and an indispensable means of access to the world of ideas.

Anyone interested in a subject will be attracted by the theories which make it seem important. Until the advent of analytical philosophy, therefore, those with an interest in aesthetics were invariably tempted by idealism. As an illustration it is useful to consider the last systematic work of English aesthetics to appear before the advent of linguistic analysis. R. G. Collingwood's *Principles of Art* was published in 1938, and, despite its influence upon art and criticism, was soon to be regarded as anachronistic. Collingwood presented in a novel idiom the distinctions through which idealist aesthetics had created its subject. He distinguished imaginative understanding from subjective association, artistic insight from scientific belief, expression from representation, seeing as an end from seeing as a means. Following Croce (*Estetica*, 1902) he advocated a version of 'expressionism', according to which art is the expression of the inner life. 'Expression', (which displays the 'particularity' of its subject) is contrasted with 'description' (which, in employing concepts, must abstract from the particularity of what it describes). It is integral to this theory that we must see art as end and not as means: we must see it, in Kant's words, 'apart from interest'. True art is therefore to be distinguished from craft, from magic, from evocation, and even from representation. This is the final residue of the idealist doctrine, that art does not advise, describe or moralize, but gives immediate, and therefore sensuous, embodiment to its 'idea'.

A corollary of most idealist theories of art is that the distinction between 'form' and 'content' is thrown in doubt. It is in the nature of a work of art to give expression to the uniqueness of its subject-matter. At the same time, the work of art — being neither a description, nor a technique — must also exemplify the uniqueness which it expresses. All features of a work of art are bound up with its 'particularity', and any change in the form brings with it a corresponding change in subject-matter. If form and content always change together, it seems problematic to claim that they are distinct.

Analytical philosophers are quick to observe a paradox, and it was not long before expressionism began to suffer from their assaults. To say that a work of art expresses something is to imply the existence of a relation, and of the two terms that are joined by it. But are there *two* things here — the work of art and its content? And is there a real relation between them? To assert a relation between *a* and *b* is to suggest that we can identify *a* and *b* independently. But that is what idealism denies. If the only answer to the question 'What does Beethoven's fifth symphony express?' is 'The content of Beethoven's fifth symphony', then the term 'express' can no longer be taken to refer to a genuine relation. Moreover, the theory that we understand a work of art by grasping what is 'expressed' by it becomes entirely empty. At such a point, idealists lean on the doctrine of 'internal relations', but it was an early achievement of contemporary British philosophy to show that doctrine to be unintelligible.[1]

In the light of such difficulties it is not surprising to find that the first articles of analytical aesthetics (gathered together as *Aesthetics and Language* (1954) edited by W. Elton and *Collected Papers on Aesthetics* (1965) edited by C. Barrett) show a fairly consistent hostility towards idealist thought. Their tone is not entirely negative. Under the influence of modern logic the authors ask questions which are to some extent new to the philosophy of art — questions about the identity and ontological status of the work of art, and about the structure of critical argument. Nevertheless, it is fair to say that these early essays subtract from the subject far more than they add to it. Analytical philosophy lays great emphasis upon logical competence, and is apt to be unadventurous in searching for the comprehensive standpoint from which aesthetics can be surveyed. This failing has persisted in the articles published in the two leading journals — the *British Journal of Aesthetics,* and the American *Journal of Aesthetics and Art Criticism* — which have been at their best when devoted to detailed analysis of critical argument, and not when attempting to explore the philosophical foundations of the subject.

It is a popular view that analytical philosophy is nothing but a devious repetition of old empiricist prejudices, expressive of an unnatural isolation from cultural life, and an a-historical view of man. Unlike idealism, it seems to occupy itself exclusively with questions of meaning, conceding to science the sole authority to determine how things are. How, then, is it to provide its own substantive conclusions? By contrast, it has seemed that other ways of thought — literary criticism, for example, or speculative phenomenology — provide a perspective on the world which renders it intelligible in a way that science does not. They seem to generate an understanding of art that goes beyond the analysis of critical terminology.

In response to those sentiments, aesthetics has tended to move in two contrasting directions — in the direction of criticism, and in the direction of more speculative schools of philosophical enquiry. I shall consider each of these movements in turn.

In focusing his attention on criticism, a philosopher might take one of two attitudes. There is an obscure realm where criticism and philosophy coincide, the realm, as one might put it, of applied aesthetics, where the concepts of philosophy are used to stretch and embellish the speculative conclusions of critical argument. Since I am not sure about the nature or the value of such an enterprise, I shall simply refer to the most important analytical philosopher who has engaged in it. This is Stanley Cavell, whose essays *Must we Mean What we Say?* (2nd edn 1976) contain extended discussions of music and literature. It may well be true that these essays add something considerable to the understanding of art. Cavell is also noteworthy for an analysis of the cinema, *The World Viewed* (1974), written in a style that conceals (from this reader at least) the nature and importance of the ideas which it is designed to convey.

A clearer, and more orthodox, way of taking inspiration from criticism, is to engage in the philosophical analysis of critical ideas. As an example I shall consider John Casey's *The Language of Criticism* (1966), which sets out to examine certain philosophical preconceptions embodied in the procedures of Anglo-American criticism. Casey shows a particular interest in F. R. Leavis who, for all his rejection of universal premises, represents in a striking way the deep longing of the English mind, oppressed by its own compulsion towards empiricist scepticism, for the intellectual framework of idealism. This framework comes to Leavis not from philosophy, but from the literary tradition of which Coleridge and Arnold are the most distinguished representatives.

Leavis had shown, in a now famous analysis of Thomas Hardy's poem 'After a Journey',[2] that sincerity in literature is not simply a matter of truth-telling. Echoing a thought of Croce's (*Estetica*, p. 60), he argued that sincerity is a property of the whole manner in which a poet's feeling finds expression, being inseparable from a detailed attention to the outer world and a concrete realization of the objects there presented. (Here is the idealist doctrine, that expression in art is connected with the 'particular', the 'concrete', and so irreplaceable by the abstractions of any discursive science). Sincerity therefore necessitates thought, is incompatible with sentimentality, and reflects a mode of understanding of the world which, while not of a 'scientific' (or theoretical) kind, is nevertheless more important to a man than any understanding that a scientific training might have brought to him.

Writers like Casey argue that the connections here — between sincerity, reality, thought and emotional quality — are not merely connections of fact. It does not just so happen that the sincere expression of emotion coincides with an attention to and realization of attendant circumstances, or that a sentimental emotion is one that outruns the control of any justifying thought. Leavis's conclusions are, if true, necessarily true, and reflect an insight into the *concepts* of sincerity and sentimentality. Thus it seemed that, properly interpreted, criticism would be an extension of conceptual analysis, covering those important but elusive areas of the human mind which art makes peculiarly vivid to us.

Whatever the merits of such an approach, it cannot in the nature of things lead us to a general aesthetics. On the contrary, it redeems art for philosophy through by-passing the questions of aesthetics altogether, and seeing in criticism only instances of more general philosophical concerns. It discusses problems relating to emotion, culture, and practical knowledge. But — while these may obtain vivid exemplification in the criticism of art — they are not problems of aesthetics. Of course, it is not an accident that literary criticism forces its practitioners to confront, in this way, fundamental questions in the philosophy of mind. Nevertheless, we need a philosophical account of art that will explain why that is so. Moreover, problems remain which seem to be peculiar to the traditional subject of aesthetics and which are not, and perhaps cannot be, solved by rewriting literary criticism in philosophical terms. It is from a desire to solve such problems that writers disillusioned with the minutiae of linguistic analysis turned to other styles of philosophical reflection. It has been said, and with considerable truth, that contemporary analytical philosophy has deprived philosophy of its status as a humanity. An informed understanding of society and culture, an acquaintance with art and literature, a consciousness of history and institutions — all these seem to have no place in the studies undertaken in English and American philosophy departments. And this reluctance to engage in the activity which Matthew Arnold (noting its overwhelming importance for the German mind) called 'criticism', is rightly to be condemned as philistine. By contrast, neither phenomenology nor Marxism has, in our century, incurred that charge. Both have a large appetite for culture, and both promise to incorporate art directly and centrally into their conceptions of philosophical method. Major schools of aesthetics on the Continent — Russian formalism, Parisian semiology, the *Rezeptionsästhetik* which has recently emerged in Germany — all claim to be indebted either to Marxism or to phenomenology. Methods which seem to add so many results to a subject that is otherwise without them, naturally arouse curiosity. It seems to me that, in fact, the results proclaimed by many of these continental schools are, like the methods which create them, illusory.[3] The attempt to translate them into English has led to a great proliferation of jargon, and a massive edifice of scholastic disputation. But it is very hard to extract a theory of aesthetics from the result. Nevertheless the claim is still frequently made that Marxism, at least, provides an indispensable clue to art, and to the mystery posed by modern man's intimate relation to it.

It is difficult to give any general assessment of that claim. But there are, I believe, grounds for scepticism. Consider the Marxist theory of history, which divides base from superstructure, hoping thereby to achieve a scientific view of both. Such a theory confines art to the superstructure, explaining its character in terms of the economic conditions under which it is conceived. Even if true, it is uncertain what such a theory can contribute to our understanding of art. It is one thing to assign causes to a work of art, another thing to understand its content or value. If this kind of explanation can generate criticism, then we shall want to know why: hence we shall need a theory of what it is to understand and appreciate art. Which means that we shall need an independent aesthetics, relying on precisely those philosophical reflections that the theory of history sought to replace. The theory can therefore neither solve the problems nor pre-empt the solutions of philosophical aesthetics. Of course, there have been more subtle models of historical determinism, conceived within the broad spirit of Marxian materialism. But it is not *subtlety* that is required in order to make the theory of history relevant to aesthetics; the question of its relevance can be decided only from the standpoint of aesthetics, and is not a question for the theory itself to answer. It is not surprising therefore, if the attempts to give a 'subtle' version of the theory fail to make an impact on philosophical aesthetics. For example, the fairly representative discussion contained in Raymond Williams's *Marxism and Literature* (1977) proves wholly un-illuminating both as criticism, and as analysis. It says nothing persuasive about the nature of realism, about literary truth, about the value of literary expression, or the nature of our interest in it. It presents no method for the interpretation of texts, and casts no light on the crucial critical concepts — expression, imagination, form, and convention — which it is constantly forced to employ. Indeed, the author at one point expressly rejects 'Aesthetics', as a study which mystifies what he purports to explain.

A Marxist will hasten to point out that there is more to Marxism than the materialist theory of history. In particular, there is a Marxian philosophy of action, according to which it is man's essence to create his own nature in production. Partly because of the influence of Lukács, partly because of the residual Hegelianism that all modern criticism betrays, this thought has commanded considerable attention among artists and their critics. But it is again difficult to see how it can either generate or replace philosophical aesthetics. Suppose it is true that the nature of man is self-created, and has its origin in productive activity. How does that enable us to understand the results of that activity? Such a theory does not tell us how the active nature of man is distilled in art or science, or why he stands in need of these activities, or what the difference is between them. The traditional problems remain. It seems reasonable to suppose that this deficiency will attend every application of Marxist doctrine. For it is characteristic of this doctrine that it will always deny the autonomy of any activity to which it is applied, while the subject of aesthetics arises directly from the perception that the significance of art is inseparable from its autonomy — inseparable, that is, from our disposition to treat art as bearing its significance within itself. If we are to argue that art has no autonomous value, no peculiar place in the spectrum of human interests, then we shall require a philosophy that demonstrates the point, not one that merely assumes it. It is for some such reason, perhaps, that Marxist criticism so often ends in futile and scholastic battles over matters which seem irrelevant to the works of art which it discusses.

Phenomenology seems better placed to generate the answers to the questions of aesthetics. It deals directly with mental data, and seeks to explore what is essential to consciousness, without either representing it as the product of some economic 'base', or leaning on some premature 'science' of the mind. Adopting a phenomenological standpoint it therefore seems possible to inquire into the nature of aesthetic experience, and into the manner in which the world is represented through it. Sartre, in exploring such questions, had been led to a theory of imagination, in terms of which to explain not only the character of aesthetic representation, but also the deep relation between aesthetic and ordinary perception (*L'Imaginaire*, 1940). Sartre concealed his theory in extended metaphor and parenthesis. The style was characteristic of a philosopher for whom rhetoric has always been an important value: as a result it was some time before the nature of the theory was adequately perceived in the English-speaking world. Those with an interest in phenomenology stayed with the more pedestrian and commonplace thoughts of Ingarden and Dufrenne. When interest was at last aroused by Sartre's work, it was partly because its conclusions were seen to resemble those of Wittgenstein, whose posthumous *Philosophical Investigations* (1952) changed the course of analytical philosophy. One of Wittgenstein's most persuasive and original arguments, however, also seems to have the consequence that there can be no such thing as phenomenology.

Wittgenstein had argued that I cannot acquire insight into the essence of my mental states from the investigation of my own case alone. The first-person standpoint can provide no knowledge of the nature of any mental process. To suppose otherwise is to assume, however covertly, the possibility of a 'private language' — a language intelligible to one person alone. Such a language, Wittgenstein argues, is logically impossible. To suppose the possibility of a 'pure' phenomenology, a study in depth of the 'meanings' contained in every mental phenomenon, without reference to any external circumstances, is, however, to suppose the possibility of just such a language. Wittgenstein's argument was presented together with many complex and elaborate illustrations of the need for a 'third-person' standpoint in the philosophy of mind. And in the course of his discussion, Wittgenstein recognized the existence of what he called 'phenomenological problems'. In particular he was interested in problems in the philosophy of aesthetic appreciation, such as those discussed by Sartre. For example, there is the important question of the relation between perceiving an object in the street and perceiving it in a painting. In understanding a painting I see something that I know not to be there. What are the peculiarities of this kind of perception? Wittgenstein suggests an answer which, while it shares some of the spirit of Sartre's, does not stray from the third-person standpoint. He also suggests that there is an important relation between perceiving paintings and understanding music. For some time Wittgenstein's readers did not perceive that many of his reflections were directly relevant to aesthetics. Only now are philosophers beginning to appreciate that Wittgenstein's philosophy of mind enables us to take up the subject of aesthetics at the point where idealism left it.

The first major philosopher to produce work in general aesthetics that showed the influence of the later Wittgenstein was Richard Wollheim, whose *Art and its Objects* appeared in 1968. In this work, and in a series of essays collected in 1973 under the title *On Art and the Mind*, Wollheim has attempted to advance a philosophical account of the nature of art which will guarantee its central place in human experience, and so translate into the terms of modern analytical philosophy the spirit of Romantic aesthetics. He has tried to explain the concepts of representation and expression while avoiding the paradoxes which bedevil the idealist theories of their nature. Wollheim draws on Wittgenstein's remarks about 'seeing as': the concept vital to his own and to Sartre's theory of imagination. The peculiarity of 'seeing as' is that it is neither an illusion (since it involves no tendency to mistake), nor a perception of what is there. In exploring this experience Wollheim shows his debt to, and his rejection of, the work of Sir Ernst Gombrich, who, in *Art and Illusion* (1960) and *Meditations on a Hobby Horse* (1963), had discussed, from the standpoint of the psychology of art, the nature of representation and expression. But the more powerful influence at work in Wollheim's writings is Freud, both directly, and also indirectly, through the writings of Melanie Klein and the Kleinian art critic, Adrian Stokes. This leads Wollheim to speculations that are far at variance with the arguments of Wittgenstein (who rejected psychoanalysis as confusion and pseudo-wisdom). Moreover it is difficult to gather from the result either a consistent theory of aesthetic experience, or a satisfactory description of art. It seems odd, in retrospect, that anyone should seek to combine a Wittgensteinian approach to consciousness with a Freudian theory of the unconscious mind, while thinking that it is the latter, and not the former, which will generate the most plausible description of aesthetic experience.

But Wollheim abstains from generalities, and invites us to see his work as providing suggested answers to suggested questions. In this, at least, he follows the convention of analytical philosophy. There is one analytical philosopher who has been bold enough to reject this convention. Nelson Goodman's *Languages of Art* (1969) was the first work of analytical philosophy to produce a distinct and systematic *theory* of art, and for this reason it has attracted considerable attention, the more so in that the theory turns out to be an extension of a more general philosophical perspective, expounded in works of great rigour and finesse, which embraces the entire realm of logic, metaphysics and the philosophy of science.

Goodman's methods and outlook are highly idiosyncratic. But his project is a familiar one. He seeks for the nature of art in symbolism and for the nature of symbolism in a general theory of signs. This project has been promoted, both on the Continent and in certain branches of the humanities in the English-speaking universities, under the name of 'semiology'. But unlike the semiologists, Goodman advances rigorous foundations for his 'semantic' theory of art. The theory derives from the uncompromising nominalism expounded in his earlier work, a nominalism developed under the powerful influences of Carnap and Quine, but showing certain affinities with the later philosophy of Wittgenstein (in its results, if not in the methods by which it arrives at them). A major difference — crucial to the kind of aesthetic theory that each philosophy generates — is that, while both Goodman and Wittgenstein represent the relation between language and the world as largely inscrutable, and draw striking metaphysical conclusions from this, Wittgenstein's central interest is in the philosophy of mind. It is this which provides the Wittgensteinian vision of consciousness, as constituted by its outward expression, in language, in culture, and in the available 'forms of life' under which these are subsumed.

According to Goodman's general theory of signs the relation between signs and the world can be described, like any relation, in terms of its formal structure — in terms of such logical categories as symmetry, reflexivity, and transitivity — and in terms of the objects related (in this case signs and things). But apart from that formal analysis, there is nothing to be said. Words are labels which attach to things, but the attempt to describe that relation of attachment must, in using words, presuppose what it seeks to explain.

A corollary of this view is that relations of identical logical structure are one and the same. Thus, if we assume paintings, like words, to be signs, then portraits stand to their subjects in the same relation as proper names stand to the objects denoted by them. Hence representation and denotation are the same relation. We should not worry if that leads us to no new understanding of the relation — for example, that it leads to no procedure for 'decoding' the painted sign. For what we are being told is that there is nothing to be understood, or rather, to put the point in Wittgensteinian idiom, that 'understanding' is what is *given*. That is what nominalism says.

Goodman proceeds to generalize his theory of symbolism, using the word 'reference' to express the relation between word and thing (the relation of 'labelling'). Denotation is the special case of reference exemplified by proper names and portraits — the case where a symbol labels *one* individual. When a single label picks out a class of things, then we have, not a name, but a predicate. (To speak of 'properties' is both redundant and, in Goodman's view, metaphysically vicious, since it implies that there are things which are not individuals. Even to employ the term 'class' is to encourage illegitimate metaphysical expectations.)

Sometimes the process of 'labelling' goes both ways. A colour sample is a sign for the colour which it possesses — the colour red, say. It therefore 'refers' to the label 'red', which in turn refers to the sample. In this case the predicate 'red' and the sample mutually label each other. Goodman calls this relation 'exemplification', and analyses expression as a special case of it, the case where the exemplification of a predicate proceeds by metaphor.

The economy and elegance of Goodman's theory are matched only by its extreme inscrutability. On the surface, it seems to provide direct and intelligible answers to all the major problems of aesthetics. What is art? — a system of symbols. What is representation? — denotation. What is expression? — a kind of reference. What is the value of art? — that it symbolizes ('displays') reality. What is the distinction between art and science? — a distinction between symbol systems, but not between the matters which they display. And so on. And yet at every point we feel at a loss to know what we are learning about art in being told that its essence is symbolic.

The fashionable works of semiology that have succeeded Barthes' *Éléments* of 1964 leave the reader without any method for attaching 'meanings' to the literary and artistic 'codes' which are supposed to exemplify them: the reader is offered only a battery of useless technicalities. By contrast, Goodman bases his analysis of art in a serious philosophy of symbolism. Nevertheless it is also true that if one describes the forms of art as 'symbol systems', while refusing to answer all epistemological questions concerning the nature of symbolism, the subject is made more, and not less, obscure. We need to know how we would *discover* that something is a symbol, and how we would *know* what it says about its subject. Moreover, the semantic theory seems to have implications that are extremely counter-intuitive. In particular it seems to imply that the relation of a work of art to its expressive content is, like any semantic relation, a matter of convention. It is true that expression in art requires convention — but it is not determined by convention. If you could achieve expression by following conventions, then art becomes a matter of skill. It requires only facility to rival Mozart. But that is implausible. To achieve artistic expression is to use rules only to transcend them, to act as much in defiance of convention as in obedience to it.

What, then, should we put in the place of the view that all art is language? Is there any theory which so successfully combines range of application with apparent explanatory power?

It seems to me that too much of contemporary analytical aesthetics has focused on questions concerning the nature of art, at the expense of the more basic question considered by Kant, the question of the nature and value of aesthetic interest. To be sure, it would be futile to give a general theory of aesthetic interest which regarded the connection with its principal object as merely *accidental*. But to concentrate on that object without enquiring into the nature of the satisfaction that we seek through it is to risk a vast irrelevance. Fortuitous properties of art thereby achieve spurious centrality in aesthetic theory. All art is forced into the mould of 'expression', 'representation', 'convention', and 'symbolism'. These concepts, in being forced to contain so much, lose all determinate sense of their own. At the same time the lingering after-image of meaning attaches itself to them; this mirage misleads the philosopher into thinking that he has discovered the path to a general theory of aesthetic understanding.

It has seemed to me more profitable to analyse the aesthetic experience itself, and in particular that central core of 'imaginative attention' which interested Wittgenstein and Sartre. However, it is necessary to free the study of imagination from the first-personal viewpoint, and to demarcate the exact place of imaginative experience in the life of a rational being. Pursuing such a study one can find a way to uphold the idealist thesis, that there are genuine distinctions between aesthetic experience and scientific and moral understanding. It is possible to conclude that aesthetic experience also has a peculiar practical significance: it represents the world as informed by the values of the observer. In the light of a theory of the imagination we can explain why aesthetic judgement aims at objectivity, why it is connected to the sensuous experience of its object, and why it is an inescapable feature of moral life. We can then fit art into the gap that aesthetic experience leaves for it. It is, we find, the most appropriate object of aesthetic interest; moreover it possesses features — among which representation and expression are but two — which mark it out as an object of irreplaceable value in the lives of rational beings.

2 Public Text and Common Reader

What makes a critical reading of a text into a reading of *that* text? More simply: is there any objective limit to critical 'interpretation', or is all criticism *jouissance*, a kind of 'metaliterature', to be appreciated not as a commentary on one text but as the creation of another? We think of criticism as constrained by its subject-matter, but may we not be deluded? Is the relation between criticism and text ever more objective than the relation between Beethoven's 'Kreutzer' sonata and the Tolstoy novella that was inspired by it, or between the novella and Janáček's first quartet?

Recent criticism has made much of a discovery that elementary logic ought long ago to have clarified. It has discovered that its subject-matter — the work of art — is, if not identical with, at least enshrined in, texts, scores and other semi-permanent things. Most works of art (and all significant works of art) therefore have a power to outlast their creator, acquiring a penumbra of significance which he himself might never have been able to acknowledge or intend. Many thoughts have been inspired by that simple observation, and it is a small step in delirium, although a large one in logic, to the science of 'grammatology', which takes the written character of the literary object as primary, and insists that in the act of writing the author vanishes from the scene. The meaning of his work is not *his* meaning, but something imposed, discovered, or invented by the grammatologist. The text then becomes mysterious, an object to be 'deconstructed', or at least deconstrued, by a critic who is omniscient since he makes ironical display of his knowledge that he knows nothing.[1]

I shall not examine the methods of contemporary narratology, as it has come to be called, and I shall ignore the specifically structuralist and deconstructive analyses of primary texts. My remarks will be of a general kind. I shall ask what follows when the public character of the text is taken seriously, and I shall leave the reader to draw conclusions concerning the many intriguing things that have been said about the status of the 'text' as 'signifier'. If I try to avoid Saussurian jargon, this is not out of disrespect for studies which are by now widely accepted as part of the academic repertoire, but out of respect for a concept — that of truth — which many of those studies seem to overlook.

The Problem of Intention

The first move in all modern theories of critical interpretation consists in recognizing that the critic is not describing the writer's intention. (Here 'intention' means what is normally referred to in a sincere answer to the question 'Why did you do that?') We should not conclude, however, that intention is simply irrelevant to the understanding of a literary work, or that the meaning of a work, since it is not given by what the author says, is therefore entirely hostage to the critic. Even when interpreting someone's action in a way that makes no reference to his intention, the fact of intentionality will be a premise of the interpretation. A person for whom it made no difference whether a sculpture was carved by wind and rain or by human hand would be a person incapable of interpreting, indeed incapable of perceiving, sculptures. This is so, even though the interpretation of the sculpture is not the reading of an intention.

The point of under-playing intention is to insist on the public character of the aesthetic object. Interestingly enough, it is precisely the move away from 'intentionalist' criticism that has prompted some literary theorists to despair of objective interpretation. Thus E. D. Hirsch writes: 'If the meaning of a text is not the author's, then no interpretation can possibly correspond to *the* meaning of the text, since the text can have no determinate or determinable meaning.'[2] In order to save himself from scepticism, Hirsch is then compelled to distinguish interpretation from understanding, assigning to the second that common search for a public significance which he removes from the first.[3] The example is of a writer influenced by the tradition of hermeneutical criticism and by all the subtleties contained in it; yet Hirsch's words remind us that the problem of the role of intention in criticism may not really be a problem. Or at least, it is not a problem that is special to criticism. It is evident that, when I ask for the meaning of a work of art, it is no more for the artist to pre-empt my inquiry than it is for the user of an English sentence to determine, Humpty-Dumpty-like, the meaning of his words. The existence of the distinction between what a speaker means and what his sentence means in no way shows that we cannot analyse the second objectively. On the contrary, it suggests that we can and must. At the same time, we must beware of any view that sees the reference to artistic intention, *Kunstwollen,* and the like, as irrelevant to public meaning. Although the meaning of a sentence is not given by the intention with which it is used, it would not have the meaning that it has were it not for its place in the expression of intention. Likewise, it is imperative to see that the whole nature of a work of art as an object of aesthetic interest is determined by the fact that it is the product of many and complex intentions.

The Publicity of Language

Publicity means this: first, that an utterance exists independently of the utterer (one part of the distinction between *langue* and *parole*); secondly, that its meaning can be understood by more than one person. These features belong to all language, even in its most 'figurative' uses. Anyone who thinks that this publicity of language causes the vanishing of the subject from the literary text is surely suffering from a confusion. It is like thinking that Wittgenstein's argument against the possibility of a private language is an argument against the existence of the self, rather than against the Cartesian theory of the nature of the self.[4] It is not the subject which vanishes, but only a false conception of its nature. It seems to me that traces of Cartesianism can be found in 'grammatology', in particular in Derrida's endless play with the idea that: 'l'espacement comme écriture est le devenir-absent et le devenir-inconscient du sujet', from which it is supposed to follow that 'l'absence originale du sujet de l'écriture est aussi celle de la chose ou du référent'.[5]

It is thus that, by sleight of hand, the discovery of the 'text' as object leads to the conclusion that no text is really *about* anything: a fortunate conclusion for those subjectivists who want at least to start from, if not to end at, the idea that in matters of literary interpretation anything goes. But once we see that such conclusions (like the many variants of the idea that the 'signifier' is always also a 'signified', or that the sign itself is unfailingly *mise en abîme*[6], are, if true, true of language in every form, we will more easily see that they must be false, as much of literature and of figurative speech as of common usage.

Criticism and Aesthetic Judgement

What is puzzling, I contend, is not the status of the text, but rather the nature of the aesthetic interest which we have in it. The public accessibility and objective status of ordinary discourse is bound up with the fact that language is used to refer to the world, and aims at saying what is true. The whole nature of language, down to the most intricate features of its structural organization, is determined by this interest in truth.[7] If there is an objective interpretation of what men say, it is because saying is referring, and because referring is a prelude to truth.

In aesthetic endeavour, to borrow Wittgenstein's expression, words are not used in the 'language-game of information', even though it is from this 'language-game' that they derive their sense.[8] Aesthetic interest abstracts from the truth or falsehood of its object in order to address itself to the peculiar needs of the imagination. I shall put the point by saying that aesthetic interest 'fictionalizes' its object. By this I mean that it drops the requirement of veracity in favour of vividness, and that of 'truth to fact' in favour of a more generalized, and less scrutable, 'truth to life', or, as the semiologists put it, *vraisemblance*.[9] This feature is very hard to define. Unlike literal truth, lifelikeness admits of degrees ('very true' is only a way of speaking). And lifelikeness is only one aspect of the phenomenon to which I refer. The aptness of a metaphor, the appropriateness of a word, the revelatory quality of an image: all these exemplify that 'non-literal' relation to the world that is the natural object of aesthetic interest. Hence, even in a narrative of actual events, it is not, from the aesthetic point of view, significant that this is how things were. The narrative must be read as fiction, and the narrator's rhetoric is a rhetoric of fiction. This gives us a clue to the aesthetic significance of figures of speech.

Figures of Speech

When I say that a heavy, slow-moving and stupid person is like an ox, I have used a simile, and what I say might be true. When I say that he *is* an ox, then I have used a metaphor, and what I say is inevitably false. This is one reason for excluding simile from the class of rhetorical figures: unlike metaphor, prosopopoeia and all the rest, similes can be true. A metaphor may be apt, appropriate, vivid or compelling, but it cannot be true. For many metaphors, there are corresponding similes which, as it were, creep in behind them with their literal meanings intact: the aptness of the metaphor consists merely in the truth of the corresponding simile (as in the example). Most of the figures of ordinary speech have such equivalents in simile. A good many of the more interesting figures of literary discourse do not. This is part of what is meant by literary condensation, as in the following well-known example from Valéry's *Le Cimetière Marin:* 'Midi le juste y compose de feux/La mer, la mer, toujours recommencée'[10] Noon is not here being compared to anything except itself: it is personalized, but only in order to attribute to it an action that no agent could perform. Such metaphors, which occur everywhere in literature, and compose the essence of dramatic rhetoric, defy literal reading and cannot be rendered as similes. Because their effectiveness is perceivable from, and perhaps only from, the aesthetic point of view, they have an immense critical significance. And for this reason we should not be surprised to find critics turning again to the ancient science of rhetoric, in the hope that it might cast some light on their subject. There has been a renewed attempt to separate and to theorize upon all the various kinds of borrowing that are employed in figurative language.[11] It is, I believe, not necessary to digress in that direction in order to understand the central feature of every figure, which is that it is, when successful, false.[12] It is only against the background of literal falsehood that the *vraisemblance* of a metaphor can be appreciated. To understand this feature we must look not to the classificatory science of rhetoric, but to the peculiar features of the aesthetic interest which has a certain kind of falsehood as its object.

'Fictionalization'

For centuries Japanese scholars were able to mystify the readers of *Genji* with arcane readings of its hidden 'messages', through failing to specify that the primary purpose of *Genji* is fictionary.[13] In aesthetic interest, even what is true is treated as though it were not. It is this simple fact that has, it seems to me, given rise to many of the recent problems and pseudo-problems in narratology and its kindred disciplines. For example, in normal speech, where truth is the aim, the subject ought to be determinate. A man who describes some real episode may not be able to answer questions like 'What was her name?' or 'How much did she weigh?', but it is a presupposition of his discourse that those questions have an answer. In contrast, fictional discourse denies an answer. ('How many children had Lady Macbeth?') When I say that aesthetic interest fictionalizes, I mean this: that even in a narrative of real events there will be questions that are not only irrelevant, but ruled out of court by the aesthetic point of view. There is an aesthetic error in asking them. Suppose events had happened exactly as Shakespeare described them. Then still to ask the question 'How many children had Lady Macbeth?' shows an *ignoratio elenchi*. One might say that aesthetic interest *abstracts* from truth, and it does this by endowing its object with the logical indeterminacy of make-believe. The aesthetic narrative, even if it is not a fiction, contains gaps, like the unseen parts of a picture, across which the dramatic movement sparks. It will always seem, even in the most complete account of the significance of a narrative work, that the interpretation is one among infinitely many. But that conclusion is mistaken. The indeterminacy of fiction means, not that there are infinitely many answers to certain narrative questions, but that there are none, since the questions are illegitimate.

The deployment of figures of speech and the existence of the 'fictional gap' are inevitable consequences of the 'abrogation of reference' that is contained in the aesthetic point of view. They combine to form a sense that fiction has a structure all of its own and that this structure is itself that of a figure of speech. The puzzling feature of a successful narrative, that it is literally false but true to life, seems to be the same as the puzzling feature of successful metaphor. If there is need for interpretative techniques, then it is in order to understand the structure of this narrative 'figure' hidden within the contours of a text. You find this idea more or less explicitly stated in Barthes,[14] and covertly relied on by much recent structuralist criticism. The idea of fiction as a kind of extended figure is attractive, since it seems to combine the two ways in which truth and reference disappear, and makes the resulting feature a property of the text itself rather than of the interest that we have in it. So that now the notion of text as object can be combined with that of meaning as hostage, to give almost unlimited licence to critical interpretation. Yet, once having embarked in this direction, the critic seems to drift without guidance; hence the *nouvelle critique* raises the problem of critical objectivity in its acutest form.

The problem, as I see it, is best approached by returning to the abrogation of reference which is intrinsic to the aesthetic point of view. It is this which raises the problem of relevance. If we do not have the criterion of truth to guide us, what remains of the idea that there might be an 'objective' standard of interpretation? In particular, what can, and what cannot, be brought by the critic to the reading of a work? This is precisely the same question as whether there is a non-literal *meaning* of a text, which, like the literal meaning, is publicly accessible, and which provides the true object of aesthetic interest.

Meaning and Association

There is a distinction which helps to highlight the kind of objectivity for which we are seeking — that between meaning and association. Suppose someone is asked to give an account of what *The Prelude* means to him. The remarks that he might sensibly make in response to this question fall broadly into two categories: those that he is prepared to refer to *The Prelude* as descriptions of its 'meaning', and those that he is prepared to refer only to himself, as the particular reader that he is. The first he offers as part of understanding *The Prelude;* the second may be important in understanding *him.* A reader who is not prepared to make this distinction between meaning and association does not *have* a conception of the (objective) meaning of a work of art. Likewise, a critical 'method' that leaves us unable to draw the distinction is one that removes the ground from any claim that it may wish to make on behalf of its own validity. The only reason for adopting such a 'method' would then be either that it had itself some of the appealing (but undiscussable) qualities of literature, or that it gave an order to private associations which proved agreeable to those who shared in them.

In order to draw the distinction between meaning and association we must allow a public nature to the first which we withhold from the second. This means that we must be prepared to say, of literary meaning, that anyone with the right faculties will be able to understand it. And that, of course, automatically introduces an idea of right and wrong into criticism. But what are these faculties and what do they discover? It is here that we find the real distinctions among schools of criticism. Different schools propose separate ideals of the faculties of literary perception, and this is because they are motivated by different conceptions of the nature of aesthetic response. I shall examine three of the available possibilities.

Criticism as De-coding

The first kind of critical theory argues that we distinguish meaning from association in literature as we do when deciphering the literal meaning of 'signs'. We discover certain conventions, rules or 'codes', which determine the symbolic meaning of the work. Hence the capacity of the critic consists in a certain kind of skill in discovering and applying literary conventions. Of course, writers who have used terms like 'convention', 'rule' or 'code' to describe the activity of critical interpretation have not always intended these terms strictly. But it is important to construe them strictly when exploring the foundations of literary criticism. Otherwise we shall never know what they add to, or subtract from, our knowledge.

On the view under discussion, literary meaning is public because it is governed by conventions that are common to all who read with understanding. Two claims are here being advanced. First, a connection is being asserted (of the kind asserted by Frege) between meaning and understanding.[15] If a text has a public meaning, it is what is publicly understood in reading it. Hence, if there is a distinction between literal and 'literary' meaning, it is because there is a distinction between literal and literary understanding. The second claim is that literary meaning, like literal meaning, is a matter of convention. The critic is seen as the theorist of literary conventions, much as the linguist is the theorist of semantic rules. The critic uncovers the semiotic principles which govern literary understanding. Since the reader's understanding, like the text itself, is a publicly observable phenomenon, the critical 'hypothesis' can be verified in just the way that a linguist's hypothesis might be verified. It is important to add that the normal reader does not have to know what the critic knows (any more than a competent speaker of a language needs a linguist's grasp of grammar). The critic knows how to describe and to theorize what Jonathan Culler has called the reader's 'literary competence'.[16]

There is something plausible, and something contentious, in that position. What is plausible is the first claim made above; what is contentious is the second. It is plausible to say that, if there is a publicly accessible literary meaning, it is because there is a publicly accessible mode of literary understanding. Understanding is the crucial phenomenon: meaning is its outward projection. This is shown immediately by the case of music. We all know that there is such a thing as understanding and misunderstanding music. But many of us find it impossible to accept theories of music which tell us how to decipher a piece in terms of its structure, syntax, semantics or internal 'code'. Such theories describe properties of the music which are not objects of musical understanding. They describe things that are never actually *heard* by the man who hears with understanding. The description of these things as parts of musical 'meaning' is therefore totally without grounds.

The contentious claim is that the relation between a work of literature and what is understood through it is one of convention. To dispute the claim is rather difficult. Terms like 'convention' and 'code' are used in literary criticism extremely loosely, and I wish to discuss the repercussions encapsulated only in very specific uses. When critics speak of 'convention' in art, they often have in mind organization, form, genre, cross-reference, certain patterns of conformity and departure. We hear of the 'conventions' of sonata-form, of tragedy, of the recumbent nude, and equally of the 'conventions' of Renaissance imagery, of versification, of reference, even 'conventions' of belief and feeling associated with particular literary forms. Not all these things can be usefully summarized under the same label. For example, there is a distinction between convention and tradition. (Is 'sonata-form' a convention or a tradition? That question could be seen as the central one addressed in Charles Rosen's celebrated study.[17]) Tradition and convention are as distinct as custom and rule. Custom is not founded in a standard of correctness, and need be related to nothing beyond itself from which such a standard could be derived. Custom consists in the convergence on and divergence from a norm of behaviour. Convention, by contrast, lays down a rule, an 'if this, then that'. When *meaning* is a matter of convention, the rule relates the literary work to its meaning in the systematic way that grammatical form is related to reference in a common language.

It is the freedom from absolute rule that allows custom and tradition to impose genuine, as opposed to arbitrary, constraint on artistic activity. And it is through this, non-conventional, constraint, that literary meaning accumulates. The same is true, I believe, of style. Those critics who think that there is a science of 'stylistics', which can take semantics or phonetics as its model, make just the same mistake as the critical theorists for whom 'convention' is everything. This was part of the point of Buffon's famous remark: 'le style, c'est l'homme même'. One theorist has spoken of the 'urban guerrilla warfare between linguists and literary men', which he denounces as the 'two-culture myth within the humanities'.[18] He reminds us that 'the linguist attempts to explain as much of style as he can without giving up the rigour of his methods'. But if there is some part of style that is not accessible to his methods, then these methods do not provide a theory of style. (Suppose someone were to say that the behaviourist attempts to explain as much of the mind as possible without giving up his methodological assumption that mental phenomena are behavioural. The reply would be: if you can only get *so* far with that assumption, then that is because the mind is constituted by the phenomena which are inaccessible to the method.)

This is not the place to embark on the vexed question of the nature of style. My intention is merely to recommend scepticism. Custom, tradition, convention and style are all forms of artistic constraint. And because convention is the easiest to theorize, it has been prematurely offered as a model for the other three. The constraints of style and tradition surround the artist and give him the opportunity to establish his identity as something both original and legitimate: without a style an artist is nothing, and without a tradition against which to define himself his style is not truly *his*. So it is inevitable that style and tradition should determine, in however unfathomable a manner, the meaning of an artist's work. In this sense — the sense in which being part of a tradition is integral to human freedom — it is clear that there are things to be understood by the critic which go beyond the work that he is examining, and which often do have the appearance (although it is, I believe, only the appearance) of conventions governing literary composition.

Convention and Tradition

Before returning to examine the idea of a literary 'code' it is worth trying to distinguish convention and tradition a little more precisely, since tradition has been such an important term in defining our native conception of the function of criticism. The distinction is, I recognize, highly complex, and I must confine myself to a few, far from obvious, observations. Moreover, I shall not discuss the particular variety of convention that is involved in the generation of meaning.

The first point to notice is that I can obey a convention at no cost to myself: nothing of myself need be a part of it or absorbed into it. When I attend a funeral ceremony for someone about whom I cared nothing, then this conventional act requires nothing from *me*. And this is part of the purpose of the conventions of mourning, that they protect the uninvolved participant. Something similar might happen in art. When I write in the convention of the Japanese *haiku*, using the standard five-, seven- and five-syllable construction, I obey a simple rule of versification. When I perform this as a party game, nothing of myself is taken up by it. I do not belong to the tradition of the *haikai,* and while I may follow its conventions, the tradition itself can still remain unalterably alien to me. I am not immersed in it; it is not a necessity for me to express myself in this way, nor does it strike me with any inward sense of its appropriateness. We might want to say, reflecting on such an example, that convention is something that can be learned and transmitted without any cost to or change in the participant. Criticism that takes convention, or any other form of rule-guidedness, as its object assumes that all art is like a funeral ceremony, existing primarily for the sake of form.

A second consideration: convention can be studied by someone who does not really understand the artistic medium in which the convention is exercised. A completely unmusical person could familiarize himself with the conventions (if there be any) of sonata-form; he thereby enables himself to recognize the new examples and to describe the old ones. But he is no nearer to hearing the essence of sonata-form. Likewise, in the appreciation of a painting, for example, the discipline of the artist is, like the colours on the canvas, part of what is *seen.* It is not simply a matter of convention that can be grasped by anybody, whatever his attitude towards art. It is a part of visual significance. Once again there is a kind of criticism that seeks to assimilate this phenomenon to the recognition of convention.[19] But no convention changes the aspect of what is seen in the way that it is changed by a tradition. We do not 'read' pictures as we do semaphore signals. Tradition brings past and present into immediate visual relation, and can be understood only by someone with a trained and sensitive eye. Visual conventions, on the other hand, can be understood even by a blind man.

A third consideration: whereas conventions are fixed and timeless, traditions are essentially 'live' in the sense of Pound's lines on this subject. A tradition is a *spirit,* and its youth is changed by the retrospective vision of maturity. The point was made by Eliot in a famous essay; a tradition is something that is made anew by anyone who elects to join it, provided he can succeed in doing so.[20] In one extended passage of *Four Quartets,* Eliot himself succeeded in making Dante part of the tradition of our literature.[21] He did this even while ignoring almost all of the *conventions* used by Dante. He captured over the centuries, and through an amazing intervening period of literature, a tradition of which he made himself a part. In Eliot's verses, the language of the King James Bible is joined to the spirit of pre-Renaissance Florence.

The importance of the last point will perhaps justify another example. Wagner wished to give dramatic and musical expression to an erotic passion which has no fulfilment. Such a passion, which cannot sublimate itself into the intellectual love of God, remains fixated on the individual mortal being, on the here and now, and must therefore find consummation in time and in death.[22] Its expression requires wholly new musical forms. Wagner therefore extracted from the body of classical harmony a principle of chromatic quasi-resolution; he also invented a style which might be called (although the description is misleading) 'a-tonal'. To Wagner it would have seemed only that he was stretching to its limit something already there in the tradition of romantic music. To us, looking backwards, *Tristan* seems to mark not a limit, but an intermediate step between Mozart and Schoenberg. We now see Wagner's chromaticism not as the extreme point of attenuation of a practice that preceded it, but rather as one step in the logical development that it made possible. Now just as we could read that tradition forwards from Wagner into Schoenberg, so we read it backwards from Wagner into Mozart. Critics now look out for the chromatic passages in Mozart, finding in them qualities of expression prescient of *Tristan*. No contemporary of Mozart would have found those qualities; but that does not make it wrong for us to look for them and to value them. In other words, tradition always makes its object present. It aligns itself with a past only to redeem that past for our present feelings. Convention, on the other hand, is rigid, timeless. It bears its significance unchangingly, like the grammar of a dead language. An historian may elucidate convention while having no feeling for the art that exploits it; whereas an understanding of tradition is reserved for those with the critical insight which comes from the love of art, not only of past art but of the present art which has grown from it.

Codes and Syntagms

There are various morals to be drawn from that digression. In general we should beware of running together the contrasting ways in which works of literature exhibit discipline. Convention and tradition are two of these; style is another. It is wrong in principle to think that a mode of interpretation which takes the first of these as a model can discover 'methods' that will enable it to interpret the others. Yet style and tradition have a more genuine claim to be determinants of artistic significance than has convention.

What, then, should be our attitude towards the view of criticism as de-coding? We have seen the appeal of the idea that meaning, like freedom, is born of constraint. This has suggested to many critics that, if we could describe the constraints that determine literary (as opposed to literal) meaning, then we could give a *systematic* method of literary interpretation. But ideas of literary competence which take semantic convention as their model seem to disintegrate in the application.[23] There is a divorce between the claims of the theory and the simplicity of the practice, which derives not from the under-determination of the first by the second, but from the absence of any real correspondence between them. It is not enough to establish this through examples — to show, for example, that Barthes' analysis of *Sarrasine*, or Lodge's comments on Hemingway's story 'Cat in the Rain' neither require nor are required by the theoretical apparatus that accompanies them. To establish it fully is to provide reasons for thinking that *no* appropriate theory is forthcoming. I shall suggest one further difficulty, which contains, I believe, the seeds of generalization.

The origin of much structuralist and semiological criticism lies in the thought that literary meaning, like literal meaning, *develops*, and that its development is, to use the Saussurian word, 'syntagmatic'. That is to say, it moves through the successive arousal, and selective satisfaction, of literary expectations. Each point in a literary structure is defined by a class of potential substitutes (a 'paradigm'). In 'Albert eats' there are two places in which terms can be substituted without loss of syntactic form. But substitution so as to save the syntax may not save the sense; and substitution so as to save the sense may not save the truth-value. Syntactic 'equivalents' are not necessarily semantic equivalents. Moreover, complete semantic equivalents — which can replace each other without changing sense, reference or truth-value — may not be poetic equivalents. So the 'literary' structure has its own rules of substitution, and its own syntagmatic organization. Hopkins could not have written 'My heart, but you were pigeon-winged', even though this is syntactically and semantically equivalent to 'My heart, but you were dove-winged'. This points to one way in which the idea of 'literary' convention has been theorized. The problem facing this method was pointed out already by one of the earlier and more sensible semioticians:

> In admitting that the projection of equivalence relations on to the syntagmatic chain plays a major role in poetry, we encounter a serious theoretical problem, to which no one has really addressed himself: which equivalences must be supposed to be pertinent? In other words, in the name of what may we decide that this or that linguistic element is or is not pertinent from the poetic point of view?[24]

Ruwet's point is of the utmost importance. Unless the division of the literary work into syntagmatic sections generates rules of literary significance, all that is achieved by this massive apparatus is the rewriting in 'structuralese' of an ancient critical observation: that in literary contexts semantically equivalent words cannot replace each other without loss of literary meaning. At the same time, it seems to me that any attempt to *explain* literary meaning as the offshoot of convention must, at some point, deny that observation. It must say that the poetic meaning of such a term, or of such a phrase, is determined by convention; in which case a like convention could have assigned just that meaning to another term. However, literary meaning is a matter of what Frege called 'tone': it is the penumbra of significance that is *consequent* on conventional meaning. It cannot itself be the subject of convention, for any such convention would generate a new penumbra as its 'literary' offshoot.

I have suggested a contrast between convention and other forms of constraint. It is to these other forms of constraint that I wish to direct attention. I have implied that no one could really be influenced by a tradition without being taken up by it, so that his judgement, taste and perception are intimately affected by its internal constraints. From the outside these constraints may seem as arbitrary as conventions; from the inside they are felt as something else. It has been a perennial thesis of Anglo-Saxon criticism, at least since Coleridge, that these constraints form and transform the perception and judgement of the participant; moreover, they are not the property of the expert critic, but of the reader and writer of literature. They provide the framework within which literary communication occurs. It is important to bear these points in mind when I return, shortly, to examine the older ideas of the nature of criticism.

The upshot of those remarks is that we should beware of theories which suggest that criticism is a kind of skill, which has literary convention as its subject-matter. What other model should we propose?

Criticism as Hermetic

The ideal of the critic that has emerged from the ruins of that first conception is that of a man possessed not of a certain skill but of a certain language. This language is not shared with any reader of literature who is not himself a critic: nor is it one which is recognized by the writer. It is a 'metalanguage', which is designed purely for the interpretation, and not for the composing, of primary texts. The professional semiotician — the master of this language — is able not so much to discover meaning in texts as to impose meaning upon them, by rewriting them in a language that traps and encapsulates their ordinary significance. This imposition of meaning has the result that the text is shown to be 'unreadable' to the uninitiated.

That is a caricature, but it has a heuristic purpose. We must see that, to the extent that criticism approaches such an ideal, to that extent does it postulate no reader of literature other than the critic himself. Such criticism is not *addressed* to the reader of literature. There is no longer any suggestion of a 'common' or 'public' meaning, since there is no common reader to whom the requisite understanding belongs. All that remains is the 'hermetic' reading of the critic. But either the meaning of a text is publicly available, in which case such a criticism cannot provide its analysis, or else it is not, in which case there is no meaning to analyse. This suggests that criticism must be as available as the works that it criticizes. It cannot take refuge in a 'metalanguage' which has only texts as its field of reference and untheorized jargon as its terms. Every ideal of the critic corresponds to an ideal of the reader; that maxim is alone sufficient to lead us to look on the pretensions of more recent semiotic criticism with suspicion.

Criticism as Response

This leads me to turn to a third, and more old-fashioned, idea. The critic is a reader with taste or judgement, where this means a certain kind of responsiveness to literature. This responsiveness can be articulated in such a way as to persuade others to share in it; it is indeed essentially shared, since it is what is common to all who read with understanding. The critic ceases to be the theorist of 'literary competence' but becomes rather its principal manifestation. But this manifestation has a cultural quality. The critic expresses the experience of literature in terms which relate it to a literary culture. The constraints uncovered in this exercise are not of the kind that can be detached from their cultural context and given the explicit form of a convention. Rarely can the critic say '*x* means *y* by convention'. Nor would it be very important if he could. What is important is to discover the meanings that emerge when works of literature are experienced in relation to each other. Those meanings are not a matter of convention, but of felt comparison. The importance of the idea of tradition is that it denotes — ideally, at least — the class of relevant comparisons. It refers us to those works of literature, and those relations between literature and the human world, which determine, in the mind of the reader, a particular response to the particular work. This response is — again ideally — the common property of a culture, accessible to every reader for whom literature matters at all.

It cannot be denied that those ideas are vague. I shall not have space to make them more precise, even if I could do so. But I shall try to give a philosophical perspective on the problem of critical objectivity that will bring tradition and culture into the foreground. What would be necessary for the present idea — of criticism as response — to lead us towards an objective criticism? A simple parallel is provided by the philosophical problem of tertiary qualities.

A primary quality of an object is one that would be attributed to it by a true scientific account of its nature, and reference to which would be essential in describing all its causal powers. A secondary quality is one that would not feature in such a scientific account, but which is observable by creatures possessing certain sensory capacities. The secondary qualities of an object are explained by its primary qualities, but not vice versa. Shape is a primary quality, colour a secondary quality. A tertiary quality is one that is observable only to beings possessing certain intellectual and emotional capacities. From the scientific point of view such a property would be even less part of the 'real constitution' of an object than the secondary qualities which it appears to have. This is because tertiary properties, not being dependent only on the senses, are indistinguishable from the 'response' of the being who observes them.

As an example, consider the face in a picture. This is not visible to a dog, but only to a being with imagination (which is a rational capacity). There are physical features of the picture which explain the fact that I see a face in it, and which could be described in primary-quality terms. But the face is no part of them. Nor is there any law which says that, to a being with certain sensory capacities (for example, sensitivity to light rays), the face will automatically appear. It will appear only to a being with imagination, that is, to a being who can accomplish that abrogation of reference that is required for the aesthetic point of view.[25]

Because of this dependence on rational capacities, it is possible that the face can be 'argued away'. This is particularly evident in the case of the more 'emotional' among the tertiary qualities. Consider the sadness of a piece of music, or the gravity of a verse. Few of us feel tempted to follow Berkeley in thinking that secondary qualities are not really 'in' the objects which seem to possess them. But we all feel tempted to say something like that of tertiary qualities. There comes a point, we feel, when it is only a manner of speaking to refer to a property of an object. The real fact of the matter is the response of the observer. If we speak of a property of the object this is only a way of saying that the response may be justified (as when we describe a landscape as 'fearful'). If we think of meaning in literature on the analogy with 'tertiary' qualities, we see why there is both a pressure towards objectivity and a pressure in the other direction. Meaning in literature would be (at its most objective) something like the aspect in a picture, observable to a being with the requisite intellectual and emotional capacities but irreducible to any structural properties of the work itself. ('Structuralism' could then be seen as the (vain) attempt to describe meaning as a *primary* quality of the thing that possesses it.)

Such a theory could solve the problem that concerns us. For it suggests not only that, but *how* meaning is objectively determined in literature. If the capacities of the critic are publicly available, so that the reader too can share in them, then the critic's reflections on his own response will also be addressed to the reader. In which case, he is describing not some personal association, but a publicly perceivable aspect of the meaning of the work. (The search for meaning is validated as a 'common pursuit'.) Tertiary qualities, unlike secondary qualities, might not be immediately perceivable to someone who lacks the requisite aesthetic understanding. It is education that enables people to perceive musical development, for example, or pictorial balance. Hence criticism may be justified, as the education (by which I do not mean articulation) of response.

Before suggesting difficulties for such a view, I should like to draw attention to an important corollary of the discussion. I have described three kinds of critic — the critic of skill, the critic of metalanguage, and the critic, as one might express it, of 'common culture'. To each critic there corresponds an ideal reader. Only in the third case does it seem obvious that the critic addresses his remarks to readers of literature who are not also professionals. This is the reason why I can see hope for the defence of the objectivity of criticism only in the postulation of this third ideal. The critic must have certain general capacities to respond to works of literature, and be capable of entering into cultural relation with the uninitiated reader. It seems to me right therefore to reject without further examination any view of criticism that moves towards either of the rival ideals. If we cannot persuade ourselves to utter such a comprehensive rejection — if we do not allow ourselves to say 'wrong from the start' — then we shall have a lifetime of fruitless studies before us. And it would be better to devote that life to reading literature than to reflecting upon how to reflect upon it.

Some Difficulties

Introducing the objectivity of criticism through the idea of a tertiary quality is attractive, but insufficient. First there is a doubt at which I have already hinted, arising from the very notion of a tertiary quality. We can think of secondary qualities as objective partly because every normal human being unavoidably perceives them. The same is not always true of tertiary qualities, particularly of those that have to do with meaning in works of art. Only some people perceive the tragedy of *King Lear,* or the ambiguity of *Othello.* Moreover, if we say that the perception of these things is part of 'culture', then are we not in danger of saying that they are *not,* after all, publicly available, being the property of some complicitous élite? (In what way is that an improvement upon the idea that meaning belongs to the structuralist élite?) Furthermore, just *which* tertiary qualities should the critic be interested in? It is not enough to say: 'those to do with meaning'. For 'meaning' is a term that extends so widely as to embrace almost anything. Was it a critical defect in young drummer

Hodge that he 'never knew / The meaning of the broad Karoo'? Hardly. It is when we reflect on such problems, and on the 'abrogation of reference' which seems to be the condition under which literary meaning emerges, that we see that it will be impossible to establish the objectivity of critical judgement except in the context of a full theory of imagination. Studies of the nature of the 'text' will always fail to take us to the point where objectivity is an issue. In order not to end on a note of despair, however, I shall return to some of the earlier considerations of this paper, in the light of a particular critical example.

An Example

I have argued that a minimum requirement of critical objectivity is that the critic should be able to draw the distinction between meaning and association — between what is *in* the work and what is not. (The sadness is in the music; my melancholy on hearing it is not.) It is surely not implausible to suggest that part of what enables us to make this distinction lies in a 'sense of intention' with which every work of art is imbued. We do not, of course, say that a work of art means whatever the artist intended it to mean. But nor do we feel that we can impose an interpretation which is incompatible with anything that *might* have been intended. This is why I referred, earlier, to the problem of intention, and to the over-hasty elimination of intention from the concerns of the critic.

The problem is no different from that of finding a right or appropriate production for a play, or a correct style of performance for a piece of music. Although a critical interpretation is something added to a work of art, it is added in the way that the props, casting and direction are added to a play: in order to capture a 'spirit' which the work already conveys. The good production becomes part of the play, in the way that the illuminating criticism becomes part of what is read. Most people have some grasp of this relation between play and performance, and will recognize that they cannot draw the line between understanding and misunderstanding arbitrarily, even if they find it difficult to say what they are distinguishing. A production can be consistent or inconsistent with the work, and this implies that there is something *in* the work — the meaning — with which it can enter into conflict.

One example that I find persuasive is given by modern productions of Wagner's *Ring*. It seems to me absurd that the Rhine-maidens should be seen swimming in a hydro-electric dam, or that Wotan should be fitted out in the accoutrements of an *haut-bourgeois* status-seeker (as in Chéreau's production at Bayreuth). This is stretching irony into sarcasm. If Chéreau's production triumphantly vindicates itself as a rendering of the dramatic content, this is not because, but in spite, of the symbolism adduced by the décor. The setting has all the character of 'associative' criticism — it is an extended whimsy which says nothing about the content of the work. To show this is, I recognize, difficult. But I think that it can be shown. For one thing, the settings borrow all the apparatus of a 'Marxised' reading of Wagner's drama, but they do so in such a way as to conflict with the Marxian meaning that is there. There is nothing absurd or whimsical about an interpretation that sees in the gold of the Rhine the collected forces of nature, or in the forswearing of love the necessary price for harnessing those forces and converting them into the 'means of production'. The transformation of nature into the golden ring of exchange-value is a logical consequence, as is the universal pursuit of that ring, its magic and its deep deception. The portrayal of alienated labour, of commodity and capital fetishism, the dependence of leisure on the broken bond that secures access to exchange-value, the underlying 'loss of love' which gives coherence to much of the Marxian critique of capitalism — all these follow quite logically, and can be heard in the musical relations between the leitmotivs of the score. But of course the interpretation requires that the stage directions be followed. The Rhine-maidens have to be closer to nature than Alberich: their world does not contain the insignia of 'production, distribution and exchange'. In particular it contains no hydro-electric dam. When one perceives that, then it seems that the score is already *saturated* with the kind of interpretation that Chéreau's designer wishes to impose on it, and that to make room for his décor one must detract from the significance that is there.

To establish even that tiny fragment of interpretation, I should have to refer to musical relations — for example, between the Rhine-maidens' song and that of the wood-bird, which represents the 'glimpse' of nature to the free agent who can belong to nature only through initiation, and not as a matter of course. (It is significant that in the Chéreau production, the wood-bird is caged.) The capacity to hear that kind of relation, and to hear, for example, the theme of Valhalla as a development of the ring motif, is not separable from musical culture. Such a culture, and the tradition which gives sense to it, could one day be swept from the earth, and in any case exists only locally. But it exists, independently of particular listeners and particular critics, and has the only kind of public accessibility that we can hope for in criticism. At the same time, it needs only the most delicate shift of emphasis for it to become apparent that, *whatever* I said in support of the interpretation offered, it could fall on deaf ears. And how could deaf ears be persuaded?

I wish to thank Elinor Shaffer and the referees appointed by *Comparative Criticism* for many useful criticisms of an earlier draft of this chapter.

The Meaning of Music

3 The Aesthetics of Music

There is little literature in the history of modern philosophy that is more exasperating than that devoted to the aesthetics of music. When the standard of philosophical competence is high enough to be taken seriously, the standard of musical competence is usually (as with Kant and Hegel) too low for the exercise to be worthwhile. Hardly any writer troubles himself with examples or analysis, and almost all rest their case in some vast and vague abstraction, such as 'form', 'imitation', or 'expression', without explaining how a work exemplifies it, or why it would matter if it did. Musical aesthetics has shown itself almost entirely unable to account for the character of auditory perception, or to explain the simplest of musical categories, such as melody, rhythm and harmony. A grain of philosophical sense would suggest that no theory of musical expression, for example, will be illuminating if unaccompanied by an explanation of those basic things. Yet even Hanslick — after Gurney, the most competent writer in the field — failed to see that he had not given that explanation and that, without it, his theory of music as an 'absolute' art was as unwarranted as the theories which he used it to attack. Consider Hanslick's definition of music, as *tönend bewegte Formen* (forms moved in sounding).[1] What does it mean to say that the forms of music 'move' or are 'moved'? It is fairly widely recognized that, at some level, the reference to musical movement is inescapable. (What would it be like to abolish 'high' and 'low', 'fast' and 'slow', 'far' and 'near', 'approaching' and 'receding', 'hollow' and 'filled', from our description of musical experience? The result might still be a description of sounds, but it would not be a description of tones). It is also fairly widely recognized that this reference to movement is in some sense metaphorical. For nothing in the world of sounds (nothing that we hear) moves, in the way that music moves. If that is so, however, a theory which tries to explain music in terms of musical movement is not a theory of music at all: it 'explains' its subject only by blocking the path to explanation. If we allow Hanslick to get away with assuming the existence of musical movement, why not allow his opponent to get away with assuming the existence of musical emotion? For although Hanslick is right to say that what we hear is neither a sentient thing, nor anything like a sentient thing, it is also true that it is not a thing in motion, nor anything like a thing in motion. Again, consider the eighteenth-century aesthetic of 'imitation'. It is well to argue that music 'copies' the movements of the human soul, or the gestures of the body, or whatever. But if the only grounds for saying so are that music moves in a similar way, then these are no grounds at all. For music does not move, and therefore does not move 'in a similar way'. Or rather, it does move, but only metaphorically, which is just as unhelpful. (You might as well say that Batteux did prove that music imitates, but only metaphorically; or that I have refuted him, but only metaphorically). At almost every point in traditional discussions this problem emerges, and nothing has been said to solve it, partly because everything has been said to prevent it from being perceived.

A related oversight of traditional musical aesthetics has been the failure to explain the all-important notion of musical understanding. Since eighteenth-century writers first began to replace the idea of musical 'imitation' with that of expression, the thought has been prevalent that music — or at least significant music — has a 'content , and that this content is what is understood by the receptive listener. The attraction of the theory is evident: it enables us to say, for example, why music moves us, and why it is important. (By contrast it is almost impossible to say why we should be interested in the fact that a piece of music imitates, say, a clock, a cuckoo, or a pair of rutting camels.) But the disadvantage of the theory of expression, in all its forms, is that it means nothing until accompanied by an analysis of musical understanding. Only Hegel, Hanslick and Wittgenstein seem to have recognized this point, and to have seen that it is crucial. If you take the point seriously, you see at once how inadequate are the currently fashionable 'semantic' and 'semiotic' theories of musical meaning. Anybody who is ingenious enough can interpret music as a language, or a code, or a system of signs; for example, by taking individual parts, structures, motifs and connections, and then correlating them with the objects, feelings and attitudes that they are supposed to symbolize. All that is required for this exercise is that the music should display syntactic structure (i.e., separately meaningful 'elements' which can be combined into meaningful wholes), and a 'field of reference' with which it can be conjoined. To express would then be to signify or stand for some item in the field of reference, according to rules of musical semantics. But of course, while the correlation of musical signs and musical 'meanings' is a task that any critic can set himself, it is not at all clear that it bears on the understanding of music. The real question is not whether this programme can be carried through (say, in the naive and illuminating manner of Deryck Cooke, or in the sophisticated and vacuous manner of Nattiez[2]), but whether it provides a genuine description of what is understood by the cultivated listener. An account of musical semantics must also be an account of musical 'competence': but without a theory of understanding, it is quite uncertain what musical competence amounts to. Maybe it has nothing whatsoever to do with the semantic analyses that have been proposed for it; maybe the relation between them is no closer than the relation between the ability to ride a horse, and the semantic interpretation of piebald markings (which could be dressed up, if you chose, as a kind of horsey syntax).

What, then, should a serious musical aesthetics attempt to do? It seems to me that it ought first to tell us what sounds are; the preoccupation of modern philosophy with the visual has been so overwhelming that the nature of sounds, as objects of perception, remains almost completely obscure. It ought also to tell us what tones are, and how, if at all, they are distinct from sounds. It should tell us what it is to perceive tones as organized, in the way that music is (or appears to be) organized: into rhythms, melodies, and harmonies. (What for example, is a harmony, and what distinguishes it from a cluster of simultaneous tones?) It should also attempt to display the nature of musical understanding, and its relation to musical experience, to musical analysis, and to aesthetic interest. Only then, when all those foundations are laid, will it be possible to make sense of such terms as 'expression', 'emotion' and 'form' as applied to music. However, a real beginning could then be envisaged, in this subject which has been for so long the victim of philosophical impetuosity. The chapters in this section explore some of the problems presented by such a 'foundational' approach to musical aesthetics. The first three — reprinted from the *New Grove Dictionary of Music* — describe major difficulties presented by the available ways of interpreting and criticizing Western music. They survey the history of music theory, and attempt to summarize the present perspectives which a philosopher might take. There follows an article on representation in music, which argues that there are grounds for treating music in terms which distinguish it from literature and painting. It emerges that the crucial notion to be analysed in a foundational aesthetics of music is that of musical understanding. The final chapter is devoted to a consideration of that idea.

4 Absolute Music

The term 'absolute music' denotes not so much an agreed idea as an aesthetic problem. The expression is of German origin, first appearing in the writings of Romantic philosophers and critics such as J. L. Tieck, J. G. Herder, W. H. Wackenroder, Jean Paul (Richter) and E. T. A. Hoffmann. It features in the controversies of the nineteenth century — for example, in Hanslick's spirited defence of *absolute Tonkunst* against the *Gesamtkunstwerk* of Wagner — and also in the abstractions of twentieth-century musical aesthetics. It names an ideal of musical purity, an ideal from which music has been held to depart in a variety of ways; for example, by being subordinated to words (as in song), to drama (as in opera), to some representational meaning (as in programme music), or even to the vague requirements of emotional expression. Indeed, it has been more usual to give a negative than a positive definition of the absolute in music. The best way to speak of a thing that claims to be 'absolute' is to say what it is not.

It is not word-setting. Songs, liturgical music and opera are all denied the status of absolute music. For in word-setting music is thought to depart from the ideal of purity by lending itself to independent methods of expression. The music has to be understood at least partly in terms of its contribution to the verbal sense. It follows that absolute music must at least be instrumental music (and the human voice may sometimes act as an instrument, as in certain works of Debussy, Delius and Holst). Liszt and Wagner insisted that the absence of words from music did not entail the absence of meaning. Liszt's *Programm-Musik* and Wagner's *Gesamtkunstwerk* both arose from the view that all music was essentially meaningful and no music could be considered more absolute than any other. This view gives rise to a further negative definition of the 'absolute' in music: it is music that has no external reference. So the imitation of nature in music is a departure from an absolute ideal; Vivaldi's concertos the 'Four Seasons' are less absolute than the *Art of Fugue*. The symphonic poem is also tainted with impurity, as is every other form of programme music.

The yearning for the absolute is not yet satisfied. Having removed representation from the ideal of music, critics have sought to remove expression as well. No music can be absolute if it seeks to be understood in terms of an extra-musical meaning, whether the meaning lies in a reference to external objects or in the expression of the human mind. Absolute music is now made wholly autonomous. Its raison d'être lies entirely within itself; it must be understood as an abstract structure bearing only accidental relation to the movement of the human soul. Liszt and Wagner claimed that there could be no absolute music in that sense; it is possible that even Hanslick might have agreed with them.

It is at this point that the concept of absolute music becomes unclear. Certainly it no longer corresponds to what Richter and Hoffmann had in mind. Both writers considered the purity of music — its quality as an 'absolute' art — to reside in the nature of its expressive powers and not in their total absence. For Richter music was absolute in that it expressed a presentiment of the divine in nature; for Hoffmann it became absolute through the attempt to express the infinite in the only form that renders the infinite intelligible to human feeling. To borrow the terminology of Hegel: music is absolute because it expresses the Absolute. (On that view, liturgical music is the most absolute of all.)

The notion of the 'absolute' in music has thus become inseparably entangled with the problem of musical expression. Is all music expressive, only some or none at all? The answer to that question will determine the usage of the term 'absolute' in criticism. To define the term negatively leads at once to an intractable philosophical problem. A positive definition has therefore been sought.

An analogy may be drawn with mathematics. Pure mathematics can be defined negatively: it is mathematics which is not applied. But that is shallow; for what is applied mathematics if not the application of an independent and autonomous structure of thought? One should therefore define pure mathematics in terms of the methods and structures by which it is understood. Similarly, it might be argued that music is absolute when it is not applied, or when it is not subjected to any purpose independent of its own autonomous movement. Absolute music must be understood as pure form, according to canons that are internal to itself. Unfortunately, such a positive definition of the term raises another philosophical problem: what is meant by 'understanding music'? And can there be a form of art which is understood in terms that are wholly internal to itself?

Attempts by the advocates of absolute music to answer those questions have centred on two ideas: objectivity and structure. Their arguments have been presented in this century most forcefully by the Austrian theorist Heinrich Schenker and by Stravinsky.[1] Music becomes absolute by being an 'objective' art, and it acquires objectivity through its structure. To say of music that it is objective is to say that it is understood as an object in itself, without recourse to any semantic meaning, external purpose or subjective idea. It becomes objective through producing appropriate patterns and forms. These forms satisfy us because we have an understanding of the structural relations which they exemplify. The relations are grasped by the ear in an intuitive act of apprehension, but the satisfaction that springs therefrom is akin to the satisfaction derived from the pursuit of mathematics. It is not a satisfaction that is open to everyone. Like mathematics, it depends on understanding, and understanding can be induced only by the establishment of a proper musical culture.

It is such a conception of the absolute in music that has figured most largely in modern discussions. It is in the minds of those who deny that music can be absolute, as of those who insist that it must be. It has inspired the reaction against Romanticism, and sought exemplification in the works of Hindemith, Stravinsky and the followers of Schoenberg. Indeed, the invention of twelve-note composition seemed to many to reveal that music was essentially a structural art, and that all the traditional effects of music could be renewed just so long as the new 'language' imitated the complexity of the classical forms. (Schoenberg did not share the enthusiasm of his disciples for such a theory: for him music had been, and remained, an essentially expressive medium.)

It should be noted that 'absolute' music, so defined, means more than 'abstract' music. There are other abstract arts, including architecture and some forms of painting. To call them abstract is to say that they are not representational. It is not to imply that they are to be understood by reference to no external purpose and no subjective state of mind. An abstract painting does not have to lack expression. Yet 'absolute' music is an ideal that will not allow even that measure of impurity.

As an ideal it certainly existed before the Teutonic jargon of its name. Boethius and Tinctoris gave early expression to it, and even Zarlino was under the influence of its charm. Paradoxically, however, the rise of instrumental music and the development of Classical forms saw the temporary disappearance of the absolute ideal. Only after Herder and his followers had introduced the word, and Wagner (through his opposition to it) the concept, did the ideal once more find expression in serious aesthetic theories.

The advocacy of absolute music has brought with it a view of musical understanding that is as questionable as anything written by Liszt in defence of the symphonic poem. It is of course absurd to suppose that one understands Smetana's *Vltava* primarily by understanding what it 'means'. For that seems to imply that the grasp of melody, development, harmony and musical relations are all subordinate to a message that could have been expressed as well in words. But so too is it absurd to suppose that one has understood a Bach fugue when one has a grasp of all the structural relations that exist among its parts. The understanding listener is not a computer. The logic of Bach's fugues must be heard: it is understood in experience and not in thought. And why should not the musical experience embrace pleasure, feeling and evocation just as much as pure structured sound? Hearing the chorus 'Sind Blitze sind Donner' from the *St Matthew Passion* may provide a renewed sense of the significance of the *Art of Fugue,* and that sense may originate in a recognition of the emotional energy that underlies all Bach's fugal writing. Clearly, however 'absolute' a piece of music may be, it can retain our interest only if there is something more to understanding it than an appreciation of mere patterns of sound.

5 Programme Music

The Term and its Meaning

The term 'programme music' was introduced by Liszt, who also invented the expression 'symphonic poem' to describe what is perhaps the most characteristic instance of it. He defined a programme as a 'preface added to a piece of instrumental music, by means of which the composer intends to guard the listener against a wrong poetical interpretation, and to direct his attention to the poetical idea of the whole or to a particular part of it'.[1] Very few of the programmes of Liszt's own symphonic poems are of a narrative character. He did not regard music as a direct means of describing objects; rather he thought that music could put the listener in the same frame of mind as could the objects themselves. In this way, by suggesting the emotional reality of things, music could indirectly represent them. Such an idea — already familiar in the writings of Rousseau — was also expressed by Beethoven when he described the Pastoral Symphony as 'mehr Empfindung als Malerey' ('more feeling than painting').

The close connection in some of Liszt's thinking between 'narrative' and 'emotional' depiction has led to confusion over the use of the term 'programme music'. Some prefer to attach the term purely to instrumental music with a narrative or descriptive 'meaning' (for example, music that purports to depict a scene or a story). Others have so broadened its application as to use the term for all music that contains an extra-musical reference, whether to objective events or to subjective feelings. The responsibility for this broadening of the term lies partly with Friedrich Niecks, whose romantic enthusiasm caused him to overlook, in his influential work on the subject (1956), the vital aesthetic distinction between representation and expression.[2] It is the narrow sense of the term which is the legitimate one. The other sense is not only so wide as to be virtually meaningless; it also fails to correspond to the actual usage of composers and critics since Liszt's invention of the term.

Programme music, which has been contrasted with absolute music, is distinguished by its attempt to depict objects and events. Furthermore, it claims to derive its logic from that attempt. It does not merely echo or imitate things which have an independent reality; the development of programme music is determined by the development of its theme. The music moves in time according to the logic of its subject and not according to autonomous principles of its own. As Liszt wrote: 'In programme music ... the return, change, modification, and modulation of the motifs are conditioned by their relation to a poetic idea ... All exclusively musical considerations, though they should not be neglected, have to be subordinated to the action of the given subject.'[3]

Liszt thought of himself as putting forward a new ideal for symphonic music, an ideal that had been foreshadowed in Beethoven's Pastoral Symphony and in certain works of Mendelssohn, Schumann and Berlioz, but which he nevertheless thought to be absent from the body of classical music. He considered the idea of exalting the narrative associations of music into a principle of composition to be incompatible with the continuance of traditional symphonic forms. The term 'programme music' came to be applied not only to music with a story but also music designed to represent a character (Strauss's *Don Juan* and *Don Quixote*) or to describe a scene or phenomenon (Debussy's *La Mer*). What is common to all these is the attempt to 'represent' objects in music; but a certain confusion has entered the use of the term by its application to any form of musical 'depiction', whether instrumental, or vocal, or incidental to an action on the stage. Properly speaking, however, programme music is music with a programme. Further, to follow Liszt's conception, programme music is music that seeks to be understood in terms of its programme; it derives its movement and its logic from the subject it attempts to describe. On that view it would be wrong to call, for example, Couperin's *Le tic-toc-choc* a piece of programme music. The logic of Couperin's piece is purely musical, even if its thematic material is derived from the imitation of a clock. By contrast, the logic of Liszt's symphonic poem *Tasso* is (according to the composer) derived from the events of Tasso's life: it is the sequence of those events, and their intrinsic nature, that dictate the development of the music. (But it should be said that Liszt's own programme music did not always follow his own theoretical precepts.)

However the term is used, it is clear that the idea of music's representing something is essential to the concept of programme music. It is important to understand, therefore, what might be meant by 'representation' in music. The first distinction to make is that between representation and expression. It is only recently that attempts have been made to formulate the distinction with any precision, and there is no agreement as to the relation between the terms. But that a distinction exists seems obvious to any lover of the arts. A painting may represent a subject (the Crucifixion, say) and it may also express an emotion towards that subject. To represent a subject is to give a description or characterization of it: it is to say (in words or in images) what the subject is like. Such a description may or may not be accompanied by an expression of feeling. Furthermore, there can be expressions of emotion that are not accompanied by representation. Mozart's *Masonic Funeral Music* is certainly an expression of grief, but it contains no attempt to represent or describe the object of grief. It has been argued that all music expresses emotion. If that is so, then, unless some distinction can be made between representation and expression, all music would have to be regarded as representational. To say that would lead to the conclusion that there was no essential distinction between music and painting in their relation to the world.

It is a matter of dispute whether music is capable of literally representing its subject, in the way that painting and literature represent theirs.[4] What passes for representation might often be more accurately described as 'imitation', as when a piece of music mimics the sound of a cuckoo. That there is a difference between representation and imitation is clear. An architectural detail can imitate the curve of a seashell without becoming a representation; or a man can imitate another's manner without representing it. Representation is essentially descriptive: it involves a reference to objects in the world and an attempt to describe them. Imitation is merely copying, and its intention may be no more than decorative. Examples of musical imitation have abounded from the very beginning of music. Indeed, both Plato and Aristotle ascribed an imitative character to the music of their time. It is nonetheless debatable whether music is made representational by imitation alone. Certainly Liszt had more than mere imitation in mind when he introduced the concept of programme music.

It is seldom clear what is meant when it is said that music can represent things. The question arises whether music can actually describe the world or whether it is merely evocative. If representation in music were merely a matter of evocation, it would be misleading to class it as representation, for that would imply an unwarranted analogy with the descriptive arts of literature and painting. That is why Liszt insisted that true programme music had a narrative or descriptive element which was essential to the understanding of it. In other words, for Liszt the subject has become part of the meaning of the music; to listen to the music with false associations was, in Liszt's view, actually to misunderstand it. Whether or not there is 'programme music' in Liszt's sense, it is clear that it would provide the most plausible example of representation in music. It is further clear that in its strictest sense programme music does not include music that is merely expressive, imitative or evocative. It is doubtful even whether Debussy's *La Mer* is a description rather than an evocation of its subject, although the titles of the movements seem to suggest a certain 'narrative' component to its meaning (for example, one of the movements is entitled 'De l'aube à midi sur la mer' — from dawn to noon on the sea — which prompted Satie to remark that he particularly liked the moment at 11.15).

Programme music must further be distinguished from the 'representational' music that accompanies words, whether in lieder, in oratorio or on the stage. While all these share devices with programme music and have influenced it continuously throughout the history of music, it is still necessary to distinguish music which purports to carry its narrative meaning within itself, from music which is attached to a narrative arising independently, whether through the words of a song or through the action of a dramatic work. The distinction is not absolute, but, unless it is made, the idea of programme music as a separate genre must remain entirely illegitimate.

History of Programme Music

When Liszt invented the term 'programme music' he was aware that he had not invented the thing that he sought to describe. Berlioz's symphonies are essentially narrative in conception; so too is Weber's *Konzertstück* for piano and orchestra, a descriptive work in one continuous movement (made up of several sections in different tempos) which was one of the first Romantic examples of the symphonic poem. One of the difficulties involved in tracing the history of programme music lies in the elusiveness of the distinctions discussed above: whether all 'representational' music should be considered programme music; whether 'imitation' should be counted as a species of representation; and whether a deliberate expressive character is sufficient to rank as a 'programme' in Liszt's sense. Clearly there are many different ways of deriving a history according to the way in which those fundamental critical (and philosophical) questions are answered. For example, the French harpsichord composers of the seventeenth and eighteenth centuries were in the habit of giving titles to their pieces. To some writers on this subject the presence of a title is sufficient to bring a piece under the rubric 'programme music'. But to others that way of thought involves a confusion, for it seems not to distinguish a piece that expresses some emotion suggested by the title from another that either evokes its subject or (in some more concrete sense) actually attempts to describe it. Many critics of Couperin's music, for example, would prefer to speak of the relation between his keyboard pieces and their ostensible 'subjects' as one of expression and not one of representation. The borderline between expression and representation is a hazy one, and it is often impossible to say of a piece by Rameau or Couperin on which side of the borderline it might lie.

If mere imitation is not regarded as a sufficient criterion of programme music, it must be concluded that the history of the genre is considerably shorter than might otherwise appear. It seems to have no medieval examples. Even Jannequin's famous chanson 'La bataille' or 'La guerre' (published in 1529 and thought to refer to the Battle of Marignan of 1515), is hardly to be considered true programme music: while it imitates the sounds of battle, there is no narrative sequence to those sounds and no attempt to subordinate the musical structure to the evolution of an extra-musical theme. Less certain cases are provided by suites in which the titles of each piece form a narrative sequence. Byrd's *Battel,* a suite for keyboard of fifteen pieces — entitled (for example) 'The Marche to the Fight', 'The Retraite' and 'The Burying of the Dead' — does, in a sense, have a programme, but the programme serves to unite the separate musical units and to explain their expressive characters; only in a very limited sense do the pieces attempt also to describe the scenes referred to.

Other puzzling cases are those in which a composer declares himself to have been inspired by some literary or artistic source. Again there are Renaissance and Baroque examples of composers who have written pieces under the inspiration of pictures. Biber, for example, wrote in about 1671 a set of fifteen mysteries for violin and keyboard after copperplate engravings of Bible themes; there is an earlier instance by Froberger. Such cross-fertilization between a representational art (such as engraving) and music is a familiar feature of more recent music. Mussorgsky's *Pictures at an Exhibition* provides a Romantic example of the same kind of musical device. Here, though, there is the added representational refinement of a 'promenade' linking some of the pieces, indicating the presence of a 'narrator' in the music, a kind of 'reflector' in Henry James's sense, who remains the true subject matter of the narrative. By that device Mussorgsky's work comes nearer to the central examples of programme music such as the symphonic poems of Liszt. An even more remarkable example of cross-fertilization is the quartet by Janáček composed after reading Tolstoy's novella *The Kreutzer Sonata,* itself inspired by Beethoven's violin sonata. The mere fact that Janáček's quartet was so inspired no more makes it into a programmatic narrative of the events in Tolstoy's story than it makes Tolstoy's story into a 'representation' of Beethoven's sonata. Inspiration, even when consciously referred to, cannot suffice to make music into programme music.

There is no doubt that programme music was established by 1700, when Johann Kuhnau published his six Bible sonatas. Each of them is preceded by a summary of the story that the music is meant to convey, and each is divided into recognizable parts, corresponding to the events of the narrative. The pictorialism is naive compared with the symphonic poems of Liszt and Strauss, but there is no doubt that the music lays claim to a narrative significance or that the composer intended that significance to be a proper part of the understanding of the music. Later examples of similar narrative music are Vivaldi's concertos the 'Four Seasons', which are prefaced by short 'programmes' in verse, and Couperin's *Apothéoses*, extended representations of Lully and Corelli ascending to find their proper places of rest upon Parnassus, in which each section refers to a separate episode in their apotheosis. Comparable pieces were written by Telemann and other French-influenced composers. The development of such programme music was affected by the French *ballet de cour*, which required just such pictorial accompaniments to its solemn and dramatic performances; but by the mid-eighteenth century programme music had emancipated itself from any suggestion of a balletic meaning. A notable example is the long orchestral work by Ignazio Raimondi called *Les aventures de Télémaque dans l'isle de Calypso*, based on Fénélon's epic poem. This, published in 1777, includes one of the first attempts to diversify the 'narrative' by representing its several characters in different ways: Calypso, for example, is represented by a flute, and Telemachus by a solo violin.

By the time of Beethoven even the most abstract and classical of musical forms had become capable of bearing a programmatic meaning. The Pastoral Symphony is but one example of a piece that seems to be straining to break free of the constraints imposed by its Classical format in the interests of a pictorial idea. The 'Lebewohl' Sonata Op.81a is another. Both have precedents, in the eighteenth-century depictions of Nature and in Bach's capriccio for his departing brother. Like Vivaldi's 'Four Seasons' and Dittersdorf's symphonies based on Ovid's *Metamorphoses*, they attempt to combine a narrative depiction with a rigorous musical form. This led Beethoven's admirers to suppose that the idea of a 'purely musical' structure was after all an illusion, and that the greatness of Beethoven's symphony, in particular its architectural perfection, was of a piece with its profound extra-musical meaning, and that great symphonic writing was but the expression of an independent poetic idea. This impression was enhanced by Beethoven's hint that an understanding of his sonata Op.31 No.2 could be induced by a reading of Shakespeare's *The Tempest*. Schering (1936) attempted to explain Beethoven's entire output as programmatic reflections on themes from Shakespeare and Goethe.[5]

Whatever one thinks of those speculations, which have been further extended to the symphonies of Haydn and Mozart (the French theorist Momigny even set a verbal text to a Mozart quartet movement as an interpretation of it[6]), there is no doubt that the greatest step towards true programme music in the Romantic sense was made not by Beethoven but by Berlioz, who introduced into musical representation for the first time a distinction vital to any true narrative portrayal of things in the world, the distinction between subject and object. By his use of the solo viola in his symphony *Harold en Italie* and by his exploitation of its deeply subjective tones he was able to create a sharp division between the individual protagonist — the feeling, suffering and rejoicing being at the centre of the narrative — and the external circumstances of his experience. Berlioz also introduced the device of the *idée fixe*, a melody representative of a character or feeling, which reappears in a variety of forms and develops with the changing circumstances. This was a substantial step towards the Wagnerian *leitmotif*, through which device the narrative pretensions of music were to receive their most striking confirmation. The *leitmotif*, a theme which is associated with a character, a circumstance or an idea, and which develops sometimes out of all recognition in order to convey the evolution of its narrative theme, permitted representation in music without a hint of imitation. By means of this device later composers, in particular Liszt and Richard Strauss, were able to associate specific themes with a fixed representational meaning. The traditional devices survived, and with Strauss imitation was carried to extremes never previously envisaged. But it was through the leitmotif above all that music was able to emulate the descriptive range of language and that Liszt was able to approach the ideal he had set himself, the ideal of a music that could not be understood even as music unless the correct poetic conception was invoked in the hearer's mind.

It is possible to doubt that Liszt ever realized that ideal, or indeed that it is capable of realization, because the conception of musical understanding underlying the theory of programme music may not be a coherent one.[7] Nonetheless, once the theoretical foundations of the genre had been laid, programme music became highly important. Indeed the 'programme' survived as a basic determining idea in symphonic music until well into the twentieth century, receiving no serious intellectual setback until the reaction led by Schoenberg in Vienna, by Bartók in Hungary, and by the cosmopolitan Stravinsky. It gave rise to many of the great works of Czech and Russian nationalism, to the symphonies of Mahler and to the French school of orchestral writing.

The concept of programme music also led to the impressionism of Ravel and Debussy. But it is doubtful that their music should be regarded as truly programmatic in the Romantics' sense; impressionism may rather have constituted a partial reaction against the narrative pretensions of the symphonic poem — it was another attempt to put evocation in the place of narrative. It would be better therefore to compare Debussy's *Préludes* with the *ordres* of Couperin, and to consider that the titles (which Debussy was at pains to put not at the beginning but at the end of the pieces) serve to indicate an expressive atmosphere rather than a definite descriptive significance. Indeed, it seems that Debussy did not intend a knowledge of the subject to be essential to an understanding of his music. It is from Debussy's pure style and clean textures that much of the most abstract of modern music has taken its inspiration.

By the end of the nineteenth century the increasing afflatus of Romanticism had served once again to destroy the distinction between representational and expressive intentions in music. So long as music aims to capture a particular episode, a particular sequence of events or a particular human character, then its representational claims are not in doubt. When, however, it attaches itself to a programme phrased entirely in emotional or quasi-religious abstractions, it is doubtful that it can be considered to be a depiction rather than an expression of its subject matter. For example Tatyana Schloezer wrote a programme for the Symphony No.3, 'Le divin poème', by Skriabin (whose mistress she was) beginning:

> *The Divine Poem* represents the evolution of the human spirit, which, torn from an entire past of beliefs and mysteries which it surmounts and overturns, passes through Pantheism and attains to a joyous and intoxicated affirmation of its liberty and its unity with the universe (the divine 'Ego').

That is an example of the 'programme' at its most self-important. It is also an example of the degeneration of the concept from something relatively precise to something entirely vaporous. For Skriabin, Mahler and their contemporaries the 'programme' was on the verge of becoming irrelevant to an understanding of the music. The entire burden of the musical movement lay now in expression; representation had been cast aside. In so far as the programme continued to exist it was a source of exasperating literary preciosities rather than of genuine musical ideas. It is hardly surprising that composers soon began to turn their backs on programme music and find their way to expression through more abstract musical means. In the 1960s and 1970s, however, some revival of programmatic or semi-programmatic devices could be noted, for example in the works of Maxwell Davies, Leeuw, Norby and Schafer.

6 The Nature of Musical Expression

In its simplest sense, the term 'expression' is applied to those elements of a musical performance that depend on personal response and which vary between different interpretations. In this sense a piano teacher may enjoin his pupil to 'put in the expression', i.e. to play a piece with a certain articulation, tempo and phrasing. It is not clear how this use of the term relates to the concept that occurs in music criticism (as when a piece of music is said to express some emotion, outlook or idea). What does it mean to say of a piece of music that it has expression, or that it expresses, or is expressive of, a certain state of mind? The question is a philosophical one, and reflects the profound uncertainty in contemporary aesthetics over the most important concept bequeathed to it by the Romantic movement.

Understanding of the Term 'Expression'

In every age it has been accepted that there is some relation between music and the passions — a relation, say, of instruction (Plato), of imitation (Aristotle), of arousal (Descartes[1], Mersenne), of 'fusion' (Santayana[2]) or simply of some mysterious 'correspondence' about which nothing further can be said (St Augustine). It was from a sense of the emotional power of music that the Greek philosophers debated its political significance, that the Council of Trent considered how to subdue its influence in the liturgy, and that Calvin warned against its appeal in his preface to the Geneva Psalter. Yet the relation between music and emotion has remained obscure, and even when, partly under the influence of Rousseau and Diderot, the term 'expression' began to be preferred as the proper name for this relation, philosophers remained baffled as to its detailed character.[3]

'Expression' must be distinguished from 'evocation'. To say that a piece of music expresses melancholy is not to say that it evokes (or arouses) melancholy. To describe a piece of music as expressive of melancholy is to give a reason for listening to it; to describe it as arousing or evoking melancholy is to give a reason for avoiding it. Some kinds of popular music, being musically blank, express nothing, but still arouse melancholy. Expression, where it exists, is integral to the aesthetic character of a piece of music, and must not be confused with any accidental relation to the listener. For similar reasons 'expression' must not be confused with 'association', despite the strong arguments for the confusion given by the eighteenth-century followers of John Locke (among them Alexander Malcolm, J. F. Lampe and Joseph Addison).[4]

It may be said of a performance that a certain passage is played 'with expression'. When it is said of a piece of music (say, of Schubert's *Erlkönig*) that it has 'expression', it seems natural to ask: what does it express? There is thus a presumption that expression in music is transitive: to have expression is to express something (in this case a feeling of terror). The piano teacher (or the critic), however, seems to be talking of expression in some intransitive sense, that is, in a sense which forbids the performer's question: 'what am I expected to express?'. That there are these two senses of the term 'expression' is made clear by the example of a face: a face may bear an expression of anguish, grief, etc., or simply the 'particular expression' visible in its features. Two faces with an expression of anger would, in the transitive sense, have the same expression, since they express the same thing; but in another sense they might have quite different expressions, and in this intransitive sense it is impossible to give rules of expression. It is impossible to say which physical features in a face are responsible for its expression. If any feature is responsible then all are.

The Impossibility of Rules

This feature of expression — that similarities in expression do not follow physical similarities in any easily specifiable way — can also be observed as a feature of 'expression' in music. Consider ex. 1, from the last movement of Beethoven's Ninth Symphony. Often one may hear the fourth and fifth

Ex. 1

etc.

quoted bars hummed or whistled as on the lower staff: a very small change, but one that destroys the expression of the melody — its character (for example, as an answer to the passionate voices that had preceded it) is lost

in such a rendering. Conversely, there may be similarities in expression between passages radically different in their physical character as sound: compare, for example, the passage from the 'Eroica' Symphony (ex.2a) with that from Stravinsky's Symphony in Three Movements (ex.2b).

One fact might seem to become apparent from such examples: that there are no definite rules of expression in music, no rules of the form 'if the music has features A, B, C then it will be expressive'. For to be expressive is to have a certain character, and that character is not determined by any one physical feature of the music but rather by the totality of its features operating together. It is therefore difficult, perhaps impossible, to say, in advance of the particular case, which features can be altered with impunity and which are vital to the effect. Sometimes the opposite seems true. Consider, for example, the 'Todesklage' from Wagner's *Ring* (ex.3a). This theme contains a tense, tragic and yet questioning expression. One might

Ex. 3
(a) (transposed)

(b)

(c)

wish to attribute that expression to the accumulated suspensions, together with the final chord of the 7th which gives to the whole an air of incompleteness. And it might seem that in so diagnosing the effect one has made reference to rules: suspensions introduce tension, 7ths uncertainty, and so on. Remove the suspensions, as in ex.3b, and the tension goes. Alter the final cadence and we have (changing the rhythm slightly) the serene introduction to Mendelssohn's 'Scottish' Symphony (ex.3c). But could one really have predicted that expressive transformation outside the context provided by Wagner's melody? And could one have known, in advance of the particular case, that, in removing Wagner's suspensions, one would arrive at an effect of serenity rather than insipidity, or that in adding suspensions to Mendelssohn's theme one would arrive at an effect of tragic tension rather than, say, cluttered portentousness? Clearly not. By all the 'rules' of composition a descending scale, for example, ought not to wear any particular expression; it ought to be an emotional blank, as in the banal theme from Beethoven's Trio in E flat Op.1 No.1 (ex.4d). But consider the slow descent of an E minor scale (changing to A minor) in the third movement of Bruckner's Eighth Symphony (ex.4b). Here, because of the context provided by the cello theme that precedes the passage, the effect is of sublime tranquillity. A detail that could never have acquired expression because of any rule gains it from its context.

Idealism

Insistence on the distinction between transitive and intransitive notions of expression naturally risks the question: why use the term 'expression' if there is not something important in common between them? This raises one of the most plausible of the Romantic theories of art, that of the Idealist Hegel.[5] For Hegel, art could only be expression, on account of its character as an embodiment of the human mind. Art derives aesthetic, and indeed moral significance, from its relation to 'ideas', from the fact that it can be understood only as a characteristically human product, as something that gives embodiment to mental life and conceptions. In some such way, Hegel might have argued, the expression on a face is understood, and even if the face is not associated with any particular state of mind, one is still justified in describing it as having an expression. For it must be treated as a sign of mental possibilities: there is no other way of seeing it, and the idea of studying the geometry of a face and disregarding its character as a revelation of mental life is intrinsically absurd.

Such a view helps to explain how it is that, even when referring to an expression in the intransitive sense, one may still go on to describe that expression in mental terms without implying the existence of any particular state of mind. For example, a face might be said to have a sad or a puzzled expression without any implication that it expresses sadness or puzzlement. Similarly, even in the case of the critic's or the teacher's concept of expression — which is clearly intransitive in the sense we have been considering — one may go on to describe the expression, saying, for example, that a particular passage should be given a mysterious or a melancholy or a wistful air.

All that seems to suggest a close connection between the transitive and the intransitive notions of expression. And indeed it has been charac-teristic of the Idealist tradition in philosophy that it has attempted to run together the transitive and the intransitive concepts, claiming, for example, that even if art does express feeling, the feeling expressed can be defined only through the expression, so that feeling and expression are inseparable and, being inseparable, incapable of being joined by any contingent relation. If there were such a relation, then expression would be governed by rules, rules which state how to express feeling A, how to express feeling B and so on; and that, as we have seen, contradicts one of our deepest intuitions about the nature of art. The argument belongs to the Italian Idealist Benedetto Croce.[6] It was borrowed by the English philosopher R. G. Collingwood in formulating his celebrated distinction between art and craft, according to which craft is a means to an end and must therefore be conducted according to the rules laid down by that end, whereas art is not a means but an end in itself, governed by no external purpose.[7] But since art is also, for Collingwood, essentially expression, expression cannot be construed as the giving of form to separately identifiable feelings or ideas. The feeling must reside in the form itself and be obtainable exclusively in that form. If it were otherwise, art would be simply another kind of craft, the craft of giving expression to pre-existing and independently identifiable states of mind.

It was Wittgenstein who first distinguished the transitive and intransitive senses of such terms as 'expression' and who pointed out the importance of the distinction for musical theory. Obscurely, however, an awareness of that distinction underlay much of the nineteenth-century dissatisfaction with Romantic aesthetics. For the Romantic theory — according to which music was an expression of something, of an idea (Hegel), of the Will (Schopenhauer), of 'intuitions' (Croce) or of feelings (Collingwood) — seems to try to have it both ways, saying that there was indeed something expressed by music, something which would perhaps explain the value of music, and yet, at the same time, refusing to allow that that thing could be identified except in terms of the particular piece of music that embodied it. In other words, it seems to want artistic expression to be both transitive and intransitive at once. In doing so it comes close to self-contradiction. In reaction to the Romantic theory, Edmund Gurney attempted to re-establish the view of musical expression as essentially intransitive, and indeed as equivalent to the critic's or the teacher's concept. He wrote:

> we often call music which stirs us more *expressive* than music which does not: and we call great music *significant*, or talk of its *import*, in contrast to poor music, which seems meaningless and insignificant; without being able, or dreaming we are able to connect these general terms with anything expressed or signified.[8]

Gurney went on to emphasize the teacher's concept of expression, arguing that one does not look for passion in music in order to know how it is to be played; an understanding of expression is constituted by a desire to play in this way or that way, and it is that which must be taught. Such a thought comes close to a view that may (with some hesitation) be attributed to Wittgenstein: the view that a theory of musical expression is primarily a theory of the understanding and appreciation of expressive music.

Expression, Understanding, Emotion

It seems wrong to imagine that one could give an account of meaning in language while saying nothing about understanding language. Similarly, to follow Wittgenstein, it would be wrong to give a theory of expression in music which was not a theory of understanding musical expression; and that requires a total theory of understanding music. There is an essential connection between grasping the expression of a passage and understanding the passage, and, in a performer, 'understanding' means 'playing with understanding'. A consideration of what that involves entails, for example, considering what it would be to play the violin theme of Bach's aria 'Erbarme dich' (ex.5) with understanding. A player who understands puts the right emphasis on the slide at the beginning of bar 1, lingers just slightly on the D, perhaps leaves a breath at the end of the second bar. He does not necessarily possess knowledge of some emotion, intention or idea that the music is purporting to communicate. His knowledge is essentially a practical knowledge, not a species of theoretical insight. A grasp of expression is no more than part of the complex activity of understanding music, an activity which has as its aim not the insight into particular states of mind but rather the performance and enjoyment of music.

Ex. 5

etc.

Such a view of musical expression accommodates readily the sense, which many people have, that there is never only one way of describing musical expression, that every piece is open to new interpretation, and that no critic can fix for all time the meaning or expressive value of a particular musical work. For there will be, on this theory, as many 'expressions' to a piece of music as there are ways of understanding it, and just as a present-day way of understanding the Bach example need in no way correspond to the way in which it was understood by his contemporaries, so also may the 'expression' which the music wears today differ from that which was familiar to listeners in early eighteenth-century Germany.

However, despite all the scepticism that has been heaped on Romantic aesthetics, the popular view remains essentially that of Rousseau and Diderot: music evokes emotion because it expresses emotion. Music is the middle term in an act of emotional communication, and it is by virtue of that role that music acquires its value. Nor is this view — which involves a commitment to a transitive theory of expression — the exclusive property of Romanticism. It was foreshadowed, for example, in the *Musurgia* of Athanasius Kircher (1650), and to a certain extent even earlier in the works of Zarlino and Galilei.[9] Moreover, while the influence of French eighteenth-century thought is certainly apparent in Romantic music, it could hardly be said that any true break in the actual practice of composition was brought about by these theories. Whatever might provoke descriptions of Beethoven's late quartets in terms of the expression of feeling must surely provoke similar descriptions of the music of Josquin, Victoria or Dowland. And there is ample evidence that in all ages composers themselves have wished to characterize their music in mental and emotional terms. This we can see, for example, in the titles given by Lully, Couperin and Rameau to their keyboard pieces, or in the letters of Mozart and Beethoven; even Bach is said to have admired Couperin for the 'voluptuous melancholy' of his themes. Of course, there have been exceptions. The most notable was that great devotee of the 'classical', Stravinsky, who regarded the treatment of music as expression as nothing short of a conspiracy to subvert true musical values by measuring music against a standard extrinsic to its aims and inspiration.[10] But Stravinsky, eloquent as he was, did not succeed in establishing his view of the total autonomy of musical practice, and his severe 'classicism' sorts ill with the deeply expressionist tendency of eighteenth-century aesthetics, the aesthetics of that period when music, according to Stravinsky, existed in its purest and least adulterated form.

Criticism, Analysis

Can the popular view answer the challenge in the preceding section — 'Expression, understanding, emotion'? That is, can it be incorporated into an acceptable theory of musical understanding? If not, then it will lead to a concept of expression that plays no part in describing the appreciation or evaluation of music, a concept that is musically irrelevant.

In fact, musical criticism may provide an understanding of music and yet never mention expression. Consider, for example, the criticism of Tovey, or the structural analysis of Schenker and his school.[11] Such criticism and analysis leads to understanding by drawing attention to musical relations, details of structure and development, thematic similarities, and so on. It is true that structural criticism may also refer to the 'mood' of a piece; and it is also true that, since the work of Tovey and (more recently) Charles Rosen, critics will describe the structural axioms of Classical music in 'dramatic' terms.[12] However, each of those ideas seems rooted in a firmly intransitive notion of musical significance. The 'mood' and the 'drama' are there in the notes, and cannot be described in terms extraneous to the musical movement. Among the works of Romantic criticism, the most valuable passages are not those where the critic attempts to diagnose an emotional state but those where he reflects on musical structure. And surprisingly, not only in E. T. A. Hoffmann, but even in Wagner, emotional diagnosis is only a part, and often a very small part, of the critical description.[13]

But the argument is inconclusive. There has been important musical criticism of a wholly expressionist nature: perhaps Kierkegaard's long essay on *Don Giovanni* provides the most striking example.[14] Moreover, it could be that the relative silence of critics on the subject of emotion merely reflects the truth of another Romantic dogma — that emotions are in any case difficult to describe in words, and more properly the subject of manifestation than of analysis.

There are further difficulties for the popular view. The first, though not serious, deserves mention on account of its frequent occurrence in the literature. To speak of music as expressing states of mind might seem to imply that those states of mind must be attributed to the composer, in which case the judgement becomes open to refutation from the facts of the composer's life, facts that would normally be considered irrelevant to an understanding of the music. (Thus it would be wrong to describe the first movement of Mozart's Symphony No.41 as an expression of joy when we come to learn how unhappy the composer was at the time of writing it.) Such an objection would be misguided. Dramatic poetry, for example, is bound to be expressive of emotion in some transitive sense, and yet it would be absurd to say that it expresses the emotions of the poet. We cannot think that Shakespeare shared the sentiments of Iago or Racine those of Phaedra. In dramatic poetry the words express the imagined feelings of an imaginary character, and the poet attempts to create for his audience both the feeling and the personality who suffers it. Why should the same not be true of music?

A more serious objection may be found among the many relevant points raised by Hanslick.[15] This objection asks: what are the objects of the feelings expressed by music? Most forms of art said to express emotion are also representational: they describe, depict or refer to the world. It is indeed difficult to see how emotions can be expressed in the absence of representation. For every emotion requires an object: fear is fear of something, anger is anger about something, and so on. Any attempt to distinguish emotions one from another must be in terms of their characteristic objects and in terms of the thoughts that define those objects. It would seem to follow that an artistic medium which, like music, can neither represent objects nor convey specific thoughts about them is logically debarred from expressing emotion. Such was Hanslick's argument, and it is marked, like the rest of his short but influential treatise, by a philosophical seriousness and competence that have few rivals in the field of musical aesthetics. It is the inability of music to describe and represent the world — its narrative incompetence, as it were — that has most of all given rise to misgivings over the concept of expression in music, misgivings seldom felt in the discussion of poetry or representational art. For, when the objection is made, that the feelings conveyed by music can never be put into words, and so no serious agreement can ever be reached as to their quality or nature, the point is really that, since nothing can be said about the objects of musical feeling, nothing can be said about the feeling itself. To say, as Mendelssohn did (letter of 28 October 1842), that musical emotion is indescribable because it is too precise for words, is not an answer to Hanslick's objection. Precision of emotion is always and necessarily consequent upon precision of thought. In other words, a precise emotion requires a precise situation, and that in turn requires a precise representation. Moreover, the complementary view — espoused by Mahler when he asserted that the need to express himself in music, rather than in words, came only when indefinable emotions made themselves felt[16] — risks once again a return to the intransitive notion of expression: how can one distinguish music's having an indefinable 'expression' from its being mysteriously related to an indefinable thing?

Language, Reference, Information Theory

It is perhaps an awareness of this last difficulty that has led musical theorists to seek for ways of construing music as a vehicle of discursive thought. The most popular suggestion has been to interpret music as a language. Among those to have attempted such an interpretation is Deryck Cooke, who drew up a kind of 'lexicon' for classical music, citing examples of correspondences, persisting over a prolonged period of musical history, between particular shapes of phrase and particular kinds of expression.[17] In terms of this musical lexicon he has offered interpretations of entire movements, interpretations which attribute a narrative development to the music and offer a continuous 'meaning' to the movement as a whole. Such a theory is open to serious objections. For example, it is not clear how one is supposed to discover that the descending minor triad signifies, as Cooke says, a 'passive sorrow'. The examples given suggest that the connection be discovered through the study of vocal music, by understanding a common reference in the accompanying words. In that case, one may object, the rules of 'meaning' are derived extraneously, and not from any linguistic capacity of the music. It may be that the descending minor triad is appropriate to the setting of certain feelings; but does that relation of appropriateness have to be described in linguistic terms? After all, black is the appropriate colour to wear at a funeral, burgundy the appropriate thing to drink with roast duck, anger the appropriate response to an insult. Does every human practice, then, amount to a language? To accept that would be to remove from the idea of language everything that is distinctive of it. In particular, meanings can be assigned to the words of spoken language only because what is said can be interpreted in terms of the true and the false. But the concepts of truth and falsehood, even on Cooke's view, are not properly attributed to music. Some such objection can be raised against philosophers (the most striking example among contemporaries being Nelson Goodman) who have attempted to describe the 'language' of art in terms of such concepts as reference or denotation.[18] There are powerful arguments, derived from Frege, which tend to show that, if the connection between reference and truth is severed, then it is not reference in any genuine sense that is being discussed. William Crotch had some inkling of Frege's insight when, writing in 1831, he complained that music could not be a language since, if it were so, it would have to be a language without substantives — a language, therefore, in which nothing could ever be said.[19]

Perhaps, however, music could be interpreted in some such way, as a language just in the sense that English is a language, a system of signs which both refers to objects and describes them. It would still not follow that music — as commonly understood — is an expressive idiom. In other words, the objection of the preceding section remains. For until the kind of understanding proper to actual musical experience can be shown to be already and intrinsically an understanding of music as a language, it will not be clear how the possibility of a linguistic interpretation enables one to appreciate, as a part of musical experience, the expressive character of works of music. The listener could find the music beautiful, and understand its character as art, and yet not dream that it is also a code that could be given independent meaning. Nobody has yet shown that ordinary musical understanding is linguistic in form, and it is doubtful that it could be shown.[20]

Some philosophers have attempted to develop notions of reference which allow for the possibility of 'reference without description', in other words which break the connection between reference and truth. One such is Susanne Langer, who attempted to generalize the 'picture' theory of meaning given by Wittgenstein in the *Tractatus* to cover the special kind of meaning characteristic of musical works.[21] Music, for Langer, consists of 'non-discursive' or 'presentational' symbols; it stands in direct logical relation to human feelings while at the same time saying nothing about them. This theory has been criticized, not only because the 'picture' theory of meaning has been thought (by Wittgenstein himself among others) to be fundamentally mistaken, but also because it seems that no theory of meaning could admit, as Langer wishes to admit, the possibility of a medium in which reference occurs continually but description never. Furthermore, in common with many philosophers who have discussed these matters, Langer assumes a view of the emotions as private, introspectible states of mind, consisting essentially of 'dynamic' episodes of an internal nature. This seems inconsistent with the acceptance of the general belief that an emotion is a disposition to act, based on a perception and understanding of the world. One's emotions no more consist in internal tremors and fluctuations, than do one's beliefs, intentions or desires (on this point see, for example, Ryle).[22]

The failure of the linguistic view of music might seem to spell the doom of the transitive theory of expression. But there is another transitive view which attempts to escape the consequences of the objection attributed above to Hanslick. This view asserts that music expresses thoughts and emotions, but that such thoughts and emotions are 'purely musical'. In other words, it asserts that the emotions or thoughts expressed by music cannot be characterized independently. In listening to music, we experience the tensions, resolutions and developments that are characteristic of music, and while music has an effect on the emotions it is an effect which is peculiar to it and of which it is the sole proper object. Such a view will of course be merely empty until some means are found of describing the musical 'thought'. Those drawn to the view have therefore attempted to give general theories of musical tension, and of the significance of tension in music, so as to be able to describe the logic of musical development and its emotional significance. A notable example is Hindemith; but perhaps the most ambitious attempt in this area has been that of Leonard Meyer, who has sought to characterize the meaning of music in terms of 'information theory', that is, in terms of a general theory of predictability.[23] A musical event has meaning, according to Meyer, because it points to and makes us expect another musical event. The more predictable a particular note, for example, then the higher its 're-dundancy', and the lower the tension that it adds to the musical line. By the analysis of redundancy, Meyer hoped to describe the progress of musical emotion, relating emotion to the development of tension in the musical structure.

While such a theory has an ingenious aspect, it is hard to know what it proves. Meyer's account of 'emotion', like his theory of 'meaning', depends on premises that many philosophers would wish to reject. The least that can be said is that Meyer does not make it clear why such terms as 'expression' and 'emotion' should be used in describing the movement of the musical line. It may be an interesting fact that, looked at in one way, the 'redundancy' of classical music tends to maintain a certain constant figure; but that does not reveal anything important about ways of understanding classical music. The concept of 'redundancy' belongs not to the theory of meaning but rather to the theory of prediction, and the theory of prediction has nothing to do with the appreciation of music.

Conclusion

A return to the intransitive concept of expression does not dispose of the philosophical difficulties. Consider again the example of a face. A face can be said to bear an expression, in the intransitive sense, only, surely, because it sometimes expresses (transitively) the states of mind of its owner. It is because the face is the sign of independent thoughts and feelings that it can be called an 'expression' at all. Can the same be said of music? The considerations discussed seem to imply that it cannot. But what, then, entitles one to describe music as having expression even in an intransitive sense? If it has no expression in any sense, it is difficult to explain the role of music in song, dance and drama, or to explain such remarks as that of Saint-Evremond, who asserted that Lully's operas were successful because their composer 'knows the passions and enters further into the heart of man' than the writers of the librettos. What Saint-Evremond said is clearly true; and it is evident too that as much can be learnt about the 'passions' and about the 'heart of man' from music, as from poetry, painting or prose. Until there is an adequate theory of musical understanding it will not be possible to show how that can be.

7 Representation in Music

Music may be used to express emotion, to heighten a drama, to emphasize the meaning of a ceremony; but it is nevertheless an abstract art, with no power to represent the world. Representation, as I understand it, is a property that does not belong to music.

The word 'representation' has many uses, and may often be applied to music. Therefore I shall discuss not the word, but the phenomenon, as it occurs in poetry, drama, sculpture and painting. Being common to both painting and poetry, this phenomenon cannot be identified with the semantic properties of a linguistic system, for painting, unlike poetry, does not belong to such a system. How, then, is it to be characterized? I suggest the following five conditions, not as an analysis, but as a partial description of the aesthetic significance of representation:[1]

1 A man understands a representational work of art only if he gains *some* awareness of what it represents. His awareness may be incomplete, but it must be adequate. He may not see Masaccio's *Tribute Money* as a representation of the scene from the Gospel; but to understand it as a representation he should at least see the fresco as a group of gesturing men. If a man does not see the fresco in some such way — say because he can appreciate it only as an abstract arrangement of colours and lines — then he does not understand it.

2 Representation requires a medium, and is understood only when the distinction between subject and medium has been recognized. Merely to *mistake* a painting for its subject is to misunderstand it; so too is there misunderstanding when a man is unable to extract the features of the subject from the peculiarities and conventions of the medium. (A varnished painting of a man is not a painting of a varnished man, however much it may look as though it were).

3 Interest in a representation requires an interest in its subject. If an interest in the Masaccio depends in no way upon an interest in the scene portrayed, then the fresco is being treated not as a representation but as a work of abstract art.

4 A representational work of art must express thoughts about its subject, and an interest in the work should involve an understanding of those thoughts. (This is an ingredient in condition 3.) I mean by 'thought'

roughly what Frege meant by *'Gedanke':* the sense or content of a declarative sentence. In this sense thoughts may be spoken of as true or false, although of course it is not always the truth-value of a thought that is of interest in aesthetic understanding. It is clear that a representational work of art always conveys thoughts, in this Fregean sense, about its subject. Among the thoughts that give rise to my interest in *King Lear,* and which give a reason for that interest, are thoughts about Lear. These thoughts are communicated by the play, and are common property among all who understand it. Something similar occurs in the appreciation of a painting. Even in the most minimal depiction — say, of an apple on a cloth — appreciation depends on determinate thoughts that could be expressed in language without reference to the picture; for example: 'Here is an apple; the apple rests on a cloth; the cloth is chequered and folded at the edge'. Representation, in other words, is essentially propositional.

Sometimes we feel that a work of art is filled with thought, but that the thought cannot be detached from the work. It is impossible to put it into words (or into other words). Such cases, I should like to say, are cases not of representation but of expression. Why I should make such a distinction, and why I should make it in that way, will be apparent later.

5 Interest in representation may involve an interest in its *lifelike* quality; but it is not, for all that, an interest in literal truth. It is irrelevant that the depiction be inaccurate; what matters is that it be convincing. To require accuracy is to ask for a report rather than a representation.[2]

I shall rely on an intuitive understanding of these conditions: they tell us what it is to treat something as a representation, rather than as a report, a copy, or a mere inarticulate sign. On this account, what makes a passage of prose into a representation is not so much its semantic structure as the specific intention with which it is composed. The semantic structure is relevant only because it provides the means whereby that intention is fulfilled. Representational literature is literature written with the intention that conditions 1—5 should be satisfied. Thus one may treat as a representation something that is not a representation; one may achieve representation by novel means; one may create a representation that is never understood, and so on.

Now some philosophers — those who think that music is a language — will give an account of musical representation on the model of description in prose or verse. But such an approach is surely most implausible. Anything that we could envisage as a semantic interpretation of music (a theory of 'musical truth') would deprive music of precisely the aesthetic aims for which we admire it, turning it instead into a clumsy code. Furthermore, all attempts to explain music in such terms end by giving rules of reference without rules of truth. We are told that a certain passage carries a reference to love; but we are not told what the passage is supposed to *say* about love. And to speak of language where there is 'reference', but no predication, is simply to misuse a word. We are in fact leaving the realm of representation altogether and entering into that of expression. But there is no need to prove that music is a language in order to assign to it the expressive properties that are mentioned, for example, by Deryck Cooke.[3]

A better attempt to prove that music is a representational medium begins by comparing music to painting. It can be said with some truth that music, like painting, may deliberately 'imitate', or 'copy' features of an object. Is this not, then, a kind of representation? Examples are familiar: Saint-Saëns' *Carnaval des Animaux*, 'Gretchen am Spinnrade', *La Mer*. And it is natural to consider such pieces as attempts to 'depict' the objects referred to in their titles. But perhaps what is meant here by 'depiction' is not what is meant when we refer to the visual arts. A few observations about painting will therefore be appropriate.

It is a commonplace that depiction is not simply a matter of resemblance.[4] Nor is it enough that the resemblance be *intended;* nor even that the artist should intend the resemblance to be noticed. No doubt Manet intended us to notice the resemblance between his *Olympia* and Titian's *Venus of Urbino*. But that is certainly not a case of one painting representing another. It is for such reasons that we might wish to lay the burden of our analysis of depiction on the notion of an 'aspect'. The artist intends that the spectator should *see* the painting *as* its subject, not merely that the spectator should notice a resemblance between the two. In other words, the painter intends that we should have the experience of a certain aspect — that we should feel that seeing his painting is importantly *like* seeing its subject — and not merely that we should notice a resemblance. Thus a painter may intend to copy the *Mona Lisa*, but he does not (as a rule) intend that his painting should be seen as Leonardo's; rather, he intends that it should be seen as the woman in Leonardo's painting. On this view, the intention in depicting is not to 'copy' an object, but rather to create a certain visual impression. And surely, it will be argued, precisely the same process, and the same intention, may exist in writing music. Sounds are created which are meant to be *heard as* other things, as the babbling of brooks, the warbling of birds, the roaring and plodding of animals.

However, a difficulty now arises. We find that, after all, it is not sufficient for the truth of '*A* depicts *B*' that *A* should be intended to be seen as *B*. Imagine, for example, a painting designed to illustrate the scene in Hamlet in which the prince questions Polonius about the shape of a cloud, saying 'Do you see yonder cloud that's almost in shape of a camel?' Suppose that the painting represents a cloud that has the aspect of a camel.

The artist will then intend that a certain part of his canvas (the part which is to be seen as a cloud) should also bear the aspect of a camel. But he does not intend the painting to contain a representation of a camel. Rather, the painting represents something which may be seen as a camel, but which is in fact a cloud. If this example should appear far-fetched, consider instead the many paintings of paintings: in Dutch interiors, for instance, one may often see a picture hanging on the wall. The Dutch painting does not depict the subject of the wall-picture; rather, it represents the picture of a tree, say, and in doing so may itself have the aspect of a tree.

Taken in isolation, therefore, a part of the canvas may have many aspects, each of which is intended, and only one of which is fundamental to the subject of the painting. This seems to suggest that the parts of the painting acquire their representational status only from the context provided by the total representation. Out of context the aspect is indeterminate: it can serve as a representation only when completed, for only when completed will the aspect convey a thought, and it is the thought which is the heart of depiction.[5] Representation is not like ostension; to represent an object is to convey a thought about it. In representing Mr Smith's house I also characterize it; but I may point to the house and say nothing whatever as to its properties or nature. To understand a representation is to understand the thought which it conveys; it is therefore to have some grasp of the context which completes that thought. In the absence of such a context representation is vague and indeterminate, and if the context is *always* absent, then representation is impossible.

Representation can be begun, therefore, only where it can also be completed. If music is to be representational, then its subject must be not only picked out, but also characterized. But that requires a context, and in music the context seems to add no further precision to the 'representational' parts. A certain passage in *Der Rosenkavalier* 'imitates' the glitter of a silver rose. But what more does this passage say about the glitter, except that it is a glitter (and even that may go unnoticed)? The context adds nothing to the thought, and while there is *musical* development, the development of a *description* seems scarcely to be in point. So too, when the imitation of birdsong in Messiaen is given musical development, there is no thought about the birdsong which is made more determinate by that process. The birdsong is absorbed into the musical structure and takes on a meaning that is purely musical. But, it might be said, does not the music none the less convey a thought about the birdsong, in the sense of a purely *musical* thought? Why should it matter that the thought cannot be put into words? Such a retort gets us nowhere. For whatever is meant by a purely musical thought, we can envisage also a purely painterly thought — a thought that finds its only expression in lines and colours, but which cannot be put into words, and which consequently cannot be regarded as true or false. And it is part of the point of calling painting a representational art that the thoughts involved in its appreciation are *not* all purely painterly, that, on the contrary, an experience of a painting will involve thoughts about its subject, thoughts that could be put into words. This 'narrative' element is an essential feature of the phenomenon of representation. If we insist none the less that there is a type of 'representation' that is purely symbolic (which contains ostension but no description) then we are simply denying the role of representation in aesthetic interest.

It is true, all the same, that I may hear a passage of music as something that I know it not to be. I may hear a passage as forest murmurs, for example, as rushing water, as an approaching or receding horse. Should we lay any emphasis on this phenomenon? One problem is that a man may hear and appreciate 'representational' music *without* hearing the aspect. And while it is true that I may also hear poetry without knowing what it says (as when I listen to the reading of a poem in Chinese), to do so is not to appreciate the poem as poetry. An interest in poetry is not an interest in pure sound; a genuine interest in music, on the other hand, may by-pass its representational pretensions altogether. Therefore we cannot assume that a composer may sit down with the honest intention of creating a piece to be heard as, say, the quarrel between Mr Pickwick and Mrs Bardell's lawyers. For he cannot be sure that it *will* be heard in that way; his intention is vitiated, and must be replaced by what is at best a hope or a wish. If the intention endures none the less, it is because there is available to the composer some independent way of specifying his subject: for instance, through the words of a song, or through action on the stage. Thus, in the more adventurous attempts at representation, such as we find in the symphonic poem, the composer is apt to depend on a specific literary reference in order to secure the hearer's complicity in what is better described as an imaginative endeavour than as an inevitable perception. It is thus with *Don Juan* and *Don Quixote,* with *Taras Bulba* and the anecdotal works of Charles Ives.

The argument is of course by no means conclusive. But certain facts are significant all the same. It is significant, for example, that, while a man may look at an untitled picture and know immediately what it represents, it is most unlikely that he should do the same with an untitled symphonic poem. Significant too is the indefiniteness of the relation between music and its 'subject': the music does not determine some one natural class of interpretations, and can usually be fitted to widely contrasting themes. A quarrel between Mr Pickwick and a lawyer may be 'represented' by music that serves equally well the purpose of 'depicting' a forest fire. We see this ambiguity evidenced in the ballet, where the action is usually left so far indeterminate by the music that several incompatible choreographies may exist side by side as accepted members of the repertoire; as in *The Rite of Spring*. Hence, while the aspect of a painting, and the meaning of a sentence, are publicly recognized facts, which make possible the intention characteristic of representational art, there are no similar facts to enable the intention to be carried over into the realm of music.

It might seem that there is another argument against the possibility of musical representation in the following: in music nothing can be represented except sounds; for no sound can be heard *as* anything that is not itself a sound. But sounds are not, strictly speaking, properties of objects. They are individuals, with a history and identity separate from the objects which emit them. A sound is not a property; nor is it an appearance; rather, it is something that *has* an appearance. Of course, the question of the identity of sounds is a difficult one: it is not certain whether sounds should be identified as events or as event-types; it is not certain that they have a precise spatial location, and so on. However, we do say, and for very good reasons, such things as the following: 'There has been a noise in this room all afternoon, and I think that it is getting louder', a sentence that both identifies an individual, and also re-identifies the individual through change.[6] This seems to suggest that a sound is detachable from the object that emits it, and that it is capable of independent existence. However, it is the sound, not the object, that 'appears' in the music. How, then, can the music represent the subjects that are normally ascribed to it, when those subjects share no appearance with the music? A painting presents a certain appearance, and an appearance can be described only in terms of some object that normally possesses it. An appearance is not an individual, but rather an intentional object; it has no properties that are not properties which an object *appears* to have. This means that, in characterizing an appearance, I am automatically engaged in describing how an object might appear. Object and appearance cannot be detached in thought. In so far as one sees the aspect of the painting, therefore, one will be led inevitably to the thought of the subject represented. Music, however, 'imitates' not the appearance of a thing, but a sound which the thing emits. How then does the sound of the music lead us to the thought of the subject represented?

There is, however, a certain narrow-mindedness in this objection which we must try to overcome. Why can we not hear a passage of music as something that is not itself a sound? Surely the operative factor here is the extent to which a subject can *make itself known* in auditory terms. Sadness, which is not strictly a visual property, can make itself known in the face: in such a case I may see the sadness in the face.[7] In a similar way emotions can be heard in the tone of a voice. And it is certainly true that, whether rightly or wrongly, people speak of music as 'depicting' such things as fights, journeys, movements and attitudes. Wagner attempts to represent not only the clap of thunder, but also the stroke of lightning that precedes it, and the shimmering rainbow that follows in its wake. There are even musical 'representations' of things that are not events, whose relation to the temporal series is wholly unlike that of sound: for example, 'representations' of character *(Don Quixote)*, of objects (the *Sinfonia Domestica*), of light and darkness *(The Creation)*. It would be wrong to insist that we cannot *hear* these things in the music. Indeed, the contrary view seems closer to our intuitions. When we learn of a piece of music that it *is* supposed to represent something, then its 'auditory aspect' (the way it sounds) may change for us, even when what is 'depicted' is not a sound. On learning of its subject we may come to 'hear it differently', despite the fact that the subject is not something audible. Consider Debussy's prelude, *Voiles*, which may be said to depict the slow drift of sails in a summer breeze. Learning that, I may begin to hear in the musical line a leisurely and day-dreaming quality that I did not hear before, as though I were watching the to-ing and fro-ing of sails on a calm bright sea. But here, of course, what is 'depicted' is not something heard. May we not say, all the same, that we *hear* the music *as* the drifting of sails?

Even if we grant the force of those remarks, however, we find ourselves facing another, and yet more serious objection to the view that there is 'representation' in music. The objection is that one can understand a 'representational' piece of music without treating it as a representation, indeed, without being aware that it is supposed to have such a status. On the other hand, the very suggestion that one might understand — say — Raphael's *St George* (National Gallery of Art, Washington) while being indifferent to, or ignorant of, its representational quality, is absurd. To suggest such a thing is to suggest treating the Raphael as a work of abstract art; it is to ignore the feature of representation altogether, because it is thought to be insignificant, or because it is thought to play no part in aesthetic interest. But to take such a view is simply to dismiss the problem. If I recognize the existence of a problem about music it is partly because I think that there *is* an aesthetically significant notion of representation employed in the discussion and enjoyment of painting.

Now someone might object to the view that one cannot both understand the Raphael and also have no knowledge of its subject. He might claim that at least a *partial* understanding of the painting could be achieved by studying it as a piece of abstract art. One may understand the composition of the painting, he will say, the balance of tensions between ascending and descending lines, the sequence of spatial planes, and so on, and in none of this need one have an awareness of the subject. But such a reply is wholly misguided. For it seems to suggest that these important aesthetic properties of the Raphael — composition, balance, spatial rhythm — are quite independent of the representation; whereas that is clearly not so. For example we perceive the balance between the upward thrust of the horse's hind legs and the downward pressure of the lance only because we see the two lines as filled with the forces of the things depicted — of the horse's muscles and the horseman's lance. Take away the representation and the balance too would dissolve. And the same goes for the composition. Alter the representational meaning of the horse (close its eye, for example, or attach a bangle to its hoof) and the composition would be utterly destroyed. Nothing here is comprehensible until the representation is grasped.

Let us return, then, to our example. When a passage from *Voiles* reminds me of drifting sails I do indeed hear an aspect of the music. But the *important* part of this aspect — the part that seems essential to a full musical understanding — can be perceived by someone who is deaf to the 'representation'. It is possible to hear the relaxed and leisurely quality of the musical line while being unaware that it depicts the movement of sails. The 'reference' to sails does not determine our understanding of the music in the way that representation determines our understanding of the visual arts.

We should consider here the normal case of representational art, as we know it from painting and literature. In such a case it goes without saying that an understanding of the work depends on a grasp of its representational quality. For, in such a case, aesthetic interest depends on certain thoughts which are expressed only through the representation. In music, on the other hand, the 'representation' is of little relevance to understanding. We can have considerable understanding of a 'representational' piece of music, while being ignorant of, indifferent to, or contemptuous towards, its representational claims. Thus, not only does our interest in music fail to answer to the fourth of our conditions for a representational art; it also fails to answer to the first. To understand a representational painting, one must have some knowledge of the subject; but the same has never been honestly claimed for music. It has always been conceded that a major part of musical understanding is independent of depiction. It is wholly natural to listen to and appreciate the music of the *Ring* long before one has a complete — or even a partial — understanding of its representational claims. And later, one's understanding of the music is enriched primarily through an increasing grasp of thematic, harmonic and structural relations, rather than through knowledge of its representational framework. There is a story that Bruckner, having stared rapturously into the orchestra pit throughout a performance of *Die Walküre*, looked up during the final scene to ask 'Why are they burning that woman?' The story is credible; few, however, would wish to argue that Bruckner had an impoverished understanding of Wagner's music.

It follows, I suggest, that the point of 'representation' in music is not strictly comparable with the point of representation in the visual arts. But I have, in effect, defined representation in terms of its point; therefore it must be wrong to say that music is representational.

To put the argument so bluntly is, however, to open the path to a certain scepticism. Why, after all, should we define representation as I have defined it? Briefly, the answer is this: we need to make a distinction between two kinds of aesthetic interest. In either case there is one central object of interest — usually a work of art — beyond which one's attention does not wander. But in one type of aesthetic interest one does not think only of the work of art. One's *attention* may be focused on the work, even though one's thoughts are not. This happens when one's thoughts are not *about* the work of art, but are nevertheless derived from it, and remain in the work's control. One's thoughts in such a case are not mere *associations,* but on the contrary are both conveyed and developed by the work to which one attends. The true subject of these thoughts may be something quite other than the work of art: the man Aeneas, for example. But in reflecting on Aeneas and his adventures one may also be attending to the *Aeneid;* and that is why it is right to say that the *Aeneid* is a representation of the adventures of *Aeneas.* The 'subject' of a representational work of art is also the subject of our thoughts when we understand the work, and therefore to enjoy the work is to reflect upon its subject. Here we begin to see the importance of such an aesthetic interest, in which the thought of a subject is entirely within the control of a work of art. And we can see too why we should wish to distinguish the quite different kind of aesthetic interest in which an attention to the work of art is not bound up with an interest in a subject, and why we should wish to say that 'understanding' the work is a different matter in either case.

Here we should make a distinction between representation and expression, since the remarks in the last paragraph help to explain why philosophers constantly rely on that distinction. Even in the second type of aesthetic interest — where there is no narrative or anecdotal element — it is possible that our enjoyment of the work will involve us in thoughts about other things. But such thoughts have no narrative or descriptive character; they are much more like ostension than statement, consisting in a gesture towards, or reminiscence of, things that are not described. A passage of music may seem to carry some reference to grief, say, or to a flight of birds, or to something one knows not what. Characteristic of such 'reference' is the frequent difficulty one has in putting the 'thoughts' conveyed by the music into words. A man may feel that *something* is being said by the music, but be quite unable to say what it is. But this inability is in no way a sign that he has not understood the music. Here we may wish to speak not of representation but rather of expression. Characteristic of expression is the presence of 'reference' without predication. Sadness is expressed by the music but nothing is *said* about the sadness, or the flight of birds is made 'present' in the music, but is not described there. (We begin to see why Croce and Collingwood distinguished expression from description, and why they claimed that the former only *presents* things, and does not generalize about them.)

But even when this distinction is made clear (and obviously much more needs to be said), an objection will be raised. I have claimed that we do not understand music in the way that is necessary if music is to be a representational art. But it will be asked: what is meant by 'understanding' here? And it might be thought that the claims I am making are purely legislative, that I am simply trying to define away the possibility of musical representation. The objection is a welcome one, since it helps us to understand the point at issue. We are not concerned to show that music can or cannot represent objects. We are attempting to show rather that the question whether music is representational is a question about the *appreciation* of music, and not a question about music's structure. The question is: do we understand music in that way? It is clear that we could envisage definitions of 'understanding' music according to which music is interpreted as a kind of code, with a systematic interpretation the parameters of which are grasped by all who could be said to understand it. On such a view music would become an inherently information-bearing medium, and its capacity to represent the world would hardly be disputed.[8] I do not propose to argue for the notion of musical understanding that I am here assuming.[9] My point is that we do have an intuitive idea of musical understanding, and that this idea reflects our experience of music as an aesthetic object. And according to this intuitive idea — with its emphasis on melody, harmony and auditory relations — there is little place for representation in the appreciation of music. If we insist, nevertheless, that there is such a place, then we find ourselves imposing an idea of musical understanding that has no intuitive appeal, and which fails to reflect the activities of those who compose and listen to music. Suppose now that someone were to develop a musical semantics, in the full sense of a theory that assigns truth-conditions to musical utterances. Then there would still be no argument for saying that music is a representational medium. For we should still have to show that this semantic theory also provides an account of the way music is understood.

In search for examples of genuine musical representation we may be led by this argument back to the suggestion that the true subject-matter of music is sound. Sounds have properties which music, being itself sound, may share; so music ought to be able to depict *sounds*. For there will be no difficulty here in explaining how it is that the music may lead us *inevitably* to the thought of what is represented. Thoughts of a subject will therefore form an integral part of musical appreciation. But again there is a peculiarity that deserves mention, since it seems to suggest that even here, in the most plausible examples, there is yet another of our five features of understanding representation that fails to belong to music: feature 2. When music attempts the direct 'representation' of sounds it has a tendency to become transparent, as it were, to its subject. Representation gives way to reproduction, and the musical medium drops out of consideration altogether as superfluous. In a sense the first scene of *Die Meistersinger* contains an excellent representation of a Lutheran chorale. But then it *is* a Lutheran chorale. Similarly, the tinkling of teaspoons in Strauss's *Sinfonia Domestica,* and the striking of anvils in *Rheingold,* are not so much sounds represented as sounds reproduced, which in consequence detach themselves from the musical structure and stand out on their own. Nor is this an accident. On the contrary, it is an inevitable consequence of the logical properties of sounds. For sounds, as I have already mentioned, may be identified as individuals independently of the objects that possess them. In attempting to represent them, therefore, one need have no regard to the object that produces them: one represents the sound alone. But since there is nothing to music except sound, there ceases to be any *essential* difference between the medium of representation and the subject represented. Inevitably, therefore, there is a tendency towards isomorphism of the two.

The most ambitious attempts at musical representation often fail as music for this very reason. In Charles Ives's evocation of the sounds of Central Park we find a constant tendency on the part of the musical medium to collapse into the sound represented, to become absorbed in it, to cease thereby to have any independent life. All that we are left with is a succession of brass-bands, jazz groups, cries and murmurs, which stand out in the music as isolated particulars bearing no musical relation one to another, just like the sounds in Central Park. The musical medium is no longer strong enough to impose on those sounds any unity or relationship that they do not already carry in themselves. (Contrast here the *Catalogue des Oiseaux,* where Messiaen, leaning so heavily on the harmonic and textural traditions established by Debussy, has produced unfailing musical sense: the birdsong finds a proper musical reality, it does not merely remain itself, however closely it is copied in the music.) In Ives the sounds 'depicted' enter so forcefully into the music as to destroy its independent structure. Their effect is like that of the actor, who, having to simulate a murder on the stage, profits from the opportunity to kill his rival. The fundamental separation of art and reality is destroyed, and our understanding ceases, as a result, to have any aesthetic aim. In Ives, when we hear the 'representation', we cease to hear the music.

Perhaps it would be better to consider the case of a 'representation' of one musical style in the 'syntax' of another. We do indeed find in such cases interesting examples that might lead us to speak more freely of representation. Consider, for example, the dance music from Act II scene 4 of *Wozzeck*. In *Don Giovanni* Mozart had placed a light orchestra on the stage, but this orchestra did not 'imitate' the sounds of popular music; rather, it reproduced them. Representation was achieved through the purely theatrical, non-musical convention that what is on the stage is part of the *action*. The 'representational' status of the music could be understood by someone with no *musical* understanding whatsoever. In *Wozzeck*, on the other hand, we find the remarkable effect of an imitation of Viennese dance music written in the prevailing atonal idiom of the work. The music has a part to play in the total representation over and above the fact that it is performed on the stage. For the music must be *heard as* the robust tonalities of Johann Strauss, and yet, at the same time, can be fully understood only in atonal terms. The atonality of the medium renders it opaque to the tonal subject-matter, so that the sounds represented are not merely reproduced in the music.

Many of the elements of representation are here, and the analogy with painting is perhaps never more apparent. Thus: (a) the extra-musical reference (to a Viennese waltz) seems to be essential to our understanding of the music; (b) the object represented is not simply reproduced in the music, nor, given the conventions of the style, could it be reproduced there; (c) the music and its subject are related in the experience of the music, which must be *heard as* a Viennese waltz; (d) all this is manifestly intended by the composer.

Nevertheless, it is important to realize that, even here, one's understanding of the music is only partly determined by its 'representational' status, and for the most part proceeds in quite another way. Moreover, the representational character is not an autonomous property of the music, and can be fully understood only through theatrical conventions that are entirely non-musical in their origin. Thus the most important of our conditions for representation — the condition that the work of art should convey definite thoughts about its subject — is not obviously satisfied by the *music* even here. If it does seem to be satisfied it is largely because of the dramatic context, which enables us to give content to the composer's thoughts.

It is not only in dramatic music that a full understanding may require a grasp of some extra-musical relation. Consider, for example, the last of *Pictures at an Exhibition*. Here there is a deliberate imitation of two familiar sounds: cathedral bells, and a distant hymn. Their combination leads to a splendid effect of musical unity, but it is a unity that could not exist were it not for our prior disposition to associate the two kinds of sound. But to see how far even this case is from ordinary representation we need only ask ourselves what a man must lack who fails to recognize the extra-musical reference. Even *he* may experience the musical unity; and for him too the association of bells and hymn-tunes may be operating to lead him to accept Mussorgsky's combination as a natural one. In no sense must his musical understanding be diminished by his failure to entertain the thought that is here suggested by the 'representation'.

Despite all these objections, it cannot be claimed that music has no part to play in representation. In the opera, for example, where dramatic and literary conventions already determine our understanding of the work of art, music can play a part in the representation that is entirely its own, and not a mere comment on the action on the stage. Indeed, in the right context, music may go so far as to present thoughts that are conveyed neither by the action nor by the words. Consider, for example, the scene that Bruckner found so bewildering. When Wotan, having summoned the god of fire to protect the sleeping Brünnhilde, points his spear and says

> Wer meines Speeres
> Spitze fürchtet,
> durchschreite das Feuer nie![10]

the music, not the words, tells us that the oblique reference is to Siegfried, the unborn hero who was earlier the subject of Brünnhilde's pleading. Here the music plays an essential part in the completion of the dramatic thought. Without it, the full impact of the scene as drama could not be understood.

But of course, we should not attempt to prove the possibility of musical representation through citing the place of music in an operatic or theatrical context. This context no more *proves* the representational nature of dramatic music than it proves the representational nature of costumes, lighting and make-up. Clearly architecture too has a part to play in the theatre: does that make architecture into a representational art? To take such a view would be shallow indeed; it would amount, in effect, to an abolition of the very possibility of an abstract form of art.

I wish to conclude with a few remarks that are far more speculative than the arguments I have given. I have argued that music is not representational, since thoughts about a subject are never essential to the understanding of music. But, it might be said, that is all very well; but you have done nothing to show that we *must* understand music as we presently understand it, nothing to show that there could not be a new way of understanding music which yet had the character of an aesthetic (rather than, say, a practical or scientific) interest, and which accorded to music a representational status.

Throughout this chapter I have been concerned to point out specific differences between music and the other arts, specific properties of music that seem to distinguish it from the other arts precisely in respect of those features that are relevant to representation. The objection just mentioned would be answered if it could be shown that these features are not accidental features derived from our present mode of interest in music, but on the contrary essential features, arising from the very nature of music as an art of sound.

Now it would be wrong to say that sounds simply cannot be understood as representations: for what is poetry if not sound? But the representational nature of poetry is a consequence of the medium of language; poetry achieves the status of representation through exploiting pre-established semantic rules. If the sounds of music were likewise to be put to a linguistic use — if there were literally a musical language — then of course music would also be capable of representation. But then it would cease to be music. It would be poetry written in a language of absolute pitch (a kind of superlative tonic language). In contrast to such a suggestion, we need to show that there could be a representational use of music which did not depend on semantic rules. Such a use would arise if our interest in music were to involve an interest in the music as sound and, *at the same time and in the same act of attention,* an interest in some extra-musical subject. Only then could it be essential to an understanding of the *sound* that there should also be some understanding of the subject. But I doubt that there could be such a combination of interests outside the special context of the music-drama. For we should need a relation between sound and its 'subject' that was so intimate that to listen to and understand the sound *was* also to think of and understand the subject, just as to see a painting and to grasp the narrative thoughts about its subject are simultaneous parts of one identical act of attention. In other words, we should need the sound to be as intimately connected to a subject as a painting is connected to its visual aspect. But I suspect that there can be no such intimate connection, precisely because of the logical status of sounds that I noted earlier. Sounds are individuals, not properties: two sounds may stand in the same relation to two respective objects, but they are not strictly *shared* by those objects. By contrast, two objects *may* share a single appearance, and in describing that appearance one must identify and describe the objects that possess it. While we pass, therefore, without hesitation from a visual appearance to that which possesses it — and hence from a painting to its subject — we can pass with ease from an auditory appearance only to a *sound*, and not, except with difficulty, to the object which emits the sound. Thus the experience of the sound will not automatically involve thoughts about the subject represented, and the sound can acquire no direct iconic relation to a subject. Moreover, while a visual appearance may *identify* the subject — since it may be sufficiently detailed to convey an *identifying description* — a sound remains merely a sound, and will tell us nothing further about the subject to which it is referred. The subject remains hidden, as it were, behind the veil of sound, and neither its identity nor its nature is easily discovered through the veil. I suspect that such considerations, while by no means conclusive, indicate that sounds cannot be representational until they are organized by semantic rules, and therefore that music, if it is to remain distinct from poetry, simply *must* be understood as an abstract art.

8 Understanding Music

Musik... Du Sprache, wo Sprachen enden. Rilke

Words move, music moves, but only in time. Eliot

Many music critics, and many critical listeners, feel impelled to ascribe content to certain works of music, and to describe this content in emotional, or at least mental, terms. At the same time music is an abstract, which is to say non-representational, art. It has (although some have doubted this) no narrative or descriptive powers, no way of referring to and presenting for our contemplation an object independent of itself.[1] So what do we mean when we ascribe a content to music? And how could we ever be justified? By shifting from terms like 'representation' and 'description' to the vocabulary of human expression, critics and philosophers have hoped to locate an idea of content that will be compatible with music's status as an abstract art. But terms like 'expression', 'expressive', and the like are far from clear: they also have implications that many would be reluctant to accept. Their use seems to imply that the meaning of music is to be found in some state of mind (for example an emotion) that is conveyed by it. But how is this possible, if music cannot describe things? Is not every state of mind identified at least in part through its intentional object, and does that not imply that an expressive medium must also be capable of representation? To put it more trenchantly: if music has a content, how can that content be described? It was thus that Hanslick posed the problem, and despite subsequent studies, the problem remains roughly as he posed it.[2]

It is not surprising, therefore, that the discussion of expression has become dominant in musical aesthetics. But little clarity seems to me to have informed this discussion. This is largely because another, and more basic concept, has been overlooked: that of musical understanding. It is clearly wrong to think that one could explain meaning in language while saying nothing about understanding language: for the meaning of a sentence is what we understand when we understand it — it is the intentional object of a particular mental act. Likewise it must be wrong to attempt to give a theory of musical expression which cannot be rewritten as a theory of musical understanding. If music has a content, that content must be understood. This chapter explores the idea of musical understanding; at the end I return to the problem of expression, which by then should seem less intractable.

Many writers, pursuing a phantom of scientific knowledge, have overlooked — what in aesthetics you can overlook only by losing sight of the subject — that there is a kind of understanding that rests in appearance. I shall call this kind of understanding 'intentional'. A scientific understanding addresses itself to the world as material object, and seeks out the causal connections which underlie and explain appearances. But scientific explanation does not eliminate appearance: it only dispenses with it. An intentional understanding considers the world as intentional object (or, to use the Husserlian idiom, as *Lebenswelt*): it therefore uses the concepts through which we perceive the world, and makes no connections or observations that are not in some way already implicit in them.[3] When we look at the dispute between Goethe and Newton about colour, it is surely difficult to resist the conclusion that, while the first is attempting to describe appearances, the second is concerned to explain them. Helmholtz criticized Goethe, arguing that the poet, by confining himself to appearance, made it impossible to find the concepts with which appearance could be explained. At the same time, there is something to be learned from Goethe: we understand colours better after reading his account of them, for we are given a way in which to bring together and harmonize the descriptions which experience forces upon us.

Although there is a sense in which we always know how things appear to us, the study of appearance is appropriate when the concepts which inform it are outside the perceiver's grasp. Consider the curious art of bird-watching. I may know as much about the science of birds as a trained bird-watcher; and yet I perceive things differently from him. I need to relate my knowledge of the parts of birds, their flight, walk and plumage, to an experience. I have to see, for example, the rings of the plover, and its short rapid step, in the exclamatory way that can best be captured in the expression 'plover!'. Thus, because all our perception is informed by concepts, and those concepts in their turn determine our understanding and our practical reasoning, a critic or a philosopher can bring system to an appearance, by drawing out the implications of the concepts through which it is described. This description need not be one that the man who perceives with understanding can provide. But when he understands it, he will recognize it immediately as a description of the experience that is his.

Understanding music is a special case of intentional understanding. How we hear music clearly depends upon our intellectual capacities and education, upon concepts, analogies and expectations that we have inherited from a culture steeped in musical expression. Yet the understanding that we derive from this culture is manifest in our way of hearing, and not just in our way of thinking about music. I shall suggest that the ways of hearing *sound* that we consider to be ways of hearing *music*, are based in concepts extended by metaphorical transference. The metaphors are deeply entrenched in our language: but they are metaphors nevertheless, and this means that the ability to hear music is dependent upon the capacity for metaphorical transfer (a capacity which belongs only to language-users). I will try to illustrate my meaning through a study of certain fundamental musical categories.

There are certain basic perceptions involved in hearing music, and these are crucial to understanding it. For example, there is the hearing of movement — as when one hears a melody, theme, or phrase, move from one note to another. There is the hearing of tones as opposed to the hearing of pitched sounds: the hearing of one tone as higher than another; the hearing of rhythm (as opposed to temporal sequence); the hearing of harmony, as opposed to aggregates of tones, and so on. All these experiences are basic, in that a person who did not have them would be deaf to music. And all other musical experiences depend upon them: for example, the hearing of melodies would be impossible without the hearing of musical movement, the hearing of counterpoint impossible without the hearing of harmony (else it would be simply the hearing of simultaneous strings of sound). And so on. It is plausible to suggest, therefore, that whatever character is possessed by these basic perceptions will be possessed also by the musical experiences that are built on them.

I have made various distinctions — between hearing a sound, and hearing a tone, hearing succession and hearing rhythm, hearing change of pitch and hearing movement, hearing agglomerated sounds and hearing harmony. The distinctions here lie *in* the experience (in its intentional object) and not in the material object perceived. But clearly they demand further analysis, especially given the fact that to take such distinctions seriously is to conclude that no speechless creature hears music, and that no birds sing.[4] What, for example, is the distinction between hearing a sound and hearing a tone? It would be tempting to take refuge in the analogy with language, to say that a tone, like a word, is a sound pregnant with meaning. My dog hears the sound 'walk' — which for him constitutes a signal, a trigger to excitement. But he does not hear the *word* 'walk', since he is deaf to its character as language. For him it is not what it is for me, the point of intersection of indefinitely many meaningful utterances. It has not, for him, the audible character of a semantic unit. Of course I may often hear words that I do not understand — but to the extent that I hear them as words I hear them as filled with semantic and grammatical implications, even when I have only the haziest idea what those implications are.

Similarly, when I hear a tone, I hear a sound imbued with musical implications. What are these implications? It is tempting to assimilate the case to that of language, and to argue that the implications are semantic. But this misrepresents the phenomenon. The analogy with language is no more than an analogy, and to take it seriously as the basis for a musical aesthetic is to invite the greatest confusion. Common sense points us, rather, to the traditional triad: harmony, melody and rhythm. A tone has implications in these three dimensions, which correspond to three kinds of expectation that are aroused or thwarted in musical experience. A tone arouses 'vertical' and 'horizontal' expectations — the first being harmonic, the second melodic and rhythmic. To say that is not to elucidate the distinction between sound and tone. On the contrary, I shall argue that a proper description of musical expectations depends upon an account of that distinction. It must further be remembered that, in identifying the implications of a tone under these traditional categories, I have already incorporated some of the demands of a musical culture. There are musical traditions without melody in our sense (the Javanese), without rhythm in our sense (the Japanese Gagaku), without harmony (much of the music of Southern Asia). But in all these (with the possible, and highly curious, exception of the Gagaku) there are tones, and it is from the idea of a tone that I shall begin.

Tones, unlike sounds, seem to contain movement. This movement is exemplified in melodies, and can be traced through a 'musical space', which we describe in terms of 'high' and 'low'. It seems fairly clear that this description is metaphorical, and this fact has had an important part to play in the development of modern musical aesthetics.[5] The questions that I wish to consider, and which, I believe, have not been correctly considered, are these: can the metaphor be eliminated? If not, what does its persistence tell us about the character of musical experience?

It seems that, because of instrumental positions, the Greeks and the Chinese called those tones high which we call low, and vice versa. On the basis of such facts, Berlioz (to take a distinguished example) professed to find the whole description of music in spatial terms arbitrary and dispensable. This profession is consistent, but not wholly compatible, with the tone-painting exemplified in such works as *Harold in Italy* and the *Symphonie Fantastique*.[6] (It is *consistent* with the practice since the denial of a metaphor is always consistent with the facts, whether or not the facts also render it appropriate.) I doubt that it is possible to share Berlioz's opinion without also recognizing a conflict with musical experience. It is, of course, impossible to draw any conclusions from the example of Greek musical vocabulary, for this does not show us how the Greeks *heard* music. To imagine the spatial metaphor reversed is to imagine a thorough-going alteration of musical experience. If someone *heard* those sounds as high which we hear as low we might, I think, wish to deny that he heard the same *tones* as we do. For him the opening bars of *Rheingold* fall slowly from a great height; for us they rise from the depths of the universe. Is that not, musically speaking, the greatest difference imaginable? For us the solo violin in the 'Benedictus' of the *Missa Solemnis* soars like an angel above the swell of the chorus: for him it is like a murky serpent undulating in the deep.

Because the experience of 'height' and 'depth' is so irresistible, some have tried to argue that these terms are used *literally* of music, say, because they denote the position of the human larynx as it strains to encompass its range of sounds. This strange suggestion, which clearly confuses the cause of a description with its ground, has nevertheless won some favour among psychologists, and even among philosophers, of music.[7] But it is clear that it does nothing to capture the true significance of the spatial reference, and leaves the whole phenomenon of musical movement unexplained. Further examination shows, moreover, that, whether or not we accept as inevitable the designations of 'high' and 'low' in music, we must recognize that the idea of musical space, and of movement within that space, is a metaphor.

In discussing this topic, we need to know the point of saying, of some gradation, that it is, or is not, spatial. The answer seems to require examination of the difference between dimension and continuity. The colour spectrum is an example of gradation, and exhibits continuity: so too does the arithmetical continuum. We can speak of a greater or less distance between points on a continuum, and between any two points there is always a third. But neither the colour spectrum nor the arithmetical continuum is a dimension: they do not constitute frames within which we identify colours or numbers, but rather ordered aggregates of colours and numbers. The distinction here is difficult to draw. It was the attempt to draw it, I believe, which motivated much of Kant's concern with space, both in the pre-critical writings, and in the first *Critique,* and which fortified his belief (surprising in someone familiar with the Cartesian reduction of geometry) that arithmetic and geometry are wholly different sciences.

A dimension stands in a specific relation to the things that it contains. For example, an object is located *in* space; it *occupies* a certain position which might have been occupied by something else; it is also oriented in space. Now the place occupied by blue in the spectrum is not a 'space' that might have been occupied by red, say. Nor is blue oriented: it is indeed hard to know what would be meant by that. It is the feature of orientation that Kant particularly remarked on in his well-known essay on this subject.[8] Orientation is present whenever there is 'incongruity', of the kind displayed between an object and its mirror image. Kant tried to show that there is more to space than spatial relations between objects. He therefore produced an example of two universes which, while identical in all spatial relations, are not identical in their spatial properties. One consists of a left-hand glove, the other of a right-hand glove. These are asymmetrical mirror images, and are therefore incongruent; the one cannot be fitted into the space occupied by the other. This feature of orientation seemed to Kant to provide a reason for identifying space as existing independently of the objects which occupy it. The example has been generalized, for example by Wittgenstein, in *Tractatus* 6.36111, in order to suggest that incongruence can always be overcome by adding a further dimension through which the mirror image can be turned. In general, the Kantian feature of orientation is now considered to be one among several features which show dimension to be, not a metric, but a topological feature of space. It is the topological structure of space that conditions the possibility of movement in space, and secures the observed character of that movement.[9]

By Kant's criterion, the auditory 'spectrum' might seem to be a dimension: objects occurring within it possess orientation, as well as position. This is so, at least, provided we can consider a chord to be an 'object in auditory space'. For a chord can be the exact mirror of another, even though it is not possible to shift the one through musical space so as to coincide with the other—chords may make what seem to be 'incongruent counterparts', as in the following example:

Ex. 1

Here the first chord mirrors the second, but cannot be shifted through musical space ('transposed') so as to coincide with it. And just as perfectly symmetrical physical objects are congruent with their mirror images, so are perfectly symmetrical chords congruent with theirs:

Ex. 2

However, is it true that a chord is an 'object in auditory space'? Someone could easily doubt that the basic individuals in musical space (the 'place-occupiers') include chords. The first chord in ex. 1 is indeed the mirror of the second. But this means only that the distances between the component tones in the first (travelling 'upwards') are the same as the distances between the component tones in the second (travelling 'downwards'). So three points taken in one direction seem to provide the mirror image of three points taken in the other. But that is not enough. For by that criterion the ordered triple of numbers (2, 5, 7) is a mirror of the ordered triple (7, 9, 12): in which case there is orientation (and therefore dimension) in the mathematical continuum. But we have produced this orientation artificially, by arbitrarily composing objects in arithmetical 'space' out of individual numbers which, taken separately, possess no orientation at all. Such groupings of arithmetical objects cannot in themselves suffice to change the topological properties of the continuum. Likewise, there is only genuine orientation in the musical 'space' if a chord can be considered as a single musical object, spread over the 'area' which it 'occupies'. But what compels us to think so?

Of course, we *hear* a chord as a single musical object: but that is the result of our musical understanding. It is not a feature of the 'spatial' distribution of sounds. Hence, in order to construe musical 'space' as analogous to physical space, we have to construe it, not materially, but intentionally, in terms of that very capacity for musical understanding that we are trying to explain. It is a phenomenal fact about auditory space that it possesses the topological feature of orientation; but it is not a fact about sound, construed independently of the musical experiences of which it is the (material) object.

Nevertheless, have we not admitted the existence of individuals in auditory space, when we speak of the tones out of which chords are composed? Again we find serious disanalogies with physical space. First, it seems that tones have no parts, and are therefore not divisible within the 'space' that they occupy: this already deprives them of orientation. Moreover, with certain rather peculiar exceptions, the basic individuals in physical space obey the law that no two individuals can be in the same space at the same time.[10] Do tones obey this law? The question is exceedingly difficult to answer, and the difficulty is that of identifying the basic individuals that occupy auditory space. Suppose a violin and a flute play in unison. Is the result one individual or two? It seems that our answer will depend on the musical context. If the unison occurs through the crossing of two lines of counterpoint, then what we hear is *two* tones; otherwise we hear only *one* tone, with a distinct timbre due to its being sounded on two instruments simultaneously. But to talk of tones is already to talk at the sophisticated level of musical phenomenology. If we wish to speak of what is indisputably and objectively true of the auditory world, we should refer only to sounds. Suppose, however, that we retreat to this point of comparative safety; we still find that the law of spatiality — that no two objects can be at the same place simultaneously — is repeatedly and unproblematically violated. The natural way of counting sounds (the way which corresponds to their physical nature) is in terms of their manner of production. So that the violin and flute in unison produce not one sound, but two.

That suggests that there is something odd in the idea that *sounds* have a spatial order (an order, that is, other than that conferred by the *physical* space in which they occur). Perhaps we should confine ourselves to the study of tones; whatever auditory space should turn out to be, it is tones that are to be its basic occupants. But what now of musical movement? It seems to follow that no individual in auditory space can be in two places at different times. We have no way to individuate tones except in terms of their uninterrupted continuity at a single pitch. Therefore no tone can move from one pitch to another, without becoming another tone. Hence no individual in auditory space actually moves. We cannot separate the individuals from the places that they occupy, not even in thought. So there is no such thing, materially speaking, as musical movement.[11] (Unless of course, we mean to refer to the material transfer of sounds from place to place, as when a character walks singing across the stage in opera, or as in some of the orchestral extravaganzas of Stockhausen, in which orchestras 'hand' sounds to each other across the floor of a concert hall).

Even if we do not accept that radical conclusion, we must concede that hearing movement in auditory space is very different from seeing or hearing movement in physical space. It does not involve an act of re-identification: it does not require the perception of the same thing at different places, and the consequent inference of a movement from one place to the other. Of course we can hear a melody, now at middle C, now transposed upwards an octave or a fifth. And that might seem to be an example of hearing the same thing at two different places. But this would only provide us with a model for the perception of musical movement if we could think of melodies as basic individuals, whose re-identification at different places gives rise to our concept of musical movement. But that is not so. A melody is itself a *kind* of musical movement, and it cannot therefore be an example of the individual whose changing position is supposed to provide us with our conception of how music moves.

The conclusion that we should draw is that, while we hear movement in music, this is a fact about our experience, which corresponds to no actual movement in the auditory world. Musical movement is, in Gurney's words, 'ideal movement'.[12] It might be tempting then to renounce altogether the idea that there is an auditory space, and that music moves within the confines of that space. We might say that 'movement' is simply a way of describing what is in fact nothing more than a process, which changes through time, but involves no movement through space. But if we take that extreme point of view, we end by reducing the experience of music to the experience of sound: the distinction between a sound and a tone has vanished. Sounds too belong to processes — indeed, they *are* processes, and can be combined sequentially, and heard in sequence, even when they are not heard as music. If we take away the metaphors of movement, of space, of chords as objects, of melodies as advancing and retreating, as moving up and down — if we take those metaphors away, nothing of music remains, but only sound.

It seems then that in our most basic apprehension of music there lies a complex system of metaphor, which is the true description of no material fact. And the metaphor cannot be eliminated from the description of music, because it is integral to the intentional object of musical experience. Take this metaphor away and you cease to describe the experience of music. But suppose it is objected that you cease to describe, not the experience of music, but only *that* experience of music (the experience constituted by the metaphorical transfer to which I have referred). What is the reply? Why do sounds have to be experienced as I have described them in order to be heard as *music?*

It is hard to find an irrebuttable answer to that question. However, it seems to me that much of its force can be dispelled by emphasizing just how *radically* different the experience of sounds would have to be for reference to space to be eliminated from its description — so different, in fact, that it might seem justifiable to say that we are no longer concerned with an experience of tones. It may be (though I doubt it) that we ought to regard the descriptions 'high' and 'low' as dispensable, replaceable, say, by 'left' and 'right' or by some non-metaphorical predicates defined purely over the set of sounds. But what would it be like to dispense altogether with the experience of space? My argument suggests that this would involve ceasing to hear orientation in music. In which case tones would no longer move towards or away from each other; no phrase would mirror another, no leaps would be larger or bolder than others. In short the experience of music would involve neither melody nor counterpoint as we presently know them. Musical movement would have disappeared, direction having been entirely replaced by succession. In which case, why should we continue to talk of music?[13]

An important corollary should here be mentioned. It has been well argued that our perceptual field has an intrinsic orientation, including a sense of 'up' and 'down' that cannot be intelligibly subtracted from the contents of perception.[14] And this sense of 'up' and 'down' is not a purely geometrical idea — it is, rather, an idea of human movement, made available to us by our own activity. It therefore depends upon our sense of what obstructs and furthers action. At a deep level, the sense of 'up' and 'down' is a sense of the human will. And it is not implausible to suggest that it is this sense of ourselves as agents — rather than any purely geometrical idea of space — which underlies our experience of musical movement, and prompts us to describe that movement in spatial terms. This observation is perhaps obscure as yet; but below I make further remarks about rhythm which will serve to clarify it. Later I shall give philosophical grounds for thinking that it is indeed our experience of ourselves, rather than any scientific representation of the world, which both prompts and explains the metaphors which we apply to music.

If the description of music is so dependent upon metaphor, we might go on to conclude that music is not, strictly speaking, a part of the material world. By that I mean that any scientific description of the world of sound should not mention — as an independent fact of the matter — the phenomenon of music. For there is no explanatory function to be filled by the concept of music that will not equally be filled by the concept of organized sound: no scientific method need discriminate between these two (the extension of each concept in the material world being identical). Hence, by the axiom of simplicity, the concept which describes the material essence of what is heard (the concept of sound) is the only one that we need employ. If there is an additional *fact* of the matter, it is that we (beings of a certain kind) hear music. Music belongs uniquely to the intentional sphere, and not to the material realm. Any analysis of music must be an exercise in intentional rather than scientific understanding.

But, someone might object, that only shows that musical properties and relations are secondary, rather than primary properties, of the sounds that possess them. To think that they are therefore not part of the material world in some significant sense (some sense that does not merely reiterate the scientific realist's commitment to the explanatory priority of primary qualities) is to repeat a mistake at least as old as Berkeley. It is to think that because the sense of a term (e.g., 'red') is to be specified in terms of certain experiences involved in its application, its reference must therefore be intentional rather than material.

In a sense the objection is fair. It is true that the terms used to describe music *refer* to material sounds. But they refer to them under a description which no material sound can satisfy. Sounds do not move as music moves (so as to 'reach into the silence'). Nor are they organized in a spatial way (*pace*, for example, Strawson[15]), nor do they rise and fall. These are all metaphors, and one thing that distinguishes metaphors from scientific descriptions is that they are, when successful, false. The case is quite unlike that of secondary qualities for another reason. The ability to perceive a secondary quality is a sensory capacity, and depends only upon the power of sensory discrimination. Many animals may discriminate sensory qualities better than we do (bees, for example, may perceive a wider range of colours, birds a wider range of sounds, through the secondary qualities that make these features audible). This ability does not depend upon superior intellect, nor upon any other faculty that might be improved or impaired through education. It is this that leads us to think of the secondary qualities as really *inherent* in the objects that possess them. For no amount of education can persuade us to perceive, or dissuade us from perceiving them; all that is required for their perception is an apparatus of sensory discrimination. Musical qualities, however, are not, in that sense, secondary. They are more closely analogous to aspects — the man in the moon, the face in the cloud, the child in the picture — which are sometimes called 'tertiary' qualities, in order to emphasize the peculiar nature of their dependence upon our capacities to observe them. 'Tertiary' qualities are often thought not to be genuine qualities of the things which possess them: first, because of their 'supervenience',[16] secondly, because they are neither deductions from experience nor used in the explanation of experience; thirdly, because their perception requires peculiar capacities (such as imagination) which cannot be tied down to any 'sense', and which perhaps do not belong to speechless beings. It does not much matter for present purposes whether we take a 'realist' view of these qualities. What does matter is that we should recognize the peculiar dependence of our power to observe them upon our power of thought.

A consideration of aspects helps us to make sense of the metaphorical transfer that is integral to musical experience. It also enables us to incorporate into our account of musical understanding the essentials of harmonic and rhythmic perception. Consider the face in the cloud. You see the face in the cloud only when you also see that it is not there. To believe that there is a face in the cloud is not (in the relevant sense) to perceive it. It is to be the victim of an illusion, of a kind from which animals too may suffer. There is a transfer involved in seeing the face: the intentional object of experience must be described using a concept that is known not to apply to the material object of perception. This transfer is not unlike that which occurs in metaphor. This is one reason for thinking that the perception of aspects is confined to beings with imagination — beings who can extend concepts beyond the field of their literal application.

The perception of an aspect is not, then, the acquisition of a peculiar false belief. For this reason, it remains partly, or perhaps wholly, within the control of the subject. He cannot choose what to believe, but he may often choose what to 'see'. The structure of this control is difficult to describe.[17] But its musical manifestations are readily identified. They illustrate the peculiar way in which the subject is active in the perception of music, however indifferent or hostile towards it he may be. By 'active' I mean something quite specific. According to the Kantian doctrine of the synthesis, and all the many philosophies which have issued from it, all perception has an active component. But in my sense not every perception is 'active'. To be 'active' a perception must exhibit that kind of conscious participation that is involved in the perception of an aspect: it must involve an engagement of attention, an interest in surface, a transference of concepts from sphere to sphere (as in metaphor); in the limiting case it may itself be a voluntary act.

All those features of 'activity' are exhibited in the perception of musical movement. The voluntary character of this perception provides one of the foundations for structural criticism of music. It is because I can ask someone to hear a movement as beginning in a certain place, as phrased in a certain way, and so on, that the activity of giving reasons in support of such analysis makes sense. Much of music criticism consists of the deliberate construction of an intentional object from the infinitely ambiguous instructions implicit in a sequence of sounds.

Rather than dwell further on musical movement, I wish now to consider rhythm, which is the dimension of musical experience that exhibits 'activity' most strikingly. An unusually complex example of rhythmic organization is presented by the first three bars of *Parsifal:*

Ex. 3

Only the eighth tone of this phrase falls on an accented beat, and the listener hears the accent there. All that precedes this tone is, in his hearing, held in rhythmic suspension. It is extremely difficult to describe this suspension. Its impact, however, is immediate, and is understood in the very first tone. Suppose the phrase had been written:

Ex. 4

Perhaps the orchestra would have produced an identical *sound* in response to the first written note. But the instructions for hearing it have (in a sense) been changed. The rhythmic character is now altered in the ears of the beholder. It may seem rather extraordinary that one can hear the difference between ex. 3 and ex. 4 from the first tone. But we must remind ourselves that the rhythmic character of the first tone is not a feature of the material world of sound; it belongs to the intentional world of musical perception. The active listener can set his mind to changing that character: he could decide to hear ex. 4 (or rather, what ex. 4 most naturally represents) in place of ex. 3. (What I wish to say here is of course extremely difficult to express, since the content of this decision is precisely what no mode of musical notation can determine.)

It might be objected that this hearing of rhythmic implications is nothing more than a perception of temporal pattern; one simply hears the tones and the spacing between them, and then fits them, as it were, into a temporal grid. But that fails to account for the difference between the two ways of hearing the first note in ex. 3 above; it also fails to take account of the phenomenon which we might (on the analogy with tone deafness) call 'rhythm deafness'. For it seems quite possible for someone to hear regularity in sound, and to fit sound into a temporal 'grid', while having no sense of rhythm. Our musical education leads us to hear rhythm in the click of a train along the tracks. Indeed, we hear this rhythm in all kinds of sounds, and sometimes, by an act of will, make the most obnoxious repetitions bearable (and in due course unbearable) by hearing them in syncopated forms. But this act of hearing rhythm seems to be something over and above the perception of time. Rhythm may not be perceived by all who perceive sound, and who gain through that perception knowledge of a temporal order. A striking illustration is provided by the cross-rhythms of classical music. Why do we hear this:

Ex. 5

and not this:

Ex. 6

There is no material differences between the sounds, but in the first case there are two rhythms, while in the second case, there is one. The answer is that the first contains two musical movements, (albeit of the simplest kind), whereas the second contains only one. Thus our capacities for spatial and melodic perception in music guide our perception of the rhythm.

All this leads me to doubt that animals hear rhythm. Just as laughter is confined to rational beings, so too is dancing. (Only rational beings can be so perfectly without purpose.) Naturally, animals must hear temporal sequence, since this is part of perceiving. But can they hear a bar line, an off-beat, an anacrusis, a suspension, and the rest? Does the dove hear the subtle rhythm that we perceive in his call?

Ex. 7

Surely it is not only quixotic to suggest it; it also makes the entire phenomenon mysterious. If he heard that rhythm, would he not be persuaded of the merits of another? What is there in his behaviour that requires explanation in such terms? Animal experience is accessible to us only because we can describe its material causes, and its material effects. Distinctions which exist purely in the intentional realm can be attributed to an animal only in so far as they are revealed in these material circumstances. But it seems impossible to envisage what a dove's behaviour would have to be like for us to attribute to him, not only the perception of organized sounds, but also the perception of rhythm.

In changing the example, I have also changed the emphasis. When referring to musical movement I was at pains to point out that the experience of music depends upon a metaphorical transfer. In speaking of the rhythm of music, it could be argued, we are not speaking metaphorically; we are not transferring to music a term which has its proper application in some other sphere. Music is as central an example of rhythm, it might be said, as anything within our experience. Whether or not that is so is, however, not of the first importance. What matters is the nature of our perception of rhythm. In hearing rhythm we hear the music as *active*; it seems to be doing something (namely, dancing) which no sounds can do. When we hear a rhythm we hear sounds joining to and diverging from each other, exerting over one another peculiar 'fields of force', determining each other in a manner familiar from our knowledge of human movement. At the same time, we do not believe that any such thing is happening in the realm of sound: in a crucial sense, we are aware of the movement as *ours*. Hence, although we may not wish to describe the idea of rhythm as metaphorical, we must acknowledge that the perception of rhythm involves imaginative transfer of the kind involved in metaphor. We should not, therefore, be surprised that the peculiarly 'active' character of imaginative perception is also exemplified by the experience of rhythm. How we hear a rhythm is dependent upon our attention; it may be more or less voluntary, and more or less subject to imaginative activities of comparison and contrast. The experience bears the marks of imaginative endeavour, and cannot be assimilated to the perceptual capacities that we share with speechless beings.

Before proceeding to analyse the more complex instances of musical understanding, it is important to say something about the third fundamental category of musical experience, that of harmony. I remarked earlier upon the important intentional distinction between the perception of harmony and the perception of simultaneous tones. In the first case the tones are heard as *one* thing—a chord—in the second as several. The difference here is not that between discord and concord. I think it is normal to hear the following collection of tones, which opens the second section of Stravinsky's *Sacre du Printemps*, as a chord:

Here it is almost impossible to hear the tones separately, and this is not because one hears a block of undifferentiated sound, as in certain of the 'chords' of Stockhausen. The peculiar character of Stravinsky's chord (in which a seventh of E flat is squeezed as it were into the interstices of an E major triad) is that it is heard as one musical entity, spread over the whole range of the bass voice, with no tone 'emerging' as the principal bearer of musical significance. By contrast, the following famous concord from the 'Hostias' of Berlioz's *Grande Messe des Morts*, sounded simultaneously on three flutes and eight trombones, is often not heard as a chord:

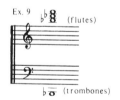

Once again it is quite easy to explain the effect: the extraordinary distance between the single bass note and the high minor triad, the agonizing difference of timbre, the absence of any intermediate parts (note how the effect disappears at once with the *pizzicato* octaves in the middle range that follow, and compare the similar example offered by the opening of Britten's first string quartet). But the explanation serves only to remind us that we can perceive consonance even where we do not perceive chords. Perhaps the best illustration of that truth is given by counterpoint, in which separate musical *movements* are heard as harmonizing, but in which at no point before the end does anything emerge that could be called a chord. One of the most important changes in the history of music is precisely that which occurred when the chord itself became a dominant musical unit, as it is in the symphonies of Beethoven, and as it remained until Schoenberg's *Pierrot Lunaire*. The Viennese school attempted to overthrow the dominance of chordal writing by overthrowing tonality: what it achieved, however, was not genuine counterpoint, but something wholly new.

One can envisage many explanations of the experience of concord. Since Helmholtz first opened this field to the methods of modern physics, the relations between sounds that had seemed so wondrous to the Pythagoreans have ceased to be puzzling. That we should distinguish concords and discords has become profoundly unsurprising; nor would it be surprising if birds and beasts distinguished them, and felt pleasure at the first and pain at the second. But the ability to make that kind of discrimination among sounds is not sufficient for the perception of harmony. The harmonic essence of musical dissonance lies not so much in the pattern of overtones that causes us to register it, as in the relations of tension, transition and resolution that it bears to surrounding chords. The following chord would be considered to be discordant, by anyone asked to classify it simply on the basis of its sound:

Ex. 10

But in the context of Chopin's Nocturne Op.27 No. 1, in C sharp minor, it is simply one of a harmonious sequence effecting a transition. Likewise, in a style like that of jazz, where accessory notes are often added to the chords, it is not normal to hear dissonance in discord: an all-pervading sweetness of harmony may be the more usual perception, so that sonorities considered highly dissonant in other contexts are felt to require no resolution. Here is how Art Tatum harmonizes the first bar of 'Aunt Hagar's Blues':

Ex. 11

From the first cluttered chord you feel the force of D flat major. The little gesture to the bass simply reinforces an existing sense of lazy consonance and delicious relaxation. Nevertheless that fairly standard jazz augmentation of a major chord would be an intolerable dissonance even in Wagner.

When considering such examples it is important to note that musical analysis often distinguishes identical sounds. Depending on context, a chord may be given several conflicting descriptions. The chord in ex. 10 would be described as a diminished seventh over an A flat pedal, forming part of a sequence which steadily increases the tension in A flat major so that the music passes with a feeling of release into D flat. Had it occurred in a Schoenberg string quartet (which is a possibility), you could not have described the chord in that way. Likewise, it is only the peculiar expectations associated with jazz improvisation that enable us to describe the first chord of ex. 11 as a seventh chord of D flat with a flattened ninth. If those sounds were to occur in Berg (which is highly likely) we would again have to alter our description. This is, of course, not surprising. But it shows very clearly that the dynamic relations that we perceive when we hear music enter into the description of what we hear. In effect we are forced to determine the criteria of identity of chords differently from the criteria for the identity of the sounds that compose them. This surely must reinforce the view that harmony belongs not to the material world of sound, but to the intentional world of musical experience. Consider the many cases in which critics cannot decide which chord a composer is using. What, for example, is the last chord of Janáček's 'On an Overgrown Path' (first series)? No answer seems right, because you cannot say what key the piece has ended in—whether the triumphant E major of the melody, or the questioning C sharp minor of the owl's call. In Debussy's early song 'Recueillement', we find the following:

Ex. 12

What is the chord in the first bar? Surely, you would say, an open fifth on C sharp. But the effect of the second bar, according to one critic, causes even this first bar to be heard as a suspension over a dominant seventh in A major.[18] Here we see a harmony feeding back into the tones that precede it, and causing us to hear and so to describe them differently. You might say, parodying Frege, that only in the totality of a musical phrase do sounds determine harmony. In which case our perception of harmony is dependent upon our musical understanding as a whole. It cannot be separated from the understanding of movement, tension, and release. Moreover, what we experience in hearing harmony is something that has to be described in metaphorical terms. Chords are heard as 'spaced', 'open', 'filled', 'hollow' (to use the basic metaphors of musical experience): harmony is described in terms of geometrical relations between parts, in terms of the coming together and separating of movements, in terms of oppositions and agreements. Just as melody involves the metaphorical transference of ideas of 'movement', 'space', 'height' and 'depth', so does harmony involve the metaphorical transference of ideas of 'tension', 'relaxation', 'conflict' and 'resolution'. Although there is a material base to the perception of these things, there is more to perceiving them than perceiving their material base.

In exploring the three dimensions of musical perception we seem to have laid bare a realm of intentional understanding which is both active in the manner of imaginative experience, and also essentially dependent upon metaphor. My aim has been to specify, not sufficient, but necessary conditions of musical understanding, in the form of constraints upon the *experience* in which understanding rests. It remains to explore how those constraints limit the experience of musical content, and so determine the form which a theory of musical expression must take. The defender of the 'absolute' in music may not agree with such an explanation. But if I am right, then even Hanslick's description of music, as *tönend-bewegte Form*, contains a description *(bewegte)* that does not literally apply to it. So why not allow that music may also be 'melancholy', 'expressive', and 'passionate'? In addressing this question I shall confine myself to a few far from obvious remarks, in the hope that the reader will see a way forward which also promises a solution to the original problem.

One way of theorizing the metaphorical character in musical perception is in terms of 'projection'. Since the movement is not literally *in* the music, it must, we are inclined to think, have been put there by the listener. It results from an act of 'projection', whereby, to borrow Hume's famous simile, the mind 'spreads itself upon objects'.[19] To say this is relatively harmless, so long as we realize that we have said nothing. For the only truth of the matter is that sounds heard as musical movement do not move. The disposition to hear them as moving is inseparable from the experience of music, but that does not mean that there is some act of 'projection' that transfers movement, as it were, to the auditory world.

Nevertheless, the language of 'projection' is useful. It presents a picture of how a theory of musical understanding might be extended from the primitive 'dimensions' that I have been discussing, to the more complex phenomena that interest the critic. According to the doctrine of projection we do not merely 'transfer a term' when we hear musical movement: we also transfer the movement. (As we might be thought to 'transfer' the face from our thought to the canvas in which we see it.) The temptation to speak in this way must eventually be resisted. But by giving way to it now, and then resisting it later, we will gain some insight into what can, and what cannot, be said by way of elucidating musical expression. So let us give way to it. Just as we transfer an experience of movement to music (which does not move), so do we transfer an experience of passion to music (which has no passions). We project into the music the inner life that is ours, and that is *how* we hear it there. This is not the same as hearing resemblances between music and feeling, any more than hearing musical movement is hearing structural relations on which the movement depends. The experience of transfer is *sui generis*. The emotion that is heard belongs purely to the intentional and not to the material realm. Such a theory would explain, for example, the enormous gap that exists between the material reality of the sounds that we hear, and the spiritual complexity of the emotions that we 'project' into them. There can be as large a gap as you like between an intentional object which is the construct of imagination, and the material object in which it is experienced. But the theory leaves unsolved the perennial difficulties surrounding the idea of musical 'content'.

In attempting to overcome those difficulties, it is useful to draw attention to another context in which 'understanding' occurs, and in which understanding has often been thought to involve 'projection': the context of human relations. It has often been said that, in order to understand the gesture, state of mind, or feeling of another, some kind of 'empathy' or *'Einfühlung'* is required, whereby I imaginatively project myself into his position and see the world through his eyes. Without that act of projection I know only his behaviour, not his mind. First in the field among theories of musical expression during this century were those that sought to extend the doctrine of *Einfühlung* from people to art.[20] In neither case is it correct: but in both cases it is illuminating.

The original picture offered by the proponents of *Einfühlung* was this: a state of mind has two aspects, that which is revealed in body and behaviour, and that which is 'subjective', captured by the contents of the subject's immediate awareness, but by nothing else. The essence of the mental state consists in the second aspect, and genuine knowledge of another's state of mind must involve knowledge of that aspect. However, that aspect is purely intentional: it is therefore the object only of immediate awareness and its nature is falsified by awareness of any other kind. To know it is also to know that you do not *discover* its nature: you know it only as 'given'. How then, can *I* know in *that* way, what is given to *you?* *Einfühlung* is invented as the faculty whereby I adopt, as it were, the vestiges of your outward expression, and so come to feel inwardly in myself the subjective awareness that is yours. I then re-create the intentional object of your awareness, and so know your state of mind in its inner essence. What I then know can be communicated only through the act of *Einfühlung*. I could not set out to describe the intentional structure of this state of mind and thereby make it available in its inner essence to you: nor could I make it available to you *simply* by acquainting you with its expression.

The claim is two-fold: that there is an objective and a subjective aspect to states of mind; and that there is a form of knowledge proper to each. These claims can each be interpreted in a misleading and in a harmless way. The misleading interpretation is the most usual, and goes as follows: there are properties of the mental which are perceivable only from the first person point of view. (This is the subjective aspect of the mental.) Those properties are knowable only by acquaintance. That way of putting the doctrine is misleading because of its commitment to a Cartesian view of the mind. The mind is represented as a subjective residue which is neither reducible to nor identical with any item in the physical world.

The harmless interpretation reads as follows. There are two modes of knowledge of the mental, which we could call, borrowing Russellian terminology, knowledge by description and knowledge by acquaintance. One is characteristic of my knowledge of your mind, the other character-istic of my knowledge of mine. The second is 'immediate' (based on nothing); hence it involves no recognition of features whereby I identify my mental state. Hence it does not involve the discovery of purely subjective properties of the mental. It is immediate knowledge of the very same thing that is known mediately and in the normal manner through the study of those physical processes which give evidence of the mental. There is a difference between being in pain and merely observing it. In the former case the pain features among the objects of immediate awareness. Even on this metaphysically harmless interpretation, however, there is an epistemological asymmetry between the first and the third person points of view. One can speak of someone not only as having theoretical knowledge of the characteristics of fear, say, but also as having another kind of knowledge associated with the 'immediate' perception about which nothing can be said. This second kind of knowledge is 'knowing what it's like'. It is an important part of the theory of imagination to show how such knowledge can be acquired by someone who does not *have* the mental state that is known. How can I know what your fear is like without feeling it? One answer is by *Einfühlung*. There is a kind of response to your face and gestures which makes available to me your first-person perspective on the mental state that I can otherwise know only by observation. I imagine what it is like to feel as you do. I then entertain your emotion within the field of my own point of view. There is nothing to be *said* about what I thereby come to know, for there is no new proposition that I know. But the experience may be of a peculiar importance, both as cementing the bond between us, and as helping me to see the force of the reasons that you offer for your action. Knowing your fear in *that* way I can see why you are compelled to flee. There is (or seems to be) a close connection between 'knowing what it's like' and the premises of practical reasoning.

'Knowledge by acquaintance' lies wholly outside the reach of any third-person perspective; it is a perspective on the mental that cannot be transcribed, a form of knowledge that contains no proposition known. If this is so, then there is no longer any paradox, either in the claim that you have to 'enter into' someone's state of mind in order to know it by acquaintance, or in the claim that what you thereby know is inexpressible.

Often *Einfühlung* has for object not a recognized emotion, but simply a facial expression, a gesture, or a frown. Such things often seem peculiarly significant, and, whether by an act of imitation, by the residue of such an act, or by whatever method (who knows, in fact, how it is done?), we 'enter into' them, and transform our observation of another's expression, into the imaginative knowledge of 'what it is like'. This might lead us to understand the place of his present state of mind in his projects and intentions. Thus *Einfühlung* may give us a picture of the complete elaboration of a state of mind which, from the third person point of view, is merely hinted at or roughly sketched.

Suppose however that someone is *not* feeling what I imaginatively feel in responding to his expression. He is feeling nothing, say, or something quite different. If he is a mimic or an actor, he may be intending to represent a character who is feeling exactly what I am prompted to 'know by acquaintance'. It is his intention that I should have just the kind of *Einfühlung* that I have. Here is a case where I might be tempted to say: behind that gesture, there is feeling. But of course I do not attribute the feeling to anyone, least of all to the actor before me. I have 'entered into' an absent state of mind. We could say, to return to the metaphor that we should now see how to eliminate, that I have 'projected' the feeling into the gesture that I see.

In the normal case, an actor will be representing a precise character in precise circumstances, suffering, no doubt, some identifiable emotion. The dramatic context will provide the thoughts through which the object of that feeling can be defined. My act of *Einfühlung* takes place against a background of knowledge by description, and so I need feel no hesitation in characterizing what is expressed. If someone says to me 'There is a quite definite emotion in these lines', then I may be able to reply to him with a description: 'It is a sentimental remorse over the murder of Desdemona'. But such descriptions, however complex and astute, never seem to give us what we are looking for. They never seem to capture what is known by the person who understands the play. We want to add; 'But of course, the important thing is the quite peculiar *shade* of remorse that is conveyed by the lines'. In answer to the question 'What shade?' the sensible critic then has recourse to ostension: '*That* shade!', and he points to the text. This way the critic also gives a reason for returning to the lines, for there is no other way of rehearsing what they tell you. At the same time it begins to look strange that we harbour the belief in an expressed 'content'. For, even in these dramatic examples, we are reluctant to identify the content independently of its form.

This problem has been discussed in aesthetics under many labels: the 'heresy of paraphrase', the 'inseparability of form and content', the contrast between 'intuition' and 'concept', or between 'expression' and 'description'. All these time-honoured phrases are ways of approaching, from rival theoretical standpoints, the area upon which our enquiry has now focused. In certain circumstances, observing a gesture of expression, we have the experience of *Einfühlung*, of knowing what it is like, whereby the gesture becomes, in imagination, our own. We then feel it, not from the observer's, but from the subject's point of view. This experience may occur, and may grant a sense of the completeness of its object, whether or not the context permits *description* of the object of the other's feeling; whether or not we believe that 'feeling' is the right term for what is known; and whether or not we even believe that there *is* another, into whose mental arena we have felt our way. It is as though we have been granted a first-person perspective on a world that we know is not ours. Neither is it anyone else's. It is a creation of the imagination, and retains the impersonality of the imaginative act. What we know from the first-person perspective can be known only from that perspective — which is not to say that it is mysterious. Or rather, it is mysterious only in the way that the first-person perspective is mysterious. (I believe that, when Schopenhauer referred our experience of music to the will, he was consciously invoking this idea of 'immediate' first-personal knowledge. The will is the inner essence of the mental, which can be known either directly, through its own activity, or else indirectly, through representation. Music is the only art that conveys that 'direct', immediate knowledge of the will that we gain through our own activity.[21])

We have now effectively eliminated all reference to 'projection'. That term stood proxy for the following ideas: a gesture can be treated as the sign or expression of a state of mind; it can also be imaginatively 'adopted' so as to enter into the first-person perspective of the observer. This adoption may occur even when the circumstances surrounding the gesture are so incomplete as to provide no description of its intentional object. There may be a sense of 'what it is like' from which all intentionality has been extruded. When I see a gesture from the first-person point of view then I do not only see it as an expression; I grasp the completeness of the state of mind that is intimated through it. That is all that should be meant by saying that I 'project' my feeling into the gesture. And only in context will my perspective on the gesture also contain some intimation of its object.

It remains to fit those observations into our earlier account of musical understanding. In dramatic use, or in the context of a song, the circumstances that surround the musical gesture give us some intimation of its intentionality. We can then say something about *what* is expressed. But this context is not normally present, and even when it is, it will not provide the 'inner meaning' of what we hear. Normally we hear musical gestures as we might see a man gesticulating to an unseen audience, perhaps guessing at the objects of his feeling, perhaps remaining entirely ignorant of them. Even in such circumstances, we may enter into gestures and see them from 'within'. For we may see them as containing spirit, character, and an outlook on the world. Just as we see spirit, life and activity in gestures, so do we hear movement, life and activity in music. And sometimes we enter into that movement as we do into the movement of an imaginary being: a first-person perspective on that movement is opened to us, and for a moment it is ours. Then comes, in addition to the recognition of expression, the sense of being acquainted with a whole state of mind, which cannot be independently described, except perhaps in lame and unformed gestures.

That is only a sketch, and of course it falls far short of giving a full account of musical understanding. In particular it leaves the *critical* question — the question, when is it right to hear music in terms of some 'content' — unanswered. But perhaps that is a merit; for it seems to me a singular defect of those theories of musical meaning which proceed by giving conditions for the application of emotion terms to music that they solve the critical question too *easily*.[22] They enable us to say what a passage expresses, only by reducing the experience of expression to a recognitional capacity, and so removing its importance. It becomes impossible to say why it *matters* that emotions should be heard in music, why this should be a part of musical understanding. To show why it matters is also to show why criticism is hard. And that is as it should be.

I have given necessary, but not sufficient conditions for musical understanding. I hope, however, that I have given some indication of how a
theory of musical understanding in terms of entrenched metaphor may be
extended to account for the more puzzling features of musical expression:
its importance, its ineffability, and the 'immediacy' which Schopenhauer
regarded as so important. Understanding music involves the active
creation of an intentional world, in which inert sounds are transfigured
into movements, harmonies, rhythms — metaphorical gestures in a
metaphorical space. And into these metaphorical gestures a metaphorical
soul is breathed by the sympathetic listener. At a certain point, he has the
experience of a first-person perspective on gestures that are no-one's. This
can be as much a part of understanding what he hears as is the hearing of a
melody. For it is no more than a continuation of the imaginative activity
which is involved in hearing music: the activity of transfiguring sound into
figurative space, so that 'you are the music while the music lasts'.

All of the following have helped me in the preparation of this chapter,
through criticisms offered at various stages during its production: Ruby
Meager, Sally Shreir, David Hamlyn, Edward T. Cone, Ian McFetridge,
Thomas Carson Mark, and Jerrold Levinson.

The Eye of the Camera

9 Photography and Representation

Critics and philosophers have occasionally been troubled by the question whether the cinema is an independent art form — independent, that is, of the theatre, from which it borrows so many conventions.[1] This question can be traced back to a more basic one, the question whether photography is capable of representing anything. I shall argue that it is not and that, insofar as there is representation in film, its origin is not photographic. A film is a photograph of a dramatic representation; it is not, because it cannot be, a photographic representation. It follows that if there is such a thing as a cinematic masterpiece it will be so because — like *Wild Strawberries* and *La règle du jeu* — it is in the first place a dramatic masterpiece.

It seems odd to say that photography is not a mode of representation. For a photograph has in common with a painting the property by which the painting represents the world, the property of sharing, in some sense, the appearance of its subject. Indeed, it is sometimes thought that since a photograph more effectively shares the appearance of its subject than a typical painting, photography is a better mode of representation. Photography might even be thought to have *replaced* painting as a mode of visual representation. Painters have felt that if the aim of painting is really to reproduce the appearances of things, then painting must give way to whatever means are available to reproduce an appearance more accurately. It has therefore been said that painting aims to record the appearances of things only so as to capture the experience of observing them (the *impression*) and that the accurate copying of appearances will normally be at variance with this aim. Here we have the seeds of expressionism and the origin of the view (a view which not only is mistaken but which has also proved disastrous for the history of modern art) that painting is somehow purer when it is abstract and closer to its essence as an art.

Let us first dismiss the word 'representation'. Of course this word can be applied to photography. We wish to know whether there is some feature, suitably called representation, common to painting and photography. And we wish to know whether that feature has in each case a comparable aesthetic value, so that we can speak not only of representation but also of representational art. (There is an important feature — sound — in common to music and to fountains, but only the first of these is properly described as an *art* of sound.)

1

In order to understand what I mean by saying that photography is not a representational art, it is important to separate painting and photography as much as possible, so as to discuss not actual painting and actual photography but an ideal form of each, an ideal which represents the essential differences between them. Ideal photography differs from actual photography as indeed ideal painting differs from actual painting. Actual photography is the result of the attempt by photographers to pollute the ideal of their craft with the aims and methods of painting.

By an 'ideal' I mean a logical ideal. The ideal of photography is not an ideal at which photography aims or ought to aim. On the contrary, it is a logical fiction, designed merely to capture what is distinctive in the photographic relation and in our interest in it. It will be clear from this discussion that there need be no such thing as an ideal photograph in my sense, and the reader should not be deterred if I begin by describing photography in terms that seem to be exaggerated or false.

The ideal painting stands in a certain 'intentional' relation to a subject.[2] In other words, if a painting represents a subject, it does not follow that the subject exists nor, if it does exist, that the painting represents the subject as it is. Moreover, if x is a painting of a man, it does not follow that there is some *particular* man of which x is the painting. Furthermore, the painting stands in this intentional relation to its subject because of a representational act, the artist's act, and in characterizing the relation between a painting and its subject we are also describing the artist's intention. The successful realization of that intention lies in the creation of an appearance, an appearance which in some way leads the spectator to recognize the subject.

The ideal photograph also stands in a certain relation to a subject: a photograph is a photograph *of* something. But the relation is here causal and not intentional.[3] In other words, if a photograph is a photograph of a subject, it follows that the subject exists, and if x is a photograph of a man, there is a particular man of whom x is the photograph. It also follows, though for different reasons, that the subject is, roughly, as it appears in the photograph. In characterizing the relation between the ideal photograph and its subject, one is characterizing not an intention but a causal process, and while there is, as a rule, an intentional act involved, this is not an essential part of the photographic relation. The ideal photograph also yields an appearance, but the appearance is not interesting as the realization of an intention but rather as a record of how an actual object looked.

Since the end point of the two processes is, or can be, so similar, it is tempting to think that the intentionality of the one relation and the causality of the other are quite irrelevant to the standing of the finished product. In both cases, it seems, the important part of representation lies in the fact that the spectator can see the subject *in* the picture. The appreciation of photographs and the appreciation of paintings both involve the exercise of the capacity to 'see as', in the quite special sense in which one may see *x* as *y* without believing or being tempted to believe that *x* is *y*.

2

Now, it would be a simple matter to define 'representation' so that '*x* represents *y*' is true only if *x* expresses a thought about *y*, or if *x* is designed to remind one of *y*, or whatever, in which case a relation that was *merely* causal (a relation that was not characterized in terms of any thought, intention, or other mental act) would never be sufficient for representation. We need to be clear, however, why we should wish to define representation in one way rather than in another. What hangs on the decision? In particular, why should it matter that the relation between a painting and its subject is an intentional relation while the photographic relation is merely causal? I shall therefore begin by considering our experience of painting and the effect on that experience of the intentionality of the relation between a painting and its subject.

When I appreciate a painting as a representation, I see it as what it represents, but I do not take it for what it represents. Nor do I necessarily believe that what is represented in the painting exists nor, if it does exist, that it has the appearance of the object that I see *in* the painting. Suppose that a certain painting represents a warrior. I may in fact see it not as a warrior but as a god. Here three 'objects' of interest may be distinguished:
1 The intentional object of sight: a god (defined by my experience).
2 The represented object: a warrior (defined, to put it rather crudely, by the painter's intention).[4]
3 The material object of sight: the painting.[5]
The distinction between 1 and 2 is not as clear-cut as it might seem: it would become so only if we could separate the 'pure appearance' of the painting from the sense of intention with which it is endowed. We cannot do this, not only because we can never separate our experience of human activity from our understanding of intention but also because in the case of a picture we are dealing with an object that is manifestly the expression of thought. Hence we will look for clues as to how the painting is intended to be seen and — such being the nature of 'seeing as' — our sense of what is intended will determine our experience of what is there.

The 'inference' view of perception, the view that there are certain things that we *basically* see (sense-data, etc) from which we then *infer* the existence of other things, is wrong both as a matter of philosophical psychology, since there is no criterion for distinguishing datum and inference, and as a matter of epistemology, since it is only if we sometimes have knowledge of the 'inferred' entities that we can have knowledge of the experience.[6] The point applies also to intention: we do not see the gestures and movements of another man and then infer from them the existence of intentions; rather, we see the gestures as intentional, and that is the correct description of what we see. But of course we cannot choose to see just what we will as a manifestation of intention. Our ability to see intention depends on our ability to interpret an activity as characteristically human, and here, in the case of representational art, it involves our understanding the dimensions and conventions of the medium. Art manifests the 'common knowledge' of a culture;[7] as E. H. Gombrich has made clear, to understand art is to be familiar with the constraints imposed by the medium and to be able to separate that which is due to the medium from that which is due to the man. Such facts lead us to speak of understanding or misunderstanding representational painting.

Although there is not space to discuss fully the concept of 'understanding' that is involved here, it is worth mentioning the following point: to understand a painting involves understanding thoughts. These thoughts are, in a sense, communicated by the painting. They underlie the painter's intention, and at the same time they inform our way of seeing the canvas. Such thoughts determine the perception of the man who sees with understanding, and it is at least partly in terms of our apprehension of thoughts that we must describe what we see in the picture. We see not only a man on a horse but a man of a certain character and bearing. And *what* we see is determined not by independent properties of the subject but by our understanding of the painting. It is the way the eyes are painted that gives that sense of authority, the particular lie of the arm that reveals the arrogant character, and so on. In other words, properties of the medium influence not only what is seen in the picture but also the way it is seen. Moreover, they present to us a vision that we attribute not to ourselves but to another man; we think of ourselves as sharing in the vision of the artist, and the omnipresence of intention changes our experience from something private into something shared. The picture presents us not merely with the perception of a man but with a thought about him, a thought embodied in perceptual form.[8] And here, just as in the case of language, thought has that character of objectivity and publicity upon which Frege commented.[9] It is precisely when we have the communication of thoughts about a subject that the concept of representation becomes applicable; and therefore literature and painting are representational in the same sense.

3

The ideal painting has no particular need for an identity of appearance with its subject. In order to present a visual account of the Duke of Wellington, it is not necessary for an artist to strive to present an exact copy of the Duke's appearance.[10] Indeed, it is tempting here to dispense with the notion of appearance altogether, to construe the painting as a conventional or even quasi-linguistic act which stands in a semantic relation — a relation of reference — to its subject, and which presents a visual appearance only as a means of fulfilling a referential function. Such a view would explain, perhaps better than all rival theories of representation, the role of intention in our understanding of art.[11]

I do not know how far those philosophers influenced by Gombrich's arguments — arguments emphasizing the place of convention in our understanding of visual art — would wish to take the analogy with language. I do not know, for example, whether a convention according to which colours were to be represented by their complements — a red object by a patch of green, a yellow object by a patch of blue — would be conceivable for such philosophers, conceivable, that is, as a mode of pictorial representation. It is undeniable, however, that such a painting would convey to someone who understood the convention as much information about its subject as another painting in which the colours copy the original. More bizarre conventions could also be imagined: a painting could be constructed entirely out of dashes and circles, arranged according to the grammar of a visual code. Given the right conventions, such a painting would count, according to the reference theory, as an extremely faithful representation of its subject. It would be read as a kind of scrambled message which had to be decoded in order to permit an understanding of what it says.

However, we cannot treat the visual connection between a painting and its subject as an entirely accidental matter, accidental, that is, to any process of representation that the painting may display. For we cannot deny that representational painting interests us primarily because of the visual connection with its subject. We are interested in the visual relation between painting and subject because it is by means of this relation that the painting represents. The artist presents us with a way of seeing (and not just any way of thinking of) his subject. (Hence the revolutionary character of such painters as Caravaggio and de la Tour.) It is this visual relation which seems to require elucidation. We cannot explain pictorial representation independently of the visual aspect of paintings and still expect our explanation to cast light upon the problem of the visual relation between a picture and its subject-matter. And yet it is that relation which is understood by the appreciative spectator.

That objection is of course not conclusive. It also seems to assume that a semantic theory of art (a theory which sees representation in terms of reference) must necessarily also be a linguistic theory. Surely there could be relations of reference that do not reflect the conventions of language, even relations that need to be understood in essentially visual terms. Let us, then, consider what such a conception of reference might be like.

It is no accident that language has a grammar. The existence of grammar is a necessary part of language and part of the all-important connection between language and truth. But there is a further significance in grammar, at least as grammar is now conceived. For the contemporary logician, grammar is primarily a 'generative' function, a means of building complex sentences from the finite number of linguistic parts. Taken in conjunction with a theory of interpretation, a proper grammar will explain how speakers of a language understand an indefinite number of sentences on the basis of understanding only a finite number of words.[12] In this way we can show how the truth or falsehood of a sentence depends upon the reference of its parts, and the concept of reference in language becomes inextricably bound up with the idea that from the references of words we may derive the truth conditions of sentences. This 'generative connection' between reference and truth is part of the intuitive understanding of reference which is common to all speakers of a language.

It is here, I think, that we find a striking difference between language and painting. While there may be repertoires and conventions in painting, there is nothing approaching grammar as we understand it. For one thing, the requirement of finitude is not obviously met. It is clearly true that we understand the representational meaning of, say, a Carpaccio through understanding the representational meaning of its parts. But the parts themselves are understood in *precisely the same way;* that is, they too have parts, each of which is potentially divisible into significant components, and so on ad infinitum. Moreover, there seems to be no way in which we can divide the painting into grammatically significant parts — no way in which we can provide a syntax which isolates those parts of the painting that have a particular semantic role. For in advance of seeing the painting, we have no rule which will decide the point, and thus the idea of syntactic or semantic rules becomes inapplicable. The means whereby we understand the total representation are identical with the means whereby we understand the parts. Understanding is not secured either by rules or by conventions but seems to be, on the contrary, a natural function of the normal eye. As we see the meaning of the painting, so do we see the meaning of its parts. This contrasts sharply with the case of reference in language, where we *construct* the meaning of the sentence from the reference of its parts, and where the parts themselves have reference in a way that it ultimately conventional.

There seems to be no justification, then, for thinking of representation in terms of reference. We could, however, insist that the relation of a painting to its subject is one of reference only by removing from 'reference' that feature which leads us to think that an account of reference is also an account of understanding. To speak of the connection between a word and a thing as one of reference is to show how we understand the word, for it is to show how the truth conditions of sentences containing the word are determined. If we speak of reference in describing paintings, therefore, we should not think that we thereby cast any light on the *understanding* of representation. What representation is, how we understand it, and how it affects us — those questions seem to remain as obscure as ever. The only thing that remains to support the invocation of reference is the fact that paintings may be true or false. It is that fact which we must now consider.

4

The fact that a painting may be true or false plays a vital role in visual appreciation. We could not explain realism, for example, either in painting or in literature, unless we invoked the concept of truth. Again we must emphasize information (and therefore the concept of reference) in our understanding of the painter's art; or at least we are obliged to find some feature of the painting that can be substituted for reference and which will show how the connection with truth is established.

Such a feature, as a matter of fact, has already been described: we may describe realism in terms of what we see *in* the painting. We therefore analyse truth not in terms of a relation between the painting and the world but in terms of a relation between what we see in the painting and the world. Goya's portrait of the Duke of Wellington is realistic because the figure we see in the painting resembles the Duke of Wellington.[13] The truth of the painting amounts to the truth of the viewer's perception; in other words, the 'intentional object of sight' corresponds to the nature of the subject. Those thoughts which animate our perception when we see the realistic painting with understanding are true thoughts.[14] Truth is not a property of the painting in the direct way in which it is the property of a sentence, and the possibility of predicating the truth of a painting does not open the way to a semantic theory of art any more than it opens the way to a semantic theory of, for example, clouds, or of any other phenomenon in which aspects may be seen.

Although distinctions may be made between true and false pictures, an aesthetic appreciation remains in one sense indifferent to the truth of its object. A person who has an aesthetic interest in the *Odyssey* is not concerned with the literal truth of the narrative. Certainly it is important to him that the *Odyssey* be lifelike, but the existence of Odysseus and the reality of the scenes described are matters of aesthetic indifference. Indeed, it is characteristic of aesthetic interest that most of its objects in representation are imaginary. For unless it were possible to represent imaginary things, representation could hardly be very important to us. It is important because it enables the presentation of scenes and characters toward which we have only contemplative attitudes: scenes and characters which, being unreal, allow our practical natures to remain unengaged.

If the concept of representation is to be of aesthetic importance, it must be possible to describe an aesthetic interest in representation. Only if there is such a thing as aesthetic interest which has representation as its object can there be representational art (as opposed to art that happens to be representational). It is commonly said that an aesthetic interest in something is an interest in it for its own sake: the object is not treated as a surrogate for another; it is *itself* the principal object of attention. It follows that an aesthetic interest in the representational properties of a picture must also involve a kind of interest in the picture and not merely in the thing represented.[15]

Now, *one* difference between an aesthetic interest in a picture, and an interest in the picture as a surrogate for its subject, lies in the kind of reason that might be given for the interest. (And to give the reasons for an interest is to give an account of its intentional object and therefore of the interest itself.) If I ask a man why he is looking at a picture, there are several kinds of reply that he might give. In one case his reasons will be reasons for an interest only in the things depicted: they will describe properties of the subject which make it interesting. Here the interest in the picture is derivative: it lies in the fact that the picture reveals properties of its subject. The picture is being treated as a means of access to the subject, and it is therefore dispensable to the extent that there is a better means to hand (say, the subject itself). With that case one may contrast two others. First, there is the case where the man's reasons refer only to properties of the picture — to pictorial properties, such as colour, shape, and line — and do not mention the subject. For such a man the picture has interest as an abstract composition, and its representational nature is wholly irrelevant to him. Second, there is the case where the reasons for the interest are reasons for an interest in the *picture* (in the way it looks) even though they make essential reference to the subject and can be understood as reasons only by someone who understands the reference to the subject. For example, the observer may refer to a particular gesture of a certain figure, and a particular way of painting that gesture, as revelatory of the subject's character (for example, the barmaid's hands on the counter in Manet's *Bar aux Folies-Bergère*). Clearly, that is a reason not only for an interest in the subject but also (and primarily) for an interest in the picture, since it gives a reason for an interest in something which can be understood only by looking at the picture. Such an interest leads naturally to another, to an interest in the use of the medium — in the way the painting presents its subject and therefore in the way in which the subject is seen by the painter. Here it could not be said that the painting is being treated as a surrogate for its subject: it is *itself* the object of interest and irreplaceable by the thing depicted. The interest is not in representation for the sake of its subject but in representation for its own sake. And it is such an interest that forms the core of the aesthetic experience of pictorial art, and which — if analysed more fully — would explain not only the value of that experience but also the nature and value of the art which is its object. We see at once that such an interest is not, and cannot be, an interest in the literal truth of the picture.

5

If I were to describe, then, *what I see* in a picture, I would be bound not merely to describe the visual properties of the subject but also to provide an interpretation of the subject, a way of seeing it. The description under which the subject is seen is given by the total thought in terms of which I understand the picture. In the case of portraiture, this interpretive thought need not be a thought about the momentary appearance of the subject: it need not be the thought 'He looked like that'. The thought may relate to the subject not as he appeared at any one moment but as he was or, rather, as the artist saw him to be. The appearance may be presented only because it embodies the reality, in which case it will be the reality that is understood (or misunderstood) by the spectator.

One of the most important differences between photography and portraiture as traditionally practised lies in the relation of each to time. It is characteristic of photography that, being understood in terms of a causal relation to its subject, it is thought of as revealing something momentary about its subject — how the subject looked at a particular moment. And that sense of the moment is seldom lost in photography, for reasons that will shortly be apparent. Portrait painting, however, aims to capture the sense of time and to represent its subject as extended in time, even in the process of displaying a particular moment of its existence. Portraiture is not an art of the momentary, and its aim is not merely to capture fleeting appearances. The aim of painting is to give insight, and the creation of an appearance is important mainly as the expression of thought. While a causal relation is a relation between events, there is no such narrow restriction on the subject-matter of a thought. This perhaps partially explains the frequently made comment that the true art of portraiture died with the advent of photography and that representational art, insofar as it still pursues an ideal of realism, is unable to capture, as the realist ought to capture, the sense of the passage of time.[16]

Of course a photographer can aim to capture that fleeting appearance which gives the most reliable indication of his subject's character. He may attempt to find in the momentary some *sign* of what is permanent. But there is a great difference between an image which is a sign of something permanent and an image which is an expression of it. To express the permanent is to give voice to a thought about its nature. To give a sign of the permanent is to create something from which its properties may be inferred. A man may remain silent when asked to defend his friend, and from that silence I infer his friend's guilt. Yet the man has certainly not expressed the thought that his friend is guilty. Similarly a photograph may give signs of what is permanent despite the fact that it is incapable of expressing it.

6

The ideal photograph, as I mentioned earlier, stands in a causal relation to its subject and 'represents' its subject by reproducing its appearance. In understanding something as an ideal photograph, we understand it as exemplifying this causal process, a process which originates in the subject 'represented' and which has as its end point the production of a copy of an appearance. By a 'copy' of an appearance I mean an object such that what is seen in it by a man with normal eyes and understanding (the intentional object of sight) resembles as nearly as possible what is seen when such a man observes the subject itself from a certain angle at a certain point in its history. A person studying an ideal photograph is given a very good idea of *how something looked*. The result is that, from studying a photograph he may come to know how something looked in the way that he might know it if he had actually seen it.

With an ideal photograph it is neither necessary nor even possible that the photographer's intention should enter as a serious factor in determining how the picture is seen. It is recognized at once for what it is — not as an interpretation of reality but as a presentation of how something looked. In some sense, looking at a photograph is a substitute for looking at the thing itself. Consider, for example, the most 'realistic' of all photographic media, the television. It seems scarcely more contentious to say that I saw someone on the television — that is, that in watching the television I saw *him* — than to say that I saw him in a mirror. Television is like a mirror: it does not so much destroy as embellish that elaborate causal chain which is the natural process of visual perception.

Of course it is not necessary to define the subject of a photograph in terms of this causal process, for the subject could be identified in some other way. But the fact remains that when we say that *x* is a photograph of *y* we *are* referring to this causal relation, and it is in terms of the causal relation that the subject of a photograph is normally understood. Let us at least say that the subject is so defined for my logical ideal of photography: that premise is all that my argument requires.

It follows, first, that the subject of the ideal photograph must exist; secondly, that it must appear roughly as it appears in the photograph; and thirdly, that its appearance in the photograph is its appearance at a particular moment of its existence.

The first of those features is an immediate consequence of the fact that the relation between a photograph and its subject is a causal relation. If *a* is the cause of *b*, then the existence of *b* is sufficient for the existence of *a*. The photograph lacks that quality of 'intentional inexistence' which is characteristic of painting. The ideal photograph, therefore, is incapable of representing anything unreal; if a photograph is a photograph of a man, then there is some particular man of whom it is a photograph.

Of course I may take a photograph of a draped nude and call it *Venus*, but insofar as this can be understood as an exercise in fiction, it should not be thought of as a photographic representation of Venus but rather as the photograph of a representation of Venus. In other words, the process of fictional representation occurs not in the photograph but in the subject: it is the *subject* which represents Venus; the photograph does no more than disseminate its visual character to other eyes. This is not to say that the model is (unknown to herself) acting Venus. It is not she who is representing Venus but the photographer, who uses her in his representation. But the representational act, the act which embodies the representational thought, is completed before the photograph is ever taken. As we shall see, this fictional incompetence of photography is of great importance in our understanding of the cinema; but it also severely limits the aesthetic significance of 'representation' in photography. As we saw earlier, representation in art has a special significance precisely because of the possibility that we can understand it — in the sense of understanding its content — while being indifferent to, or unconcerned with, its literal truth. That is why fictional representation is not merely an important form of representational art but in fact the primary form of it, the form through which the aesthetic understanding finds its principal mode of expression.

One may wish to argue that my example is a special one, that there are other ways of creating fictional representations which are essentially photographic. In other words, it is not necessary for the photographer to create an independent representation in order for his photograph to be fictional. Suppose he were to take a photograph of a drunken tramp and label it *Silenus*. Would that not be a fictional photograph, comparable, indeed, to a painting of Silenus in which a drunken tramp was used as a model?

This example, which I owe to Richard Wollheim, is an interesting one, but it does not, I think, establish what it claims. Consider a parallel case: finding a drunken tramp in the street I point to him and say 'Silenus'. It is arguable that my gesture makes the tramp into a representation; but if it does, it is because I am inviting you to think of him in that way. I have expressed a representational thought: imagine this person as Silenus. And I have completed the thought by an act of ostension toward its dozing subject. The act of ostension might on some other occasion be accomplished by a camera (or a frame, or a mirror, or any other device which isolates what it shows).

The camera, then, is being used not to represent something but to point to it. The subject, once located, plays its own special part in an independent process of representation. The camera is not essential to that process: a gesturing finger would have served just as well. If the example shows that photographs can be representations, then it shows the same of fingers. To accept that conclusion is to fail to distinguish between what is accidental and what is essential in the expression of a representational thought. It is to open the way toward the theory that everything which plays a part in the expression of thought is itself a representation. Such a view does not account for the aesthetic significance of representations. It also, however, and far more seriously, implies that there is no distinction between representational and nonrepresentational art. The concept of representation that I am assuming makes such a distinction, and it makes it for very good reasons. I am not tempted by such dubious examples to abandon it. One might put the point by saying that a painting, like a sentence, is a *complete* expression of the thought which it contains. Painting is a sufficient vehicle of representational thought, and there may be no better way of expressing what a painting says. That is why representation can be thought of as an intrinsic property of a painting and not just as a property of some process of which the painting forms a part.

Consider also the second feature mentioned above: the subject of an ideal photograph must appear roughly as it appears in the photograph. By its very nature, photography can 'represent' only through resemblance. It is only because the photograph acts as a visual reminder of its subject that we are tempted to say that it represents its subject. If it were not for this resemblance, it would be impossible to see from the photograph how the subject appeared, except by means of scientific knowledge that would be irrelevant to any interest in the visual aspect of the photograph. Contrast here the case of an electron microscope, which punches out on a ticker tape a codified indication of a crystal's atomic structure. Is that a representation of the atomic structure? If it is, then why not say that any causal relation which enables us to infer the nature of the cause from the properties of its effect provides us with a representation of the cause in the effect? Such a concept of representation would be uninteresting indeed. It is impossible, therefore, that the ideal photograph should represent an object except by showing how it appeared at a certain moment in its history and still *represent* it in the way ideal photography represents anything. How indeed could we make sense of an ideal photograph representing its subject *as* other than it appeared? We could do so only if we could also say that a photograph sometimes represents its subject as it appears; that is, if we could say that representation here is 'representation as'. But consider this sentence: *x* is an ideal photograph of *y* as *z*. It seems that we have no means of filling out the description '*z*', no means, that is, of filling it out by reference only to the photographic process and not, say, to some independent act of representation that precedes or follows it. One might say that the medium in photography has lost all importance: it can present us with what we see, but it cannot tell us how to see it.

We *must* be aware of the three features mentioned above if we are to appreciate the characteristic effects of photography. In looking at an ideal photograph, we know that we are seeing something which actually occurred and seeing it as it appeared. Typically, therefore, our attitude toward photography will be one of curiosity, not curiosity about the photograph but rather about its subject. The photograph addresses itself to our desire for knowledge of the world, knowledge of how things look or seem. The photograph is a means to the end of seeing its subject; in painting, on the other hand, the subject is the means to the end of its own representation. The photograph is transparent to its subject, and if it holds our interest it does so because it acts as a surrogate for the thing which it shows. Thus if one finds a photograph beautiful, it is because one finds something beautiful in its subject. A painting may be beautiful, on the other hand, even when it represents an ugly thing.

7

Someone might accept the general difference I have indicated between an aesthetic interest and an attitude of curiosity, and accept too the implication that something is a representation only if it is capable of carrying a reference to its subject without merely standing as a surrogate for it. He still might argue, however, that it is possible to be interested in a photograph *as* a photograph and find it, and not just its subject, beautiful.

But what is it to be interested in a photograph as a photograph? Of course one might have a purely abstract aesthetic interest in a photograph — an interest in the photograph as a construction of lines and shapes (as one is intended to appreciate Man Ray's Rayogrammes, for example). One can have a purely abstract aesthetic interest in anything; photography is only a representational art if our interest in a photograph as a photographic 'representation' is a type of aesthetic interest.

Let us return to the previous discussion of representation in painting. It appears that there is a prima facie contradiction between saying that I am interested in a thing for its own sake and saying that I am interested in it as a representation of something else. In attempting to reconcile these two interests, it is necessary first to restrict the place of truth in aesthetic interest. Truth is aesthetically relevant only insofar as it may be construed as truth to the situation presented rather than 'truth to the facts'. From the point of view of aesthetic interest, it is always irrelevant that there should be a particular object which is the object represented or, if there is such an object, that it should exist as portrayed. That is not to say, of course, that an aesthetic interest does not require things to be in general roughly as they are shown; but that is another matter.

As I have already said, this conflicts with the typical way in which we are interested in photographs. Knowing what we know about photographs, it is at least natural that we should be interested in them both because they are true to the facts and because they tell us useful things about their subject-matter. It seems, therefore, that the emotional or 'aesthetic' qualities of a photograph tend to derive directly from the qualities of what it 'represents': if the photograph is sad, it is usually because its subject is sad; if the photograph is touching, it is because its subject is touching, and so on. It is worth reflecting on why there could not be a photograph of a martyrdom that was other than horrifying. One's curiosity here would be no different from one's curiosity in the act itself. Hence it would be as difficult (and perhaps also as corrupt) to have an aesthetic interest in the photograph as it would be in the real situation. By contrast, a painting of a martyrdom may be serene, as is Mantegna's great *Crucifixion* in the Louvre. The painting has emotional qualities in defiance of the qualities of its subject. In the case of a photograph — say of the victim of some accident — one's attitude is determined by the knowledge that this is how things are. One's attitude is made practical by the knowledge of the causal relation between photograph and object. This is not to deny that one might be interested in a photograph for its own sake and at the same time maintain a proper distance from its subject, even when it depicts a scene of agony or death. But the real question is, Can we have such an interest in a photograph without having the same interest in its subject? Can I have an aesthetic interest in the photograph of a dying soldier which is not also an aesthetic interest in the soldier's death? Or, rather, can I maintain that separation of interests and still be interested in the 'representational' aspect of the photograph? If we are distanced from the photograph only because we are distanced from its subject, then the important distinction that I wish to emphasize, between interest in the representation and interest in the subject, has still not been made. It seems necessary to show that photography *can* — by itself — create that sharp separation of interests which is everywhere apparent in serious painting. Consider too the photographs of old London. How is it possible to detach one's interest in their beauty from an interest in the beauty of London as it was? Regret is here the appropriate reaction to the photograph (as it is not — or at least not normally — an appropriate reaction to a Canaletto). 'That is how it looked!' is the central index of one's emotion.

Consider, then, the reasons that may be given in answer to the question, 'Why are you looking at that?' With a photograph, one mentions the features of the subject; with a painting, one mentions only the observable aspect captured in the picture. This essentially is what distinguishes an interest in a representation as a surrogate from an interest in a representation for its own sake. Suppose now that someone wishes to argue that it is *not* inevitable that we treat photographs, even ideal photographs, as I have described. Let us see what the consequences of such a position might be.

8

Imagine that we treat photographs as representations in just the same way that we treat paintings, so that their representational natures are themselves the objects of an aesthetic interest. What are the consequences if we study photography in such a way that it does not matter whether its subject actually existed or actually looked like the thing we see in the picture? Here we are interested not in the subject but in its manner of presentation. If there *can* be such an interest in a photograph, it suggests that a photograph may sometimes be the expression of a representational thought and not merely a simulacrum of its subject.

An interest in an object for its own sake, in the object as a whole, must encompass an interest in detail. For if there is nothing *for* which one contemplates an object, as has frequently been argued, there is no way of determining in advance of looking at it which features are, and which are not, relevant to one's interest.[17] It is for this reason that we cannot rest satisfied with nature but must have works of art as the objects of aesthetic judgment. Art provides a medium transparent to human intention, a medium for which the question, Why? can be asked of every observable feature, even if it may sometimes prove impossible to answer. Art is an expression of precisely the same rational impulses that find an outlet in aesthetic interest; it is therefore the only object which satisfies that interest completely.

The photographer, then, who aims for an aesthetically significant representation must also aim to control detail: 'detail' being here understood in the wide sense of 'any observable fact or feature'. But here lies a fresh difficulty. The causal process of which the photographer is a victim puts almost every detail outside of his control. Even if he does, say, intentionally arrange each fold of his subject's dress and meticulously construct, as studio photographers once used to do, the appropriate scenario, that would still hardly be relevant, since there seem to be few ways in which such intentions can be revealed in the photograph. For one thing, we lack all except the grossest features of style in photography; and yet it is style that persuades us that the question, Why this and not that? admits such fruitful exploration in the case of painting. Style enables us to answer that question by referring solely to aspects of the painting rather than to features which are aesthetically irrelevant, or in no way *manifest* in what is seen.[18] The search for meaning in a photograph is therefore curtailed or thwarted: there is no point in an interest in detail since there is nothing that detail can show. Detail, like the photograph itself, is transparent to its subject. If the photograph is interesting, it is only because what it portrays is interesting, and not because of the manner in which the portrayal is effected.

Let us assume, however, that the photographer could intentionally exert over his image just the kind of control that is exercised in the other representational arts. The question is, How far can this control be extended? Certainly there will be an infinite number of things that lie outside his control. Dust on a sleeve, freckles on a face, wrinkles on a hand: such minutiae will always depend initially upon the prior situation of the subject. When the photographer sees the photographic plate, he may still wish to assert his control, choosing just this colour here, just that number of wrinkles or that texture of skin. He can proceed to paint things out or in, to touch up, alter, or *pasticher* as he pleases. But of course he has now become a painter, precisely through taking representation seriously. The photograph has been reduced to a kind of frame around which he paints, a frame that imposes upon him largely unnecessary constraints.[19]

In other words, when the photographer strives towards representational art, he inevitably seems to move away from that ideal of photography which I have been describing toward the ideal of painting. This can be seen most clearly if we consider exactly what has to be the case if photography is to be a wholly representational art — if it is to manifest all those aspects of representation that distinguish it from mere copying and which endow it with its unique aesthetic appeal. No one could deny that from its origins photography has set itself artistic ideals and attempted to establish itself as a representational art. The culmination of that process — which can be seen in such photographs as Henry Peach Robinson's 'Autumn' — is to be found in the techniques of photo-montage used by the surrealists and futurists (and in particular, by such artists as László Moholy-Nagy and Hannah Höch). Here our interest in the result can be entirely indifferent to the existence and nature of the original subject. But that is precisely because the photographic figures have been so cut up and rearranged in the final product that it could not be said in any normal sense to be a *photograph* of its subject. Suppose that I were to take figures from a photograph of, say, Jane, Philip, and Paul, and, having cut them out, I were to arrange them in a montage, touching them up and adjusting them until the final result is to my mind satisfactory. It could very well be said that the final result represents, say, a lovers' quarrel; but it is not a photograph of one. It represents a quarrel because it stands in precisely the same intentional relation to a quarrel that a painting might have exhibited. Indeed, it is, to all intents and purposes, a painting, except that it happens to have employed photographic techniques in the derivation of its figures. Insofar as the figures can still be considered to be photographs, they are photographs of Jane, Philip, and Paul and not photographs of a lovers' quarrel. (Of course the fact of their *being* photographs might be aesthetically important. Some ironical comment, for example, may be intended in using figures cut from a medium of mass production.)

The history of the art of photography is the history of successive attempts to break the causal chain by which the photographer is imprisoned, to impose a human intention between subject and appearance, so that the subject can be both defined by that intention and seen in terms of it.[20] It is the history of an attempt to turn a mere simulacrum into the expression of a representational thought, an attempt to discover through techniques (from the combination print to the soft-focus lens) what was in fact already known.[21] Occasionally, it is true, photographers have attempted to create entirely fictional scenes through photography and have arranged their models and surroundings, as one might on the stage, in order to produce a narrative scene with a representational meaning. But, as I have argued, the resulting photograph would not be a representation. The process of representation was effected even before the photograph was taken. A photograph of a representation is no more a representation than a picture of a man is a man.

9

It might be felt that I have begged the question in allowing only one way in which photography may acquire representational meaning, a way which inevitably leads photography to subject itself to the aims of painting. One may argue that a photographer does not choose his subject at random, nor is he indifferent to the point of view from which he photographs it or to the composition in which it is set. The act of photography may be just as circumscribed by aesthetic intentions as the act of painting. A photograph will be designed to show its subject in a particular light and from a particular point of view, and by so doing it may reveal things about it that we do not normally observe and, perhaps, that we might not have observed but for the photograph. Such an enterprise leads to effects which are wholly proper to the art of photography, which therefore has its own peculiar way of showing the world. Why is that not enough to give to photography the status of a representational art?

I do not think that such an objection need cause me to revise my argument. For exactly the same might be said of a mirror. When I see someone in a mirror I see *him*, not his representation. This remains so even if the mirror is a distorting mirror and even if the mirror is placed where it is intentionally. This intention might even be similar to the intention in photography: to give a unique and remarkable view of an object, a view which reveals a 'truth' about it that might otherwise have gone unobserved. One could even imagine an art of mirrors, an art which involves holding a mirror aloft in such a way that what is seen in the mirror is rendered by that process interesting or beautiful.

This art of mirrors may, like the art of photography, sometimes involve representation. It may, for example, involve a representation of Venus or of Silenus in the manner of the two types of 'fictional' photographs considered earlier. But representation will not be a property of the *mirror*. It is impossible that I could, simply by holding a mirror before someone, make him into a representation of himself. For after all, whether I look at him or at the mirror, in either case it is *him* that I see. If the mirror is to become the expression of a representational thought, it too must be denatured; like the photomontage, it must be freed from the causal chain which links it to its subject. One can perhaps begin to see the truth in Oliver Wendell Holmes's description of the daguerreotype as a 'mirror with a memory'.[22] It was just such a mirror that led to the downfall of Lord Lambton.

It does not matter, therefore, how many aesthetic intentions underlie the act of photography. It does not matter that the subject, its environment, activity, or light are all consciously arranged. The real question is, What has to be done to make the resulting image into a representation? There are images which are representations (paintings) and images which are not (mirrors). To which class does the photograph belong? I have argued that it naturally belongs to the latter class. Photography can be *made* to belong to the former class by being made into the principal vehicle of the representational thought. But one must then so interfere with the relation between the photograph and its subject that it ceases to be a *photograph* of its subject. Is that not enough to show that it is not just my ideal of photography which fails to be a mode of representation, but also that representation can never be achieved through photography alone?

A final comparison: I mark out a certain spot from which a particular view of a street may be obtained. I then place a frame before that spot. I move the frame so that, from the chosen spot, only certain parts of the street are visible, others are cut off. I do this with all the skill available to me, so that what is seen in the frame is as pleasing as it might be: the buildings within the frame seem to harmonize, the ugly tower that dominates the street is cut off from view, the centre of the composition is the little lane between two classical façades which might otherwise have gone unnoticed, and so on. There I have described an activity which is as circumscribed by aesthetic intentions as anything within the experience of the normal photographer. But how could it be argued that what I see in the frame is not the street itself but a representation of it? The very suggestion is absurd.

10

Here one might object that representation is not, after all, an intrinsic property either of a painting or of a description. Representation is a relation; an object can be described as a representation only if one person uses it to represent something to another. On this view, there is no such thing as 'being a representation'; there is only 'having a representational use.' And if this were the case, my arguments would be in vain. Photographs are as much, and as little, representations as paintings, as gestures, as mirrors, as labels, and as anything else that can play its part in the process of communication.

The objection is more serious, and reflects a well-known dispute in the theory of meaning. Meaning, some say, is a property of a sentence; others, for instance, H. Paul Grice, argue that meaning is primarily a relation between utterance and speaker.[23] Now, even for Grice, there remains a distinction between utterances which are articulate and utterances which are not. Sentences are to be distinguished from nods of the head in that they participate in and exemplify a grammar, and through that grammar they can be understood independently of the context of their use. By being articulate, the sentence can stand alone as the principal expression of a thought. There arises a kind of interest in the sentence (and in its content) which is independent of any direct involvement in the act of communication. Meaning can be read *in* the sentence and need not be inferred from surrounding circumstances.

Similarly, painting, being fully articulate, can attract attention as the principal expression of a process of thought. It can be understood in isolation from the special circumstances of its creation, because each and every feature of a painting can be both the upshot of an intentional act and at the same time the creation of an intentional object. The interest in the intentional object becomes an interest in the thought which it conveys. A painter can fill his canvas with meaning in just the way that a writer may fill his prose. This is what makes painting and literature into representational arts: they are arts which can be appreciated as they are in themselves and at the same time understood in terms of a descriptive thought which they articulate.

In photography we may have the deliberate creation of an image. Moreover, I may use a photograph as a representation: I may use a photograph of Lenin as a representation of him, in the way that I might have used a clenched fist or a potato or a photograph of Hitler. The question is, What makes the image *itself* into the principal vehicle of representational thought? I wish to argue that an image can be deliberate without being properly articulate. The image becomes articulate when (a) the maker of the image can seriously address himself to the task of communicating thought through the image alone, and (b) when the spectator can see and understand the image in terms of the process of thought which it expresses. To satisfy (a) we require a painterly approach to detail; to satisfy (b) we must distract the spectator's attention from the causal relation which is the distinguishing feature of photography. Either way, the persistence of that relation — in other words, the persistence of the *photographic* image — can only hinder representation. It can contribute nothing to its achievement. This is perhaps what James Joyce meant when he wrote the following in his Paris notebooks of 1904:

> Question: Can a photograph be a work of art? Answer: A photograph is a disposition of sensible matter and may be so disposed for an aesthetic end, but it is not a human disposition of sensible matter. Therefore it is not a work of art.

If Joyce meant by 'work of art' what I mean by 'representation', then he was clearly getting at the same point. The property of representation, as I have characterized it, is the upshot of a complex pattern of intentional activity and the object of highly specialized responses. How can a photograph acquire that property? My answer is that it can do so only by changing in precisely those respects which distinguish photography from painting. For it is only if photography changes in those respects that the photographer can seriously address himself to the thoughts and responses of his spectators. It is only then, therefore, that the photograph becomes a proper *vehicle* of representational thought.

11

Photography is not representation; nor is it representation when used in the cinema. A film is a photograph of a dramatic representation, and whatever representational properties belong to it belong by virtue of the representation that is effected in the dramatic action, that is, by virtue of the words and activities of the actors in the film. *Ivan the Terrible* represents the life of Ivan, not because the camera was directed at *him*, but because it was directed at an actor who *played the part of* Ivan. Certainly the camera has its role in presenting the action, much as the apparatus of production has its role on the stage. It directs the audience's attention to this or that feature and creates, too, its own peculiar effects of atmosphere. Proper use of the camera may create an interest in situations that could not be portrayed on the stage. Hence photography permits the extension of dramatic representation into areas where previously it would not have been possible, just as music, which is not a representational art, enabled Wagner to create for the first time a theatrical representation of a cosmic theme.[24] (Consider, for example, the camera in Bergman's *Persona*, where it is used to create a dramatic situation between two characters, one of whom never speaks. Such mastery is perhaps rare, but it has existed as an ideal since the earliest days of cinema.) Nonetheless, the process of photography does not, because it cannot, *create* the representation. Thus documentary films are in no sense representations of their subject-matter. (Which is not to say that they cannot involve the realization of elaborate aesthetic ideas: it is hardly necessary to mention Leni Riefenstahl's film of the Berlin Olympics.) A cinematic record of an occurrence is not a representation of it, any more than a recording of a concert is a representation of its sound. As all must agree, representation in the cinema involves an *action*, in just the way that a play involves an action. The action is understood when the audience realizes that the figure photographed is attempting to portray adventures, actions, and feelings which are not his own, and yet which are nevertheless the proper subject-matter of aesthetic interest. It follows that the fundamental constraints which the cinema must obey as an art form — those constraints which are integral to its very nature as a representational art — are dramatic ones, involving the representation of character and action. ('Dramatic' here does not mean 'theatrical', but is applied in the sense which Henry James gave to it when he spoke of the novel as a form of dramatic art.) To succeed as cinema, a film must have true characters, and it must be true to them; the director can no more sentimentalize with impunity than can the novelist or the playwright. The true source of the badness of most cinema lies, of course, in the fact that the gorgeous irrelevancies of photography obscure the sentimentality of the dramatic aim.

Photography, far from making dramatic representation more easy, in fact makes it more difficult. Indeed, the possibility of dramatic success in the cinema is a remote one, for which there are two reasons. The first, and somewhat shallow, reason is that the film director is photographing something which either is or purports to be a part of the actual world. It follows that he can only with the greatest difficulty convey to his audience an appropriate sense of detail. Typically the audience is given no criterion of relevance, no criterion which settles what must be attended to. Was the audience meant to notice the man on the street corner, the movement of the eyebrow, the colour of the macintosh, the make of the car? In every cinematographic image, countless such questions remain unanswered. There are various reasons for this. For one thing, a film is fixed with respect to all its details; although it is a dramatic representation, it cannot exist in more than one performance. Therefore features of interpretation cannot be separated from features of the action: there is no such distinction. It is only in understanding the representation as a whole that I come to see what I should be attending to. Furthermore, the cameraman operates under a permanent difficulty in making any visual comment on the action. The difficulty can be solved, but its solution is perforce crude in comparison with the simpler devices of the stage; crude because it must both create irrelevancies and at the same time persuade us to ignore them. (Consider, for example, the ritualized expressionism of *Der blaue Engel* or *The Cabinet of Doctor Caligari*. Even Fritz Lang's *Siegfried* contains reminiscences of this *commedia dell'arte* mannerism, whereby the actor attempts to divert the audience's attention from the infinite irrelevance of detail, toward the dramatic meaning of the whole. Of course more recent directors have emancipated themselves from the theatrical constraints of expressionism; as a result they have at least felt happy to ignore the problem, even if they could not solve it.)

In the theatre the situation is different. The necessary limitations of the stage and the conventions of stage performance, which derive from the fact that the play exists independently of its performance, provide a strong representational medium through which the dramatic action is filtered. Someone with a knowledge of the conventions will see at once what is relevant and what is not. Symbolism in the theatre is therefore clear and immediate, whereas on the screen it is too often vague, portentous, and psychologically remote. Consider, for example, *L'Eclisse*, where the camera, striving again and again to make a comment, succeeds only in inflating the importance of the material surroundings out of all proportion to the sentiments of the characters. The effect is to render the image all-engrossing, while at the same time impoverishing the psychology.

It is for this reason that what often passes for photographic comment in the cinema ought more properly to be described as photographic effect. The camera may create an atmosphere — it may be an instrument of expression — but it is unable to make any precise or cogent analysis of what it shows. Consider the techniques of montage, used to such effect by the Russians. Eisenstein argues that there is a precise parallel between the technique of montage and the sequential structure of verse.[25] For example, each image that Milton presents in the following passage corresponds to a precise and unambiguous shot:

> . . . at last
> Farr in th'Horizon to the North appeer'd
> From skirt to skirt a fierie Region, stretcht
> In battailous aspect, and neerer view
> Bristl'd with upright beams innumerable
> Of rigid Spears, and Helmets throng'd, and Shields
> Various, with boastful Argument portraid,
> The banded Powers of *Satan* hasting on
> With furious expedition . . .

(One may note the cinematographic device 'and neerer view' and the very Eisensteinian quality of the image that follows it.) The contention is that for each of Milton's images one may find a cinematic shot that somehow 'says the same thing'; the total montage would form a dramatic unity in precisely the same sense, and for the same reason, as Milton's lines. The director will be doing something analogous to the poet: he will be focusing attention on carefully chosen details with a view to creating a unified expression of the prevailing mood.

It should be noted, however, that each shot in the montage will also present infinitely many details that are *not* designed as objects of attention. The shot corresponding to 'Helmets throng'd' will capture that idea among others, but it will also say much more that is irrelevant. It will not be able to avoid showing the *kind* of helmet, for example, the material, size, and shape of it. By so concretizing the thought, the camera leaves nothing to the imagination. As a result the detail that really matters — the thronging of Satanic helmets — is in danger of being lost. It was for this reason that Eisenstein developed techniques of contrast and composition in order to control more effectively the attention of his audience. It is a testimony to his genius that the poetry of *Ivan the Terrible* has rarely been rediscovered by subsequent directors. Even in Eisenstein, however, comment comes primarily through drama rather than through image. The whole effort of photography lies in expression and effect. And interestingly enough the clearest examples of photographic comment in the cinema come when once again the causal relation between image and subject is replaced by an intentional one. Consider the following sequence from *The Battleship Potemkin:*

1 Title: 'And the rebel battleship answered the brutality of the tyrant with a shell upon the town.'
2 A slowly and deliberately turning gun-turret.
3 Title: 'Objective — the Odessa Theatre.'
4 Marble group at the top of the theatre building.
5 Title: 'On the general's headquarters.'
6 Shot from the gun.
7 Two very short shots of a marble figure of Cupid above the gates of the building.
8 A mighty explosion; the gates totter.
9 Three short shots: a stone lion asleep;
                            a stone lion with open eyes;
                            a rampant stone lion.
10 New explosion, shattering the gates.[26]

Here we have one of Eisenstein's most striking visual metaphors. A stone lion rises to its feet and roars. This amazing image (impossible, incidentally, outside the limitations of the silent screen) acts as a powerful comment on the impotence of imperial splendour precisely because it startles us into a recognition of the underlying thought. But we know that this cannot be a photograph of a stone lion roaring. It is, rather, the intentional juxtaposition of unconnected images; it is the intention that we see and which determines our understanding of the sequence. It is of course lamentable that such art should have subjected itself to the inane mythmaking revealed in the titles to this script; that does not alter the fact that, if there is art here, it is an art which is essentially photographic.

The second and deeper point I wish to mention is extremely difficult to express in terms that would be acceptable to the contemporary analytical philosopher. I shall try not to be too deterred by that.[27] Photography, precisely because it does not represent but at best can only distort, remains inescapably wedded to the creation of illusions, to the creation of lifelike *semblances* of things in the world. Such an art, like the art of the waxworks, is an art that provides a ready gratification for fantasy, and in so doing defeats the aims of artistic expression. A dramatic art can be significant only if it is, at some level, realistic; but to be realistic it must first forbid expression to those habits of unseriousness and wish fulfilment that play such an important part in our lives. Unless it can do that, the greatest effects of drama — such as we observe in the tragedies of the Greeks, of Racine, and of Shakespeare — will be denied to it. Art is fundamentally serious; it cannot rest content with the gratification of fantasy, nor can it dwell on what fascinates us while avoiding altogether the question of its meaning. As Freud put it in another context, art provides the path from fantasy back to reality. By creating a representation of something unreal, it persuades us to consider again those aspects of reality which, in the urgency of everyday existence, we have such strong motives for avoiding.[28] Convention in art, as Freud saw, is the great destroyer of fantasies. It prevents the ready *realization* of scenes that fascinate us, and substitutes for the creation of mere semblance the elaboration of reflective thought.

The cinema has been devoted from its outset to the creation of fantasies. It has created worlds so utterly like our own in their smallest details that we are lulled into an acceptance of their reality, and persuaded to overlook all that is banal, grotesque, or vulgar in the situations which they represent. The cinema has proved too persuasive at the level of mere realization and so has had little motive to explore the significance of its subject. It is entirely beguiling in its immediacy, so that even serious critics of literature can be duped into thinking that a film like *Sunset Boulevard* expresses an aesthetic idea, instead of simply preying on the stereotyped fantasies of its audience.

Moreover, the cinema, like the waxworks, provides us with a ready means of realizing situations which fascinate us. It can address itself to our fantasy directly, without depending upon any intermediate process of thought. This is surely what distinguishes the scenes of violence which are so popular in the cinema from the conventionalized death throes of the theatre. And surely it is this too which makes photography incapable of being an erotic art, in that it presents us with the object of lust rather than a symbol of it: it therefore gratifies the fantasy of desire long before it has succeeded in understanding or expressing the fact of it. The medium of photography, one might say, is inherently pornographic.

I have benefited greatly from discussions with Richard Wollheim, Mark Platts, John Casey, Peter Suschitzky, and Ruby Meager, as well as from the criticisms of Robert A. Sharpe and Rickie Dammann, my fellow symposiasts at a conference organized in Bristol by Stephan Körner, to whom I am grateful for the opportunity to reflect on the nature of photography.

10 Fantasy, Imagination and the Screen

Freud remarked that the artist accomplishes a passage through fantasy, back to reality.[1] He said little to illuminate the remark, although its tenor is in keeping with his admiration for the peculiar discipline of the Greek tragic stage. I want to consider a thesis which is suggested by it and which I believe to be of great interest to those who wish to understand the similarities and the differences between the stage and the screen. The thesis is this: that there is an opposition between fantasy and reality and that this opposition defines one of the ways in which art may be both the object and the cause of corruption. I shall be referring to fantasy not on the part of the artist, but on the part of his audience; and I shall not be using the word fantasy in its psychoanalytic sense (assuming that it *has* a psychoanalytic sense), but in a sense according to which fantasy bears directly on the understanding of art.

In the course of his reflections on the nature of poetry, Coleridge made a famous distinction between fancy and imagination, assigning to the second, but not to the first, the task of understanding the true nature of reality.[2] This distinction was made in terms of Coleridge's adventurous but undeniably eccentric reading of Kant's critical philosophy, and I do not propose to defend or attack it in its original form. Nevertheless, somewhere in his meaning, there are traces of a real distinction that will survive translation from the idiom Coleridge used to express it. I shall describe this as the distinction between fantasy and imagination.

My thesis will be this: that imagination is involved in the understanding of art, and that the aim of imagination is to grasp, in the circuitous ways exemplified by art, the nature of reality. Fantasy, on the other hand, constitutes a flight from reality, and art which serves as the object of fantasy is diverted or corrupted from its proper purpose. If there is a *transition* from fantasy to reality, it is because there is a discipline which turns fantasy into imagination. I shall be advancing the thesis that much interest in the cinema is a fantasy interest, and is inhibited by this discipline. Such an interest remains indifferent to the possibilities that the cinema may present, as a form of dramatic art. My thesis may be denied by arguing that the cinema is not a form of dramatic art; that is an objection that I will not attempt to answer.[3] I shall be interested only in those objections which arise from the attempt to map the difficult terrain of consciousness which is the subject of this paper.

There is an important point which must be borne in mind, if the *critical* significance of the distinction between fantasy and imagination is to appear evident from my discussion. When we speak of the satisfaction which lies in the fulfilment of desire, we might mean either of two very different things. We might be referring to the satisfaction of the desire itself, or to the satisfaction of the creature who possesses it. In the first case satisfaction is simply the completion of a motivating force. In the second case satisfaction is not related to any specific motivating force, but rather to the well-being of the creature as a whole. It is fairly obvious that satisfaction of the second kind is not necessarily the result of, and may even (depending on the desire in question) be undermined by, satisfaction of the first.

It is difficult to specify more narrowly the second idea of satisfaction; but since it is important to my argument I shall say a few things about it. These will, I hope, be sufficiently evident to prove acceptable without the full backing of philosophical analysis that they deserve. First, satisfaction of this kind is a state of the whole being; as such, it is a matter of degree. This is so whether we are talking of a person, or whether we are talking of some organism which, for whatever reason, falls short of the requirements deemed necessary for personhood. Secondly, the idea of satisfaction presupposes a state of flourishing, health, or 'success'. This state is analogous to the fulfilment of desire, since the organism or person as a whole can be thought of as in some sense striving towards it.[4] Thirdly, and in consequence of that, we must see the absence of satisfaction as a decline, a misfortune, or a corruption, whether of the organism or of the person. Which term we use will depend both upon the circumstances that engender dissatisfaction and upon the circumstances that we envisage as repairing it. Fourthly, it seems to me quite reasonable to suggest that, since not all organisms are persons, and since persons are distinguished in part by the peculiarity and complexity of their activities and aims, we should not suppose that personal satisfaction and organic satisfaction (happiness and health) are one and the same. In discussing the moral significance of things it is primarily the personal, and not the organic, that concerns us.

In our case at least, if not in the case of animals, it is an evident result of the most primitive reflections, that the satisfaction of a desire may detract from personal satisfaction. I shall be concerned with certain desires which it is normal to call corrupt. It will be possible to consider only fleetingly the considerations which justify the use of that term. But I hope that it will be apparent that, whatever persons are, they have reason to avoid both the fulfilment, and also (if possible) the possession, of corrupt desires.[5]

I shall begin by defining fantasy, as a property of desire. I shall be defining a technical term, and it is not my concern to approximate to common usage. A desire exhibits fantasy when (i) its object in thought is not the object towards which it is expressed, or which it pursues; (ii) the object pursued acts as a substitute for the object in thought; and (iii) the pursuit of the substitute is to be explained in terms of a personal prohibition. By a 'personal prohibition' I mean a prohibition that forms part of the deliberation of the person himself and which is in some sense self-imposed, or accepted. The contrast is with prohibitions thought of as imposed by some external power, having no independent or intrinsic claim to acceptance.[6]

The definition is more simple than it appears, and should become clear through an example. A morbid person may reflect intensely and aimlessly on the subject of human death and suffering. The image of agony may rise frequently before his mind and begin to exert its fascination. There is born in him the desire to witness such a scene. At the same time fear, sympathy and respect for human life make it abhorrent to him to realize this desire, either by producing the circumstance which fascinates him, or by frequenting those places where it might be found. The effect of this prohibition is to turn his desire towards a substitute: he begins to seek the 'realistic' portrayal of death and destruction — for example, in a waxworks museum, or in the cinema. (The word 'realistic' occurs in inverted commas for reasons to be made apparent.) This desire for the perfect image of suffering is an example of fantasy.

It is possible to imagine many such examples and to extract from them, and from the definition which they exemplify, a description of the 'characteristic fantasy object'. The object of a fantasy is, as I have said, a substitute or surrogate. But it is not just that: the peculiar circumstances which generate fantasy also determine the character of this surrogate. For example, a fantasy will seek to gratify itself, not in the delicately suggestive, but in the grossly obvious, or explicit. Thus a fantasy desire will characteristically seek, not a highly mannered or literary description, nor a painterly portrayal, of its chosen subject, but a perfect simulacrum — such as a waxwork, or a photograph.[7] It eschews style and convention, since these constitute impediments to the construction of the surrogate object, ways of veiling it and confusing it in a mask of thought. The ideal fantasy object is perfectly 'realized', while remaining wholly unreal. It 'leaves nothing to the imagination': at the same time it is to be understood only as a simulacrum and not as the thing itself.

The reason why I earlier placed 'realism' in inverted commas is this: that it has come to mean something quite different from the 'realization' which is pursued in fantasy. It has come to mean, in fact, the attempt to *represent* the world as it is. Now to represent an object is not to provide a surrogate for it. The 'realization' of an object in a surrogate is, in fact, one way of relinquishing the attempt to understand it; it is, in one sense, the opposite of representation.

It is useful at this stage to distinguish the fantasy object from other — perhaps more innocuous — kinds of surrogate. A man who has a great desire to visit China might be compelled, by financial or other circumstances, to content himself with pictures and descriptions of the object of his desire. And if his desire is really to visit China, to see it and to know it in the way that it is only properly known in the act of acquaintance, then it is not a representation so much as a surrogate that he requires, and again his passion may expend itself on models and photographs, rather than on the thing itself.   This is not, on my account, a genuine case of fantasy, since the 'transference' of desire (to borrow another psychoanalytic term) is motivated not by an interior prohibition but only by an external constraint. Should the opportunity to travel to China arise, then the interest of the surrogate would instantly decline. Of course, one can imagine some deep and darkly motivated prohibition against travel to some longed-for place (witness Proust's inability to reach Venice[8]). Here the search for substitutes again takes on the character of fantasy, as I have described it.

There are other innocuous surrogates that could be mentioned — the most evident being the use of models, photographs and the like in the course of instruction, where all desire, emotion and interest is still directed towards the reality, and not towards the substitute that is, fortuitously, required. I mention these things only because reflection on them might help to clarify the phenomenon with which I am trying to contrast them.

Even in the case of a docile and harmless fantasy, it must be remembered that the desire which underlies it is real. (In certain cases one may speak not of desire, but of compulsion. This does not affect the point, even if it suggests a *theory* of fantasy that may, in the end, be correct). The subject of a fantasy really does want something. This is brought out by the fact that, in the case of sexual fantasy, the sexual experience may be pursued *through* the fantasy object, and attached to it by a definite onanistic activity. The subject wants something, but he wants it *in the form of a substitute*. This desire has its origin in, and is nurtured by, impulses which govern his general behaviour. Objects can be found to gratify his fantasy; but the fantasy is grounded in something that he really feels.

So we could define fantasy, briefly, as a real desire which, through prohibition, seeks an unreal, but realized, object.

There is a common instinct that fantasy, even when gratified, does not contribute to, but is in fact more likely to detract from, personal satisfaction. I here offer a semi-philosophical reason for thinking that this instinct might be sound. It seems to me that the fantasy-ridden soul will tend to have a diminished sense of the objectivity of his world, and a diminished sense of his own agency within it. The habit of pursuing the 'realized unreal' seems to conflict with the habit, which we all, I believe, have reason to acquire, of pursuing what is real. There is no expenditure of effort involved in the gratification of fantasy, and hence the fantasist is engaged in no transformation of his world. On the contrary his desires invade and permeate his world, which ceases to have any independent meaning. The nature of the fantasy object is *dictated* by the passion which seeks to realize it; and the world therefore has no power either to control or to resist the passion. Normal passions are founded on the sense of the independent reality of their object. They do not invade, but on the contrary, are disciplined by, the world. They change as understanding changes, and come, in time, to bear the imprint both of the subject's agency and of the world's reality. Thus it is with the greatest of human benefits — love between equals. In love, all my fantasy is destroyed just so soon as it is erected, by the deeper desire to understand and respond to a being whose essence resides in his independence, in his freedom from me. It seems to be no accident that people have repeatedly described sexual fantasy as 'loveless'.

I now turn to the subject of imagination, specifically to the idea of imaginative perception. Consider a theatrical representation, say of the murder of Desdemona. This is an imaginary scene; which is to say that what is represented is not really there on the stage, nor anywhere else in the objective world. It is also perceived as imaginary, which is to say that the observer (at least the observer who understands what is going on) has no disposition to believe that what he sees is actually happening. There is something voluntary in this pattern of perception, although it is not, *pace* Coleridge, a 'willing suspension of disbelief': more like the opposite, indeed. We might say, that the episode is 'perceived in disbelief'. It is not merely that the scene is known to be unreal; it is that all pleasure and emotion derive from that belief, and from the recognition that here the unreal object is not substituting for the object of some real desire.

Of course, a man may bring to his perception of theatrical scenes just such fantasy emotion as I have described. In this case the theatrical scene performs, for him, the role of substitute. He will demand absolute lifelikeness, rather than dramatic realism. We know that the normal spectator does not demand this absolute lifelikeness of the stage and whether, like the Greeks, he expects all violence to take place off stage, or whether, like us, he merely expects gestures and language to be stylized and bound by convention, his interests are elsewhere than in the absolute reduplication of a specific object or event.

It would be wrong to say that this kind of imaginative perception is 'disinterested', if that is taken to mean that it is purged of all emotion and desire. Clearly the spectator feels something when he sees the death of Desdemona. But the object of this feeling is not the reality before him — two actors simulating murder — but the thing that is *not* there, and which he perceives unbelievingly, namely, the death of Desdemona.

There is a great difficulty in describing the nature and value of these 'imaginary' emotions. But one point needs to be made at the outset, which is that, whatever their nature, they are *responses* to a given situation, and neither pre-exist nor determine it. They arise out of the attempt to *understand* what is pictured. In this they are wholly unlike fantasy emotions. They have precisely the same character of objectivity (or response to something independent) as the healthy desires and feelings with which fantasy should properly be contrasted. They are informed, like all responses, by a 'reality principle' — which is to say that their object is also thought of as their justification.

There is a major difficulty in the description of 'imaginary' emotions. It is hard to find any real desire which is essential to them, as the desire to avoid is essential to fear, the desire to please essential to love.[9] A real desire always presupposes a background of belief, and in the present case the background is lacking. The thoughts which identify the intentional object of the feeling are imagined, not believed, and this fact determines the nature of the emotion. A desire that arises from an imaginative thought is not a real desire: I no more desire Othello not to murder Desdemona, than I desire to leave the theatre, even though murder is, in some imaginary world, as terrible as murders really are. One is tempted to speak here of a desire 'entertained in imagination'; just as one must say the same of its attendant thought.

In a sense it is even wrong to say that it is *I* who feel grief over Desdemona's murder. It is rather that I imagine this grief, and come to a conception of what, from the subjective point of view, it feels like. Then I find myself drawn into sympathy with the emotion that I have been compelled to imagine. We might say that, in imagination, there is neither real object nor real feeling. The feeling is an imagined response to the imagined object which compels it. In fantasy there is a real feeling which, in being prohibited, compels an unreal object for its gratification. These two phenomena, which seem on the surface to be so alike, turn out on inspection to be deeply opposed.

It is now possible to give some further characteristics of the imaginative emotions which will reinforce the contrast with fantasy. Since imaginative emotions are responses, they do not exist independently of those imaginary scenes which occasion them. They arise out of, and are controlled by, an understanding of their object. To exercise the under-standing is already to take an interest in objective truth. The questions: are things really like that? is it plausible? is my response exaggerated or not?, will all be apt and even unavoidable outcomes of the imaginative endeavour. Such questions are, of course, the death of fantasy, which withers as soon as its object is represented as having a reality independent of itself.

For similar reasons, we can say that 'realization', in the sense earlier considered, is not the main aim of imaginative thought, and may even impede that thought, precisely by awakening fantasy. The imagination, governed as it is by a reality principle, seeks condensation, suggestion, dramatic completeness. These are the features which make fiction into the accurate representation of an independent world. The absolute realization of specific scenes is no part of the imaginative purpose; this purpose may be better served by convention than by an explicit image.

If the contrast be granted, then we must conclude that the imagination can, while fantasy normally cannot, play a part in the education of feeling. Imagination can present us with unfamiliar situations, or with familiar situations transformed by some new radiation of thought; it generates emotion as a response to this. Its object is not, as a rule, realized according to the mechanical impulses of fantasy, but presented and completed in accordance with the 'reality principle' mentioned earlier. In not requiring our immediate practical involvement, it may, in Arnold's words, 'teach us how to feel'.

Certain kinds of convention, together with stylistic constraints, have an important part to play in this process. They discipline the imaginative thought, by enabling it to pass over irrelevancies, to ignore what may fascinate the eye and exclude the understanding, to achieve the kind of condensation without which truthful representation is impossible. Fantasy, by contrast, is killed by convention, since convention prevents the lifelike realization of the fantasy object. Fantasy precedes and commandeers its object, seeking not to understand but to veil the world by means of it. Thus the imaginative object can, while the fantasy object cannot, possess an emotional and moral character quite other than that of the real object (which is in one case represented, in the other case realized). A fantasy realization of exquisite torture has all the moral character of torture: it is horrifying, disgusting and despicable. But a painting of such a scene may — like Mantegna's *Crucifixion* — set torture in a context which makes its representation serene. It is in differences of this kind that we see the real distinction between a representation and a substitute. We might also see the purpose in distinguishing, as many have distinguished, between pornography and erotic art.

It is now possible to consider the relation between the stage and the screen. First, it cannot be doubted that, leaving aside documentaries, and considering the normal case, a film is a kind of dramatic representation. But its conventions are not theatrical. Whence comes its representational power? It seems to me that we should not attribute this power to the photographic image. I have argued above that it is only in very exceptional circumstances that a photograph can be treated as a representation of its subject: documentaries are not representations, any more than tape-recordings are representations of concerts.[10] A documentary is a special kind of substitute for the thing itself. When we speak of representation in the cinema, the instrument of representation is not the photograph but what the photograph is *of*. It is Marilyn Monroe who represents the female saxophonist. She does this just as it is done on the stage, by acting the part. If representation were not understood in this way then it would be extraordinary that we should think of films as fictions, with a dramatic significance, involving character, plot and dénouement.

It is very difficult to say anything decisive and uncontroversial about the difference that is made to dramatic representation when it is mediated by the screen. It has often been remarked that there is an increasing 'conventionalization' of the camera by serious directors, an increasing tendency to replace reproductive with painterly techniques. (A very good example is the countryside in Mizoguchi's *Crucified Lovers,* executed so as to imitate the appearance of Chinese painting, and then used to generate an expressive atmosphere not unlike that of the 'journey narratives' in the Japanese puppet plays.) One could perhaps explain this in terms of a natural tension between the 'reality principle' which governs dramatic representation, and the 'realization principle' which governs the camera. For consider how the magic of the screen arises: the photograph is so pellucid to its subject matter as to reveal it to your eyes. You see an actor, portraying a famous detective; and he is walking through the streets of London. But the streets of London are not represented: they are *there*, realized before you, with all their bustle and noise and arbitrary design. The actor is part of this scene and must behave with the gestures, the speech, and the appearance, that absorb him into it. Were he to obey dramatic conventions (as Bergman's actors used to do, thanks to highly original techniques of conventionalized photography), then in the normal case there would be a grotesque clash between the actor and his setting. The detective has to be, from the visual point of view, as realized as the street in which he walks. This is so, even when the 'reality principle' — which operates to take our attention away from our ordinary world, towards a fictional representation in which the world is condensed and comprehended — demands that the scene be, not realized, but swept up in an imaginative gesture.

The tension between realization and reality can be suppressed, kept out of mind, even eliminated. But the temptation towards the first is always there, both on the stage and on the screen. It is never more clearly apparent than in those subjects, sex and violence, for which both are most habitually condemned. And I think it is important to be aware of the greater strength of this tendency in the cinema. With the aid of a camera, you can realize violence or the sexual act completely, and so minister to the fantasy which has realization as its object. Our fantasies about such things are strong and immediate. There is therefore a danger that fantasy will take over, so as to dominate the interest in representation. The desire behind fantasy is a real desire; whereas that behind imagination is not. If fantasy breaks through the tissue of imagination, then the dramatic thought is scattered, and the imaginative emotions along with it; the value of dramatic representation is destroyed. A mechanism takes over, which imprisons the spectator in the bonds of his own untutored emotions, just as true imagination frees him from these emotions by granting an impersonal vision of a larger moral world.

What I have said is only a hint; I find it difficult to express the point precisely. But it seems to provide some explanation of the fact that many people are both quickly satiated by cinematic representations, and yet deeply disturbed and absorbed by features (violence in particular) which, from the dramatic point of view, bear little intrinsic meaning. Imagination withers when realization blooms; and understanding withers along with it.

Critics often wonder why it is that such people are unable to see their favourite film more than a few times. A lover of the theatre, of literature, and of the opera — of any other form of representation that qualifies as dramatic — can usually envisage no point beyond which his favourite works would begin to fatigue him. Perhaps my remarks contain the beginnings of an explanation. For many interests in the cinema involve no imaginative effort, and have no imaginative reward; and many films are made precisely as the objects of such interests.

I have drawn a distinction between fantasy and imagination, discussing only works of art that are 'about' the world: I have confined myself to representation. Yet are there not other kinds of art — music for example — which are without serious representational aims, and yet which demand an imaginative response from their audience? Is there an equivalent of fantasy here? Or would it be merely metaphorical to talk in such a way?

I believe that there is expressive music which gives form to a feeling and understanding to the listener. I also think that there is music which decks itself out in the colours of an emotion which it neither explores nor controls, but for which it provides a convenient reinforcement and perhaps a surrogate object. To describe the distinction is hard: but perhaps it is an instance, in the domain of expression, of a distinction which I have discussed in terms of representation alone.

The Aesthetic Understanding

11 Emotion and Culture

We often distinguish between practical and theoretical reason, and despite the many views that hold one or the other to be primary, the existence of both is seldom doubted. What is more often doubted is that we may distinguish theoretical from practical *knowledge*. Part of the distinction between the theoretical and the practical is that in the former case we are dealing with questions of truth and falsehood, whereas in the latter case we are dealing primarily with something else, with a notion of rightness that is in some way irreducible to truth. And it might seem that notions like knowledge (with its implied background of objective assessment) can be applied only where we may also speak of truth. Perhaps the principal difficulty, therefore, which the notion of practical knowledge presents, is the difficulty in making clear what is meant by 'correctness' where one cannot speak of truth. But there are other difficulties, and it is with these other difficulties that I shall for the most part be concerned.

There is a distinction, made familiar by Ryle, between knowing that (the object of which is a proposition) and knowing how (the object of which is an action). I know that my bicycle is made of steel; I also know how to ride it. But that distinction is not the one that I wish to discuss. 'Knowledge how' denotes a skill, and one might say that there is a distinction between true practical knowledge and 'knowing how' which corresponds in part to the distinction Aristotle had in mind in contrasting virtue and skill.[1] In the first of these there is more to success than the matching of means to end. There is the right knowledge of the end itself.

Ordinary language is unlikely to provide us with the concept we require. Nonetheless, it is worth pointing out that we do use the term *knowledge* in other ways, to denote what seem to be practical capacities, capacities that cannot be evaluated in terms of the truth or falsehood of some proposition that they contain. For example, we speak of 'knowing what to do'. Knowing what to do is not a matter of knowing the truth about a situation. In *that* sense one might be as knowledgeable as possible and still not know what to do, perhaps because one is so much the further from making up one's mind (which phrase seems to suggest a more than accidental connection between knowing what to do and deciding). And again knowing what to do cannot be considered simply as a matter of knowing how. For the accumulation of skills may also bring one no nearer to making up one's mind, even though a certain confidence in one's skills may, for that end, be necessary.

There is also another popular reference to knowledge which seems to have something to do with the practical: knowing what one is doing. A man may be said not to know what he is doing, even when what he is doing is an intentional act, because his activity manifests a practical confusion about his ends or means, rather than because he has the wrong description of his action. We have no trouble in our daily lives in recognizing instances of this confusion, and we cannot always (or even typically) reduce those instances to cases of ignorance over the truth-value of a proposition.

Now someone might here wish to point out that when we say, of a workman for example, that he does not know what he is doing, we are referring to a deficiency in *skill*. He does not know how to carry out the given task, even though, in some other sense, he knows quite well what he has to do: what he is aiming at. But that is not the only occasion upon which we would wish to say of someone that he does not know what he is doing. There is the more puzzling case where we might say this of someone who had no deficiency in skill and yet was employed in a task of which he had no proper understanding — as we might say of a politician or an administrator, that he does not know what he is doing.

Simplifying somewhat, we might speak here of a difference between knowledge of means and knowledge of ends, and knowledge of ends has two sides — roughly corresponding to knowing what to do (at the outset), and knowing what one is doing (when one has begun). I say that it is simplifying somewhat to make this division into ends and means for the reason that I do not think that it applies to rational behaviour with the neatness that is often assumed; nonetheless it is an honoured distinction, and one that locates as well as one can at the outset the philosophical problems that I wish to discuss. I wish to say something about what 'knowledge of ends' might consist in — something about the kind of practical knowledge that is roughly located by the two locutions to which I have referred, when they cannot be replaced by the simpler notion of 'knowing how'.

Whatever else it is, practical knowledge in the sense I am considering is the property of the individual and must be understood in terms that — while generally intelligible — make essential reference to his individual predicament. To know what to do (for example) involves knowing what *I* should do. That reference to the first person is, I think, ineliminable from the idea of rational agency. I know what to do not just by knowing what a person answering to a certain description should do (even if it is a description that I uniquely satisfy), but (typically) by making up my mind and acting accordingly. In practical reasoning one is, in the last analysis, always subject, and never object.

Now this might lead us to think that practical knowledge is simply identical with decision — with the forming of intentions. But that is surely not so, either from the objective or from the subjective point of view. If we can talk of knowledge at all it is because decisions can be evaluated, and a man who claims to know may be convicted of ignorance. A false claim to knowledge is refuted by the world — not by the way the world is, but by the way it turns out to be. It is surely the main question of ethics to determine what this 'refutation' might consist in, to determine, that is, the content of genuine knowledge, when knowledge is of ends.

Moreover, it is too simple to represent even the subjective side of practical knowledge as an intention, for the reason that a man may sometimes know what to do and yet fail to do it. This evident fact is also a well-known problem. For if practical knowledge is to be truly practical (that is, if it is to be connected with a *specific* form of action and not reducible to an act of intellectual judgment, or 'holding true'), then its connection with action must be non-contingent. And yet at the same time, because of weakness of will, the connection cannot be universal.

Despite those — by now fairly familiar — difficulties, there remains a strong tradition in moral philosophy which still sees decision (or 'choice') as containing the whole of practical knowledge. Kant would not have approved of the recent representatives of this tradition — of Sartre and Hare — but all the same he endowed it with its fundamental concept, the concept of autonomy. To express the thought of this tradition in a nutshell: decision to act is necessary for practical knowledge (of ends); commitment is sufficient. And commitment means nothing more than a reinforcement of the same decision, either by deciding at the same time on a universal principle (Hare), or by deciding not just to *do* this thing, but also to *be* the man whose decision this is (Sartre). In other words, decision becomes practical knowledge when accompanied by a second-order decision, either a decision always to act likewise, or else a decision to be, in this act, what one 'really' is.

Now it is well known that both those views find it very difficult to step out of the subjective side of practical knowledge into the objective world of real assessment. There does not even seem to *be* an objective right or wrong: the only standard is that of autonomy (or 'authenticity') and indeed, to speak of 'knowledge' is to employ a metaphor redolent of discarded moral notions. In this chapter I shall begin by concerning myself exclusively with the subjective side of practical knowledge. But I shall suggest, too, an account of something objective, something that might lead us to accept that there really is such a thing as practical *knowledge,* even when knowledge is not of means but of ends. Indeed, it seems to me that philosophers such as Hare have failed to see the possibility of an objective ethics partly because their description of the subjective side of rational agency is so impoverished.[2]

1

One feature that is left out of consideration by Hare, though not by Sartre, is that of emotion. To speak again in terms of our intuitive notions of these things: just as there is 'knowing what to do' so too is there 'knowing what to feel'. The feelings, like the will, are capable of education. Of course, it is no easy matter to say what we mean by 'knowing what to feel', or how that process of education might be brought about. But Aristotle is clearly not the only philosopher who has thought that the important thing, if one is to lead a fulfilled and proper life, is to feel the right emotion, on the right occasion, toward the right object and in the right degree.

Now if we are to speak of knowledge at all here it must be possible to describe — as in all cases of knowledge — a subjective state, an objective rightness, and some non-accidental relation between the two.[3] In the case of theoretical knowledge the subjective component is usually described as some kind of belief; characteristically, a *certain* belief. A belief that comes and goes, a belief in respect of which one has to make up one's mind afresh each time one entertains it — such beliefs fall critically short of knowledge. For they do not enable us to attribute to the subject the right kind of authority. Let us begin by asking whether there is any analogue in feelings for the certainty that may qualify belief. It might be better in this connection to speak of something's 'being *settled*' for the agent. But I shall continue to use the word 'certainty' in the hope that the discussion will make clear what is meant by it.

We all have some idea what it is to be *un*certain what to feel, as when some sudden crisis overtakes us and we find ourselves bereft of ready emotion. This state of uncertainty might, in its extreme form, bear some relation to the state variously described as 'dread' or 'anxiety,' a peculiar, objectless state, which is normally contrasted with the 'innocence' of direct and open feeling.[4] The uncertainty to which I refer comes about because, while we may know what we *ought* to feel — in the sense of what the *good* man would feel — we do not feel it. As a result we feel alienated from ourselves, from our thoughts, motives, and gestures. Something like this might happen at the death of someone close. One knows what grief is but, being overcome by the disaster, grief seems impossible: relief, indeed, seems easier. The experience is recorded by Emily Dickinson in the following verses from poem 1100 (*Complete Poems of Emily Dickinson*, 1970):

We waited while She passed —
It was a narrow time —
Too jostled were Our Souls to speak
At length the notice came.

She mentioned, and forgot —
Then lightly as a Reed
Bent to the Water, struggled scarce —
Consented, and was dead —

And We — We placed the Hair —
And drew the Head erect —
And then an awful leisure was
Belief to regulate —

Dr Johnson referred to grief as 'a species of idleness'. Clearly, that is not Emily Dickinson's meaning. The 'awful leisure' to which she refers is the punishment we must expect when, overtaken by a calamity, we do not know what to feel in the face of it.

Now, knowing what to feel is not a matter of knowing what one ought to feel, any more than knowing what to do is just a matter of knowing what one ought to do. In the normal case, at least, knowing what to feel must involve feeling: it is not a kind of opinion about feeling. If it were just that then we should have — I suggest — no special reason to value it. I think it will be conceded that there are men who know what they ought to do, and what they ought to feel, while seldom knowing what to do, or what to feel. Despite the richness of their theoretical awareness, they act and feel in ignorance. What remedy remains to them?

It is now widely accepted that all emotion involves both understanding and activity and, indeed, that nothing important is left to an emotion when those two have been removed from it. It follows that it is possible to educate an emotion, to the extent that it is possible to educate the understanding and activity that are involved in it. It is perhaps only a vestige of Cartesianism which prevents us from seeing this, and from seeing that a man ignorant of the art of emotion is a man who is in a significant way *confused*.[5] Emotions, therefore, are teachable, for one may teach a person both a way of understanding and an appropriate reaction; together these will constitute a feeling. For example, one may teach someone how to understand another's utterance as an insult. An insult may not be obvious, and becomes obvious only when a man recognizes that he is being treated in a highhanded or contemptuous way; that recognition involves the acquisition of concepts of justice, right, and denigration. The thought involved in recognizing an insult is thus extremely complex and I do not think that any philosopher has succeeded in giving a full account of it. But it is a thought that is, so to speak, publicly available. With sufficient understanding a man can learn to recognize what is insulting and what is not. But he must also acquire the appropriate reaction: how and when to treat the insult with contempt, with aggression, with violence. A man may react violently when he should have been contemptuous, or he might be contemptuous when he should have been amused. He must therefore learn the arts of anger and resentment, so that he can measure his response in accordance with his understanding of its object. There is no doubt that we all of us have, at least in the case of these emotions that arise out of and manifest our perception of social realities, a sense of what is and what is not appropriate. Thus we criticize a man for being unreasonably angry over an accident, or resentful of another's good intentions, or proud of having eaten a hundred sausages. It is a small step from such criticism to the distinction between the man who knows what to feel and the man who does not. The education of the emotions has that knowledge as its aim, and while there is a sense in which I cannot be held to blame for my present lack of knowledge, and for the present confusion of my feelings, I certainly can be held to blame for allowing myself, or another for whom I am responsible, to slip into the uneducated habits which those feelings exemplify. (Which is why Kant's attempt to eliminate feeling from the sphere of moral assessment ought to be firmly rejected.) It is hardly surprising that the principal concern of honest parents is to see that their offspring acquire the proper feelings — sympathy, pride, remorse, and affection. I teach my child not just to avoid fire but to fear it, not just to consort with others but to love them, not just to repair wrongdoing but to suffer remorse and shame for its execution. There should be nothing puzzling in that.

There is a distinction to be made at this juncture that, while not essential to my argument, bears on it indirectly. It seems to me that we ought to be able to distinguish between emotions with a universal or abstract, and those with a particular or concrete, object. A few remarks about that distinction will help to isolate more clearly the emotions that I wish to discuss, emotions like love and grief which have a special place in determining the quality of individual experience. These emotions have particular objects. Others, such as contempt, admiration, and indignation, have universal objects. If I feel contempt for James, for example, it is because of something that is true about James; if that thing were true of William then I should feel contempt for William too. The object of my contempt is the particular — James — as an instance of the universal. What I despise is James's cowardice, say, or childishness, and I would feel just the same toward anyone else who showed the same defect. Or if I did not feel just the same, then there would have to be an explanation, an explanation in terms of the intentional object. Merely to say 'I despise James for his childishness, but not John, although I can see no relevant difference between them' is either to misuse the words or to speak insincerely.[6] It is not difficult to see how one might educate such 'universalized' feelings. Having shown a man what is contemptible in one instance of cowardice, and having brought him to feel contempt towards it, one will necessarily have brought him to feel contempt on like occasions. In educating such emotions one is educating a man's values, and providing him with a sense of what is appropriate not just here and now but universally.

It is more difficult to see how we might educate emotions of the particular variety, emotions like love, hatred, and erotic desire, which impose upon the subject no universal logic, as it were, no obligation to respond likewise on like occasions. Although there is no doubt some feature of James which is the reason why I love him, I am not obliged to love William as well, just because he shares that feature.

The important point about such 'particular' emotions is their intimate connection with one's sense and conception of *oneself*. These emotions lack the postulated objectivity of their universal counterparts, which abstract from the individual situation and attach themselves to impartial notions of what is just and right. While it is *I* who feel contempt and indignation, I do so in obedience to an imperative that is applicable beyond my present situation, in accordance with a universal law. Such emotions seem to abstract, not only from the particularity of their object but also from that of their subject: it is only accidentally *I* who am feeling this indignation — the call to indignation might have been addressed to and taken up by another. The emotion is, as it were, impersonal. Learning its proper exercise involves acquiring conceptions of justice, appropriateness, and right which propose themselves as universally valid, and which remove the object of emotion from the sphere of any merely personal resentment or dislike. One might say, therefore, that the education of these universalized emotions is an essential part of moral development.

It is not so with love, liking, and delight. From the point of view of individual existence these emotions are indispensable. I cannot regard the call to love someone as addressed only accidentally to me without losing all sense of myself as an agent in my situation. These emotions — love, hatred, grief, and the rest — are irremediably personal. The obligation to feel them cannot be shifted; if a man tries to shift it, then automatically he puts his personality at risk. It may seem strange to talk of 'obligation' here, and of a personal 'risk'. In using such language I am trying to sum up a very complicated phenomenon, a phenomenon so often explored by Shakespeare in his tragedies and sonnets that it would be presumptuous at this stage to describe it more concretely. But my remarks will become a little clearer if we address ourselves to the questions: 'What is it, in the case of these essentially particular emotions, to know what to feel? And how is that knowledge acquired?' I shall approach those questions from the subjective side: my interest will be in the kind of certainty that would have to be involved. I wish to describe how the question what to feel can be *settled* for me, in the case of an emotion that is, as it were, inalienably mine.

2

Let us return for a moment to the case of grief. Grief is not an easy thing to feel; every man has a reason to avoid it, and may well try to avoid it, even in the presence of its proper object, which is the death of someone loved. A sort of busying anxiety, a haste to clear away the debris and turn to something new, is a familiar reaction in the face of death. So too is the 'awful leisure' that is consequent on that avoidance of emotion. Such anxiety is the natural consequence of not knowing what to feel, at a time when it is important to feel something, and yet when one has, as it were, no precedent: the feeling concerns me, here, now; it is not detachable from the imperatives of my individual life and present situation.

Our account of the general structure of emotions suggests that two things might be required in this predicament: first, a way of understanding the world in terms that invite emotion (I shall call this — for reasons that I hope to make clear — an 'intentional' mode of understanding); secondly, recognized patterns of appropriate behaviour. What I have in mind can be understood from considering the anthropological idea of a 'common culture' — the system of shared beliefs and practices that tell a man how to see the situation that besets him (where 'seeing' is a matter of recognizing the appropriate occasions of emotion), and which may also tell him what to do in response to that perception. Consider — to take an ancient example — Elpenor's plea to Odysseus in *Odyssey*, Bk XI, ll. 66-78:

> Now I beseech you, by all those whom you left behind, by your wife and by the father who reared you as a child, and by Telemachus your only son whom you left within your halls, that you will, sailing from the Kingdom of Hades, put in with your good ship at the isle of Aeaea. And there my lord I beseech you to remember me and not to leave me there unwept and unburied, lest I should become a cause of divine wrath against you. But burn me there with all my arms and raise a mound for me by the shore of the grey sea, in memory of an unfortunate man, so

that those yet to be will know the place. Do this for me, and on my tomb
plant the oar that I used to pull when I was living and rowing beside my
companions.

Odysseus shares a common culture, in my anthropological sense, with his
band of *hetairoi,* and Elpenor reminds him of shared beliefs and practices.
In the hurry to leave Circe's palace Elpenor (who while drunk had fallen to
his death) had been given little of the sympathy that was his due. Now,
however, Odysseus can bewail him. There is something that it is correct to
do in response to this death. Odysseus can burn Elpenor's body, he can
mourn his passing, and erect a monument for the eyes of 'those who are yet
to be'. His doing these things is connected, in a way that is immediate to
Odysseus's perception, with Odysseus's own love for his family and
respect for the father who had reared him. The common culture embraces
these complex feelings and obligations and makes them alive together in
the single episode of a servant's death. Indeed, it would be impossible to
give a statement of all that is suggested to Odysseus by Elpenor's words: to
attempt that would be to attempt to describe their entire social bond.

All this is of course subtly suggested by Homer: but its truth to life is
surely unquestionable. It is not simply that Elpenor is asking to be buried:
he is asking too to be mourned. 'Do not leave me,' he begs, 'unwept and
unburied' *(aklauton kai athapton)*. Now of course I am not suggesting that
Odysseus did not know what to feel when Elpenor fell from the roof of
Circe's palace. I wish rather to suggest that there is an intimate and perhaps inextricable connection between that knowledge and the practical
knowledge enshrined in the practices to which Elpenor refers. If we accept
the account of the emotions that I have been suggesting, then it must be
that there is an intimate connection between knowing what to feel and
knowing what to do. So that a practice that intimates what to do might also
be instrumental in determining one's knowledge of what to feel. This is
especially so if the practice is, as it were, wholly occasioned, and wholly
exhausted, by the proper object of the corresponding emotion. To explain:
the proper object of grief is the death of someone loved. A practice that
tells one what to do solely and exclusively on the occasion of such a death is
a practice that takes its meaning from the emotion of grief. It exists as an
imperative in those circumstances when grief is appropriate. If the
ceremony is of the right kind it serves to direct the subject's attention to
those features of his situation which make grief the appropriate reaction.
In telling him what to do, it insistently brings him back to the point of what
he must feel. But, being a ceremony, of universal application, it reminds
the sufferer of his participation in a common lot. It tells him what to feel,
while at the same time rendering his feeling objective, independent of his

own situation. His grief becomes part of a continuing activity in a public and objective world, and ceases to be a private anxiety to be borne by himself alone. That 'awful leisure' of which Emily Dickinson speaks is overcome. The privacy of grief is removed from it, the subject becomes aware, not as a theoretical insight but as a practical matter, that this emotion, the grief that he feels, is also something 'universal', something that it is right and proper to feel, that others too would feel to the extent that they engage in like activities and obey like ceremonial constraints. This sense of 'universality' is present whenever some idea of the validity of a sentiment becomes an active and serious part of the sentiment itself, informing not just the behaviour of the subject, but the very description under which the object is perceived. (This is perhaps what Goethe had in mind in speaking of the 'elective affinity' that is felt in the most particular, and least 'transferable', form of love.) In being the complete subject of his emotion, a man feels it also as an objective law.

To participate in a common culture is therefore, one might suggest, to be gifted with a certainty in one's feelings, a certainty which the uprooted, alienated, and disenchanted may not have and may not want to have. By certainty I do not mean crass impetuousness: there are occasions when any man must hesitate. Certainty comes when the matter is, in the last analysis, settled for the agent, when he sees his situation in terms of objective imperatives rather than subjective choices, imperatives that record for him the fact of his shared humanity, even in the midst of a predicament that is uniquely his. In this way the question what to feel becomes 'settled' in a manner that no mere 'authenticity' could achieve. The question is, then, why that certainty should be considered valuable, and also whether it is available not only to Odysseus but also, for example, to Leopold Bloom (which was, I think, the main point of Joyce's comparison).

3

To show the value of practical certainty (or, at least, of certain certainties) is to make the bridge from certainty to knowledge. It is to move out of the sphere of subjective choice into that of objective assessment. To speak of practical knowledge is to presuppose some practical analogue of truth, some basis for assessment. For the purpose of this analogy, the salient feature of truth is that it constitutes a kind of success, success in belief or assertion. (Hence the view, made familiar by Dummett, that assertion *aims* at truth, and derives its nature from that aim.[7]) But if we are to speak of knowledge, success cannot be an accident — it must be the sign of some authority; the man with knowledge owes his success to his own reliability. In looking for the practical analogue of truth, therefore, we must look for a notion of success in action which is at the same time capable of being achieved non-accidentally.

In the case of 'knowledge of means', or knowing how, this is not difficult. Success here lies in the end attempted; and the non-accidental achievement of the end is what we mean by skill. That is all there is to 'knowing how'. The case of 'knowledge of ends' is more difficult to describe: the notion of 'success' here indicates a gap in accepted theories of practical reason, a gap that philosophers have been unable or unwilling to fill. The unwillingness stems from Kant, who took so seriously the idea of the 'autonomy' of practical reason that he could not acknowledge a validity in practical reason that was not, as it were, internal to it: in particular, he could not acknowledge that the rightness of practical thought could derive from the success of its application. In that he was consciously opposing the 'ancient' system of philosophy (meaning Aristotle), which proposes some idea of happiness, well-being, or fulfilment as the cornerstone of practical reasoning. Roughly speaking, however, the practical equivalent of truth must be some such idea of fulfilment, of finding satisfaction in what is achieved. Clearly, there is more to rational fulfilment than achieving one's ends, for not all those ends will bring satisfaction: practical knowledge consists in the ability to aim at those that do. In other words, for there to be practical knowledge, the satisfaction that is the outcome of a man's activity should not be accidental (a dispensation of fate) but the natural result of his state of mind and character. A fortunate man is not necessarily a happy one.

This is not the place to describe the kind of fulfilment to which I refer; nevertheless, there may well be a part to be played in it by the emotional certainty that I have described.[8] For it is difficult to imagine how a self-conscious being can be fulfilled when he is at variance with his own emotions. A large part of happiness lies in the vanquishing of guilt, and in the achievement of a proper organization in one's feelings. It is true that not every common culture will provide that freedom and control, but a common culture is the kind of thing that does so, and the healthy culture is the one that succeeds. To partake of such a culture, to be educated in the constraints and perceptions that it embodies, is to transform certainty into knowledge. It will not be an accident that a man who partakes of such a culture will be fulfilled. His sufferings will be external — such calamities as the death of someone loved; he will not also suffer in his own self-opinion, or experience his personal life as something alien and confused. His sufferings, in other words, will be misfortunes, but not faults.

Much more needs to be said if that bridge from certainty to knowledge is to be constructed. We should need to know more about the nature of happiness, and more about the character of human emotion. But a small digression may show more clearly why the certainties of culture might in the end be indispensable. Consider, then, the view of human nature which sees all human fulfilment in terms of the freedom of choice of the individual, and the subjective side of practical knowledge in terms of the willed 'authenticity' of the agent. Of course, the dangers for society which that notion enshrines are by now familiar enough. It is important to realize, however, that the dangers for the individual are equally great. According to the defenders of 'authenticity', certainty comes only through the deliberate adoption of an aim or purpose — a sort of ideological imposition of the will, whereby all one's future conduct will be governed. There results from this neither the objective fulfilment that is the aim of knowledge, nor even the subjective certainty that is its initial reward. For, however authentic, a choice can lead to certainty only if it is thought capable of succeeding, only, that is, if it accompanies some understanding of the world as an arena of rational activity, an understanding that enables the agent to envisage how the world might be affected by what he chooses to do. Let us consider what that might involve.

In discussing Elpenor's appeal to Odysseus I referred to an intentional mode of understanding. By that I meant an understanding that represents the world through the concepts that inform our aims and attitudes, concepts that characterize the 'intentional objects' of our states of mind. That such an understanding is possible, and that it is not necessarily identical with the kind of understanding fostered by science, should be evident. Consider three strips of material, one of wood, one of an artificial fibre with similar strength and cutting properties, and another of some isotope of the same artificial material, which has none of the plastic properties of wood, being soft and flabby. A scientific classification would assimilate the second to the third. But such a classification would have no part to play in the practical understanding of the jobbing builder, for whom the first and second would fall under concepts proper to his aims, being for practical purposes indistinguishable. Nor is the contrast here merely that between a natural and a functional kind.[9] Concepts that play an important part in practical thinking may have their basis, for example, in aesthetic experience. It used to be the practice for stone merchants to class together (as 'ornamental marbles') such stones as marble (a carbonate), onyx (an oxide), and porphyry (a silicate), while limestone (chemically identical to marble) had no part in the classification. An intentional mode of understanding is one that fills the world with the meanings implicit in our aims and emotions. Not only is it indispensable to us as rational agents, it may also be irreplaceable by any understanding derived from natural science.

The last point is of some significance, I believe, not only in understanding the nature of culture but also in clarifying the feature of emotions that has been called their 'intentionality'. Emotions are classified partly in terms of the conceptions under which their objects are presented. The object of fear is 'something harmful', that of jealousy 'a rival', that of envy 'coveted success', and so on. These conceptions define what has been called the 'formal object' of each emotion — that is, they define the description under which any object of some given emotion must fall (or be thought to fall).[10] To the extent that some putative object of jealousy, say, can be shown not to be an instance of the formal object (not to be a rival), then jealousy can be not only criticized but actually *refuted* — for it can be shown to be founded on a mistake.

There remains, however, a further dimension of criticism, associated with the idea of an 'appropriate' or 'proper' object. Although Timothy is a rival, and therefore a 'possible' object of jealousy, there is more to jealousy than the thought that he may be so described. There is also the activity that is based in that thought, and which may be criticized in terms that belong to accepted modes of practical reason. A man may be enjoined to master his jealousy, on the grounds that its object is proper but trivial, or on the grounds that it is unjust or heartless to pursue it.

Now it is tempting to try to understand the intentionality of the emotions simply by following our previous division. On the one hand there is the province of theoretical reason, which provides the thoughts and beliefs on which an emotion is founded: these thoughts and beliefs determine the intentional object. On the other hand there is the province of practical reason, which governs the activity of which that object is the 'target'. However, the activity will play its own part in determining the content of the accompanying belief. For it may provide the classifications in terms of which that belief is formulated. (It is the activity of the sculptor which gives sense to the classification 'ornamental marble'; it is the activity of human competition which gives sense to the conception of a rival). Were we completely to separate the theoretical and the practical, then we might find that much of the emotional life that we need and esteem as rational beings would become alien to us. For, construed in isolation from human practice, a belief is a purely theoretical thing, the essence of which is the claim to truth. To make that claim is to commit oneself to the pursuit of truth, and it is the essence of that pursuit to spill over into theory, and into the consequent classification of the world in terms of natural kinds. Yet there is no reason to suppose that such a classification will provide sufficient basis for all rational activity, just as there is no reason to think that the chemical classification of stones will provide a sufficient basis for the activity of a sculptor.

Consider the most elementary human relations. All the people I know are members of a natural kind — the kind 'human being' — and behave in accordance with the laws of that kind. Yet I subsume people and their actions under concepts that may not figure in the formulation of those laws. Indeed, the hallucination of those laws (for so it must be described in our present ignorance) often seems to distract people from genuine human intercourse. If the fundamental facts about John are, for me, his biological constitution, his scientific essence, his neurological structure, all those aspects that constitute the 'empirical self' of Kant, it may be that I shall find it difficult to respond to him with affection, anger, love, contempt, or grief.[11] So described, he may be mysterious to me, for it is not obvious that those classifications make contact with the ruling interests of personal feeling. The intentional object of love, of anger, of resentment, cannot, one feels, be so 'neutrally' described.

Suppose that we acknowledge that the intentional object of an emotion is specified by some belief or thought. Then we must acknowledge that the concepts used to formulate this thought may not be the concepts of any theoretical inquiry, and that they may not be wholly 'transparent' to the pursuit of scientific truth. They will reflect the forms through which our emotions are enacted, and will bear the stamp of shared human interests. Our emotions lose their certainty when our 'intentional' modes of understanding lose authority; and this authority is not bestowed upon them by some act of 'autonomous' choice. If I see a special significance in common culture, it is precisely because it provides concepts that classify the world in terms of the appropriate action and the appropriate response. A rational being has need of such concepts, concepts that bring his emotions together *in* the object, which enable him — as the Idealists might say — to find his identity *in* the world and not in opposition to it. Culture, far from creating the separation between subject and object that is (on one plausible view) characteristic of theoretical understanding, represents the world as entirely circumscribed by the agent's sense of what it is like to experience it and act on it.

But of course, precisely because the 'intentional' mode of understanding is deeply intertwined with action, it is difficult to delineate the concepts that it involves. Indeed it is often easier to speak of the intentionality of an emotion as though it were a matter not so much of thought as of perception: the object of hatred is *perceived* hatefully. Moreover, not only may we not be able to disentangle the intentional classifications from the culture in which they are embedded, but also we might find it difficult to describe the ends of the conduct which they serve to rationalize. Understanding the emotion of another as it is felt — understanding its true intentionality — may require the imagination of a poet. Consider again my example. Elpenor referred to a connection between Odysseus's own longing for his wife and family, and the need to erect a sepulchre to Elpenor. The reality of this connection is not stated: it is *present* in the language that Elpenor uses, and if Odysseus responds to it, it is on account of what is more easily described as an immediate perception than as an explicit thought. The funeral rite is perceived, not as fulfilling a specific aim, but as lying at the point of intersection of many existing satisfactions. These satisfactions are to be found *in* human relations and cannot be imposed on them from the outside, as willed external aims. If one were to try to encapsulate the shared perceptions of Odysseus and his *hetairoi* in a formula or recipe one would in all probability misdescribe their experience. Was Odysseus performing the rite *in order to* give rest to Elpenor's soul, *in order to* escape divine displeasure, *in order to* appease his own feelings toward his wife and father, *in order to* remember Elpenor — or what? It is the phrase 'in order to' that is here misleading: the action is not a means to these ends, but an embodiment or reminder of them. It is chosen, as a work of art might be chosen, as the appropriate sign of ends that cannot all be clearly stated, and which are not, in any real sense, *pursued*. But the motives referred to are not for that reason irrational. On the contrary, we have here an instance of practical knowledge, of the ability to achieve order and satisfaction where there might have been chaos and dread.

I am grateful to John Casey, Mark Platts, David Hamlyn, Moira Archer and Amélie Rorty for comments on earlier drafts of this chapter.

12 Laughter

1

Man is the only animal that laughs, but it seems that laughter belongs also to the immortals. A starting point for all enquiries into laughter must therefore be the hypothesis that it is an attribute of reason (which is the quality that distinguishes men and gods from animals). That gets us no further than our definition of reason. If all we can say is that reason is the feature which distinguishes men and gods from the humourless animals, then it gets us nowhere. As a matter of fact, however, it has become clear in recent years that much can be said about the concept of the 'rational being'. Although analytical philosophy has yet to give a theory of rationality that has the grandeur and consequence of those of Aristotle, Aquinas or Kant, it can nevertheless make gestures which carry some promise of system. In this chapter I shall make such a gesture, and hope that the intimation of a distant theory will compensate for the sketchiness of my account.

It is evident that a theory of sensation that said nothing about the nature of sentient beings would not be a theory of sensation. It should be equally evident that no theory of laughter can dispense with an account of the being that laughs. It is not a misfortune of animals that they are so humourless. The cackle of the hyena would not be turned into laughter by a little more effort on his part. However hard he tries, the day will never come when that dismal sound is irradiated by the spirit of amusement. It is not that he should try harder at what he is doing, but that he should do something else. And this something else lies outside his nature. The discussion of animal mentality frequently brings to light these mental capacities that are 'outside nature'. It is this which compels us to recognize the vastness of the gap between the animals and ourselves. To possess reason is not to possess a further sense or 'capacity': it is to be systematically different in *kind*. Reason permeates our nature, and transforms even our pains and pleasures into states that are peculiar to us.

2

'Laughter' is a misleading term. We use it to refer to the sounds emitted by someone who is being tickled, to certain expressions of scorn or dismay, to the 'hollow laughter' that accompanies the perception of one's ruin. In this broad sense (in which it denotes a sound produced through the mouth of a sentient being) we even use the term of hyenas. Hence the preference among philosophers for less symptomatic labels: 'amusement', which denotes a state of mind, and 'humour', which denotes one of its objects. Neither of these terms is fully satisfactory: an amusing holiday, like an amusement arcade, may contain little humour, and no amusement. To feel our way towards the mental phenomenon that concerns us, we must recognize that common usage will be an inaccurate guide.

The first step towards imposing order on this usage is to stipulate that the phenomenon which we seek to describe has intentionality. It is not laughter, but laughter at or about something, that interests the philosopher. Given intentionality, 'laughter', 'amusement' and 'humour' may designate a single state of mind. Laughter is its full expression, amusement its essence, and humour its intentional object. As we shall see, this is not quite right; but it serves to introduce the topic in a more or less orderly manner.

3

One familiar account of intentionality is in terms of thought. A state of mind is intentional if it contains, or is founded on (recourse to metaphor is difficult to avoid) a thought. 'Thought' here means what Frege meant by '*Gedanke*': the content of a declarative sentence; the bearer of a truth value. In certain cases this thought may be a belief. I am afraid of you because I believe that you intend me harm. But not all thoughts are beliefs; some are merely entertained, in whatever mode of imagination or suspended judgement.

One explanation of the humourlessness of animals might be that amusement contains, or is founded on, a thought of which animals are incapable. Thoughts that involve self-consciousness are peculiar to rational beings (which is why animals are never sentimental); so too are thoughts that involve morality (which is why animals never feel remorse). And so on. I make this suggestion not in order to endorse it, but in order to suggest an *easy* way in which rationality and amusement might be brought into connection. It is not the way that I shall recommend.

Is it true that all intentionality involves, and is explained by, thought? Unfortunately there seem to be intentional states that do not (in the sense intended) involve thoughts. The nearest a dog ever gets to laughing is, I suppose, barking. But we make the distinction between barking *simpliciter* (a useless activity which most human beings deplore), and barking *at* an intruder or a friend. Is this second not an example of intentionality? It certainly seems that reference to the object of a bark can require an intensional context; in which case barking satisfies the most favoured criterion of intentionality. If a dog barks at a cat, it does not follow either that there is an object at which he is barking (he might be barking up the wrong tree), or that, if there is one, it is, so to speak, as he 'barks' it to be (it may be a mechanical cat with jaws of invincible steel, and he was certainly no such fool as to bark at *that*). Thus things barked at need not obey Leibniz's law; nor can one always quantify into a bark. Confirmation of the 'intentional in-existence' of the barkee is to be found in George Eliot:

> The sincere antipathy of a dog towards cats in general, necessarily takes the form of indignant barking at the neighbour's black cat which makes daily trespass; the bark at imagined cats, though a frequent exercise of the canine mind, is yet comparatively feeble. (*Felix Holt*, ch. 15).

Whatever we say about the case, however, it is clearly not likely to provide us with a model for amusement. In the same sense in which dogs bark *at* cats, we can imagine hyenas laughing *at* each other. But it is quite another thing to say that hyenas thereby express their amusement (although we may hear them as expressing ours). This must lend weight to the theory that amusement is an expression of thought. So is there any specific thought, characteristic of amusement as such? If so, we will be able to characterize the 'formal object' of laughter — the description under which anything must be thought to fall if it is to be laughed at.

4

The case for the formal object has been admirably set out by Michael Clark in an article which also offers a theory of amusement.[1] Clark rightly criticizes those, like Schopenhauer and Bergson, who have tried to provide sufficient conditions for something's being funny, and to explain amusement as the perception that those conditions are fulfilled. If there is a place in the analysis of amusement for such a perception it is, Clark argues, as a necessary and not as a sufficient condition. That is to say, it may be necessary to perceive, think of, or imagine an object in a certain way in order to laugh at it: but one might well so conceive it and not laugh. Clark argues that the traditional theories are more acceptable if regarded as attempts to give the thought that is characteristic of amusement — the 'description under which' an object is laughed at — rather than the whole character of laughter.

Clark rightly points out that the thought which characterizes amusement does not have to be a belief: I can be amused by what is merely imaginary. Following Schopenhauer, he proposes the 'incongruous' as the formal object of amusement, and argues that whenever I am amused, I must 'see' the object 'as' incongruous, in a manner that he tries to specify. That is not sufficient for amusement, but it is necessary. In order to be amused I must also enjoy this incongruity, the incongruity must be the cause of my enjoyment, and (I here paraphrase radically) I must enjoy the incongruity at least partly *for its own sake*. I shall return to these further observations later.

5

I wish first to examine the suggestion that the formal object of amusement is to be captured by the idea of 'incongruity'. Clark, following Munro, distinguishes three common accounts of amusement: superiority theories (exemplified by Hobbes's view of laughter as 'sudden glory'), 'relief from restraint' theories (such as Freud's explanation of jokes), and 'incongruity' theories, of the kind given by Schopenhauer.[2] He rejects the first two kinds — rightly I believe. For either they cover all examples of amusement by being made so vague as to be insignificant; or else they are given a precise meaning only to exclude many of the things at which we are prone to laugh. But why is the incongruity theory not open to a similar objection? Clark, inspired by Schopenhauer, explains incongruity as 'incongruous subsumption under a concept', which amounts to some kind of striking discrepancy between the object subsumed and the standard instances with which it is thereby brought into relation. Is it likely that such an idea could be made precise without also excluding central cases of amusement? In order to test the theory I shall return to Schopenhauer, and attempt to gloss the idea of 'incongruity' in terms which are not Clark's but which capture, I think, Clark's meaning.

Schopenhauer explains incongruity thus: 'two or more real objects are thought through *one* concept, and the identity of the concept is transferred to the objects: it then becomes strikingly apparent from the entire difference of the objects in other respects, that the concept was only applicable to them from a one-sided point of view. It occurs just as often, however, that the incongruity between a single real object and the concept under which, from one point of view, it has been rightly subsumed, is suddenly felt. Now the more correct the subsumption of such objects from one point of view, and the greater and more glaring the incongruity with it from another point of view, the greater is the ludicrous effect which is produced by this contrast'.[3]

This is not the place to embark on an interpretation of Schopenhauer. However, the passage makes several suggestions about incongruity: for example, that it is revealed or understood through a conflict of points of view; that it lies, or can lie, in an incongruity between object and concept. Neither suggestion is clear. I suspect that the real incongruity of which Schopenhauer speaks lies not between object and concept but between points of view: the reference to concept and object being no more than an attempt to squeeze his analysis into the brave metaphysical system of which it is designed to form a part. There is an instance, however, that could be held to illustrate Schopenhauer's meaning: that of the mimic. Mimicry is amusing partly because of its successful presentation of *two* things in one — the mimic, and the person mimicked. The 'funny man' presents his victim at the same time as distorting him, with the odd result that one sees the victim *in* the distortion.[4] You might say that this is like the simultaneous subsumption of an object under, and exclusion of that object from, a single concept. From one point of view the mimic's gestures fit the concept 'indolent man'. From another point of view (that which does not penetrate to the representation), the subsumption is absurd, for the very exaggeration of the gestures denies it.

But the language of 'concept and object' belongs to the metaphysical theory, and looks plausible only because of its vagueness. Consider a caricature of the Prime Minister: it may represent a non-deviant example of a woman, but still be a caricature of *her*. So what is the concept with which this instance is compared? Should we say: the concept of Mrs Thatcher? Should we refer, that is, to the Leibnizian 'individual notion' which she uniquely satisfies and from which the caricature, in however minute but significant a way, departs? It may seem so, since what is funny in a caricature is its simultaneous proximity to and deviation from an individual. But then the reference to 'concepts' is no more than a ruse. And when this reference is dropped, it is no longer clear that we have a case of incongruity. The caricature amuses, not because it does not fit Mrs Thatcher, but because it does fit her, all too well. It is true that it must also contain an exaggeration: but the exaggeration is amusing because it draws attention to some feature of *her*. If one wishes to describe the humour of a caricature in terms of incongruity it must be added that it is an incongruity which illustrates a deeper congruity between an object and itself.

If that is vague, it is because the word 'incongruous' is vague. The point of the example was merely to draw attention to the general difficulty: either you make the concept precise, and then risk leaving out important cases of amusement, or you leave it vague, and content yourself with a vacuous characterization of the formal object of laughter — vacuous because to know what is meant by the 'incongruous' you would have to consult, not some independent conception, but the range of objects at which we laugh.

Further examples can be adduced to confirm that thought. Consider the action which is so much *in character* that we cannot but laugh. Wit may not be quite what Pope said it is — what oft was thought but ne'er so well expressed — but satire at least possesses, when successful, the quality of accuracy, and satire has its equivalent in everyday life, when a character acts true to himself. What amuses us, it could be said, is the total congruence between the idea of the man and his action. We might be enraged or hurt by it: but I do not see why we might not also be amused.

It would be wrong to expand those observations into a 'congruity' theory of amusement. For that would be to risk just the same kind of censure that I have been expressing. Rather I wish to suggest that the problems with Clark's analysis stem, not from a faulty identification of the formal object of amusement, but from a misleading implication in the idea of a formal object.

6

I have taken for granted a certain understanding of the phrase 'formal object' — a medieval term of Aristotelian provenance, recently applied to the discussion of intentionality by Kenny.[5] When describing states of mind we transfer the idea from the material to the intentional realm. The relation between emotion and object is — to use the misleading term — 'internal'. It is not a material relation. In the material sphere the idea of a formal object is not so hard to understand: only what is wet can be dried, only what is solid can be thrown, and so on. But you can *try* to dry what is not wet: 'trying to dry' designates an intentional relation, and its object is characterized by what Brentano called 'in-existence'. So too with emotions. If the formal object of fear is 'what is harmful', then this designation must be understood to qualify only the intentional object. It specifies a limitation not on the material object of fear, but on the thought through which the material object is presented. I can fear only what I *think* to be harmful. It has been argued that many emotions have formal objects, since they are identified in terms of the beliefs on which they are founded. For example, we distinguish jealousy from envy by referring to the belief, present in the first, but not in the second, that the subject is *cheated* by another's possession of some good. Some, Clark included, go on to construe the existence of the 'formal object' of emotion as a product of our classifications of states of mind.[6]

It is necessary to distinguish formal from proper objects. The formal object of fear (say) is given by the description under which something must be thought if it is to be feared: it is what *can* be feared. The proper object is not what *can* be feared, but rather what it is right, proper or justified to fear. The 'harmful' is (perhaps) the formal object of fear; its proper object is the fearful. To justify the description 'fearful' is to justify fear. Confusion between formal and proper objects leads many — including Sartre — to consider emotions to be a kind of judgement. Fear then becomes the recognition of the fearful, anxiety the recognition of the *angoissant*, amusement the recognition of the amusing. It begins to seem as if nothing of the *emotion* remains, other than this act of (admittedly passionate) appraisal. The characteristic of a formal object is that someone may think something to be an instance of it, and yet feel no prompting towards the emotion which it partially characterizes. The formal object is given by a description which falls short of embodying the peculiar emotional characteristics which it serves to focus. The proper object is not so given. It is my belief that the temptation to build into the description of the formal object ideas that belong to the proper object is responsible for many fallacies in ethics, aesthetics and the philosophy of mind. In particular it seems to have precipitated renewed sympathy for the philosophy of 'moral realism', according to which the possession of values resides in an ability to recognize peculiar (and peculiarly elusive[7]) features of reality.

7

Does amusement have a formal object? How do we settle the question? We could, I suppose, list all the possible candidates and attempt to find counter-examples. One pleasing candidate is offered by Bergson: the formal object of amusement is life overcome by mechanism, or mechanism perceived in the heart of life (a special case of the incongruity theory).[8] This seems vulnerable at once to the counter-example of the character who amuses because he is true to himself. But perhaps there is some better method than that of listing proposals and then attempting to demolish them. If the formal object is a *merely* nominal feature, if it results *only* from our attempts to classify, then the question would hardly matter. We could arbitrarily designate amusement as that form of enjoyment which has the situation described by Bergson as its object, and use *Le Rire* as a kind of extension to our dictionary entry on 'laughter'. But the subject would hardly have aroused such interest if there were not some real basis to our classifications, and if the choice of a formal object were not restricted by some independent reality that we are attempting to describe.

It is important to understand, in this connection, a peculiar feature of amusement, which serves to distinguish it from the common examples of emotion: it is a matter of indifference whether the object of amusement be thought to be real. Most of our emotions are founded not just on thoughts, but on beliefs. We may also suffer them in imagination; but the imagined version is a derived case, to be understood in terms of the real, active emotion of which it is the shadow. Consider jealousy. There is no doubt that jealousy has a formal object: in order to be jealous of Alfred I must believe Alfred to be a rival. (That is only one part of the full description of the formal object, but it will do.) Without that belief I may hate Alfred, despise him, or envy him; but I cannot be jealous of him. The formal object is given by this belief. I can also entertain the thought of 'Alfred as rival' in imagination; and I may then feel some imaginative simulacrum of jealousy. But it is quite clear that real jealousy and 'imagined' jealousy are different states of mind. The first is necessarily terrible; the second may be titillating, even pleasant. The first involves a definite stance towards the world, and a tyrannical invasion of experience; the second is sealed off in a private reserve of fantasy.

In the case of amusement no such distinction between the real and the imagined can be sustained. If I laugh at someone's remark, and if I imagine the remark and laugh, then in each case my laughter has the same object, and expresses genuine amusement. Whether the object of my amusement be believed or imagined, my amusement remains the same; it has the same consequences, and the same place in my experience as a whole. Belief seems to be irrelevant. Or at least, what relevance it has is not that of distinguishing imagined amusement from the genuine article.

I think that this 'indifference to belief' is an important feature, and explains our reluctance to describe amusement as an emotion. In the case of normal emotions the belief which identifies the formal object has an important role in determining the structure and significance of the feeling. For normal emotions are also motives to action. Jealousy seeks not just to interpret the world but to change it. Amusement may cause us to do things, but it is not itself a motive. (I do things *for* amusement, but not *from* amusement.) We classify emotions not arbitrarily but according to their role in the explanation of behaviour. As motives they are intermediaries between belief and action. Human nature being what it is, we have fixed expectations concerning the actions that will follow upon certain beliefs. Our classifications of emotions therefore stem from our perception (however indistinct) of real and recurrent causal relations between certain beliefs and the desires and projects which express, confirm and purge them. It is not merely a nominal matter that jealousy has the particular formal object that it has. It is a matter of the real essence of a state of mind active in the generation of human conduct, in which a belief is found locked in the heart of a perduring motive to action.

The indifference of amusement to belief suggests that we should not expect it to exhibit the kind of structure that we observe in fear, anger and jealousy. Sometimes, it is true, belief plays a role in precipitating amusement: amusement (if it is indeed such) that expresses *Schadenfreude* arises only in response to a belief that one's rival, enemy, or thorn in the flesh has suffered injury. The mere thought of him doing so is never satisfactory. But we hesitate to call *Schadenfreude* amusement, and this suggests that my thesis is correct. Such examples could not possibly establish, either that a belief is necessary to normal amusement, or that any *particular* belief is always active in producing it. It is partly this that makes it so difficult to attribute a formal object to amusement: for we lack the motivational structure that is present in normal emotions, and hence can never feel confident that anything is *explained* by our identification of this or that predicate as the description under which an object must be laughed at. We should therefore hesitate to elucidate the intentionality of amusement in terms of some single directing thought common to its instances. It *may* be that there is such a thought; but it is hard to say whether its designation is a merely nominal matter, or whether, on the contrary, there is some real (and explanatory) essence that is being picked out by means of it.

8

Nevertheless the intentionality of laughter is not like the intentionality of a bark. Amusement *is* a mode of thought. What mode of thought? It is noteworthy that the traditional theories were not theories of the formal object of laughter. They were, for the most part, attempts to specify its proper object (the ridiculous): that at which it is appropriate to laugh. Laughter and amusement were described in terms, not of some basic thought that is necessary to them, but in terms of the pattern of thought which renders the object ridiculous in the subject's eyes. This is fairly obvious in the passage quoted from Schopenhauer: it is also evident in Bergson. Perhaps there *is* no formal object of amusement. Perhaps there is no general study of the intentional object that stops short of saying when it is right to be amused.

There is a trivial sense in which every intentional mental state has a formal object: only the believable can be believed, only the thinkable can be thought. And these empty tautologies may be given content by a theory of the 'understanding', such as was envisaged by Kant. The *Critique of Pure Reason* offers a disjunctive account of the thinkable (you can think X only if you think it under the categories). But if this is all we mean by referring to a formal object — i.e. the *a priori* conditions of the thinkable — then the assertion that amusement has a formal object is highly uninformative.

We should, I think, recapture the motivation behind the traditional

theories. We should look for a pattern or structure of thought characteristic of amusement, without concerning ourselves too much with the
single necessary proposition in which all our laughter is based. It may be
that there is such a proposition, but, since amusement is not an emotion, it
is hard to say how we might discover it. When we seek the pattern of
thought characteristic of laughter, two peculiar features impress themselves on us. The first is that, while everybody likes to laugh, nobody likes
to be laughed at. The second is that a direct connection exists between
amusement and the aesthetic point of view. The second feature is
illustrated by the contrast between comedy and tragedy. There is no
difficulty in explaining why we laugh in the theatre: any theory of humour
is also a theory of comedy. Aesthetic representations are as much objects of
amusement as anything else, and amusement enters into the enjoyment of
comedy without doing any violence to the aesthetic point of view.
Tragedy, by contrast, creates a notorious problem for the philosophy of
aesthetic interest. Why do we enjoy the representation of suffering? There
seems to be no normal ('extra-dramatic') state of mind of which tragic
feeling is a species: we do not feel grief, dismay or horror in the theatre (else
why should we go there?). The experience of tragedy is, or seems to be, *sui
generis;* some mysterious alchemy is at work in accommodating the
representation of terrible things to the aesthetic point of view from which
they become enjoyable. Hence philosophers have felt obliged to give some
special account of tragedy, in order to explain the transformation effected
by the stage. Comedy, however, has never seemed problematic in quite
that way. I wish to comment on these two features and suggest a theory of
amusement that will explain them.

9

To be amused by someone is not the same as to be amused at him; while the
first is gratifying to its object, the second is not. Why is that? Here we
should reflect on the peculiar importance of the human among the objects
of amusement. One can be amused at animals, and even at inanimate
things (for example, mechanical dolls). But there is a temptation to think
that these kinds of amusement are anthropomorphic. One sees the object
in human terms, either as a human being, or as the expression of human
thought and action. (Thus there are amusing buildings, but not, I think,
amusing rocks and cliffs, even though many rocks and cliffs are quite
bizarre.) If I were to propose a candidate for the formal object of
amusement then the human (in its widest significance) would be my
choice. But I am certain that I should be quickly forced to withdraw the
suggestion, and to content myself merely with emphasizing the impor-

tance of the human, its centrality, among the objects of laughter, and perhaps hazarding the guess that someone who could be amused at nothing human could be amused at nothing.

If people dislike being laughed at it is surely because laughter de-values its object in the subject's eyes. This de-valuing may be much needed and it may even be desired by the object. It is difficult to love a great man with the warmth that characterizes normal human relations. In order to do so, it may be necessary to find in him that which can be (however gently) laughed at. A truly great spirit will no doubt be willing to exchange the absolute security of the unlaughable for the comfort of human affection. Else, like Christ, he must think of himself as divine, in order to bear his inner isolation. Without the mitigation of friendship it is painful to be the object of laughter. It is possible not to be afflicted only by feeling such contempt (or pity) for those who laugh as to count it a virtue to be de-valued in their eyes (cf. Christ's attitude to those who mocked him).

'Laughing at' has many modes. Absolute mockery and reviling scarcely constitute amusement. Here every merit is stripped from the victim in the subject's eyes, and the laughter has that quality of malice which can be heard or overheard only with revulsion. Sarcasm likewise de-values and rejects in an unkind way, and again we feel that this 'unkindness' distances it from the normal cases of laughter. But sarcasm must be distinguished from irony. Irony de-values without rejecting: it is, in that sense, 'kind'. For example, Joyce's ironic comparison of Bloom with the wily Odysseus de-values the former only to insert him more fully into our affections. His shortcomings are part of his pathos, since they reflect a condition that is also ours. Irony of this kind causes us to laugh at its object only by laughing at ourselves. It thus forces upon us a perception of our kinship. Flaubert called it 'l'ironie qui n'enlève rien au pathétique'; it is the laughter between familiars, without which no domestic affection could arise.

In referring to a process of 'de-valuing' that is integral to laughter I have spoken very imprecisely. But I am not sure how to remedy the defect. 'De-valuing', however it is to be analysed, seems to be neither a precondition of amusement nor the result of it. It is, rather, the amusement itself. It is difficult to encapsulate it in the form of a judgement or thought which might have existed without the disposition to laughter. This 'pattern' of thought is constitutive of laughter. Amusement may thus be described as a kind of 'attentive demolition'. It is no accident that this pattern of thought should be enjoyable to us, since it reconciles us to our own condition. The connection between attentive demolition and enjoyment is real. The conjunction of the two in the definition of amusement is not the arbitrary specification of a nominal essence, but an attempt to isolate the causal process which structures a part of our mental life.

10

It is open to the defender of the formal object to find some way of translating my 'pattern' of thought — attentive demolition — into a specific proposition entertained about its object. If that *could* be done, then I concede that amusement has been provided with its formal object. But I am sceptical. For I am impressed by the complexity of this 'attentive demolition', which resides in no single thought, and which feeds insatiably on everything that serves to approximate the condition of its object to our own.

What matters, in any case, is the peculiar complexity of the thought that underlies amusement, and its distance from the thoughts which focus our emotions. There is no 'discovery' at the heart of amusement. Amusement is, rather, a mode of reflection, which presents its object in a certain light. It might now be thought that I have committed myself to the traditional 'superiority' theory mentioned earlier. But my remarks about irony were intended to deny that charge. To lower the object is not necessarily to raise the subject; it might be to lower both together. It is by the universal lowering that one may come to feel 'kinship' with the thing at which one laughs. The mistake, of 'superiority' and 'release' theories alike, is to find the meaning of humour in what it does for the subject, rather than in how it represents the object. Humour is not, normally, self-directed. Indeed one of its values lies in the fact that it directs our attention unceasingly outwards. If we are repelled by the humourless person it is often because we think of him as interested only in himself.

11

I turn now to the second feature of amusement: its ready subsumption under the aesthetic point of view. We laugh at real scenes, and at their dramatic representation, but there seems to be no transformation in the nature or quality of amusement as we proceed from life to art. Whether we are interested in an amusing episode, in the recital of it, or in its theatrical representation, we laugh always at the same thing and for the same reason. If the last is an example of aesthetic pleasure, then so is the first. Conversely, if amusement at real situations is not aesthetic pleasure, then laughter in the theatre ought not to be so either: in which case, there *would* be a problem of comedy after all. We should have to explain just how and why amusement is transfigured in the contemplation of imaginary scenes, and how it becomes part of an aesthetic interest in what is observed.

It seems to me that it is most plausible to say that amusement *is* a kind of aesthetic interest — or at least, that it belongs to the genus of which aesthetic interest is a species. This is suggested by the thought (which I attributed to Clark, although the words are not his) that amusement is a mode of enjoying an object 'for its own sake'. My suggestion can be formulated in four propositions:

1 Amusement is a mode of reflective attention to an object.
2 It does not have the purpose of discovery (it does not concern itself with the acquisition of new beliefs, or the verification of old ones).
3 It is not a motive to action (it does not regard its object as the focus of any project or desire).
4 Enjoyment is to be explained by the thought of the object, and it is not felt (as Clark puts it) *'for some ulterior reason'*.

It is, I believe, one of the major tasks of aesthetics to make that last proposition clear. We know that there is a difference between the laugh of triumph, which enjoys the sight of another's misfortune because of what it seeks in it, and the laugh of amusement, which takes pleasure simply in what it sees, and for 'no other reason'. But it is hard to say anything systematic about the contrast.[9] But the task is a general one for aesthetics. To the extent that amusement satisfies the four conditions, to that extent is it already a mode of aesthetic interest. For the conditions are precisely those which must be invoked in order to elucidate that peculiar kind of 'disinterest' that has — since Baumgarten — been called 'aesthetic'.

12

The argument has touched on a subject that lies beyond its scope. So I shall end with a suggestion that returns us to the opening remarks of this chapter. It is only rational beings who can be attentive without a motive; only rational beings who can be interested in that in which they have no interest. Whatever explains that fact explains why only rational beings have aesthetic pleasures, and why only rational beings are moral. I shall offer no theory. But it remains to point out that the humourlessness of animals is of a piece with their incorrigible lack of taste, and with their total indifference to questions of morality.

13 Art History and Aesthetic Judgement

It is sometimes argued that aesthetic judgement is subjective, in the sense of admitting no procedure or constraint that can overrule the untutored preference. It is also argued that every academic discipline requires a method, and that no method can be subjective. Any art historian who holds both those views will have a strong motive for believing that the discipline of art history does not require aesthetic judgement. I shall try to give reasons for doubting that belief, but I shall not argue against the two views from which it derives, for, while they are false, it lies beyond my present scope to disprove them.

Art history rose rapidly out of eighteenth-century connoisseurship to become one of the most important and popular of those subjects that we should now classify as humanities. This meteoric rise inspired both enthusiasm and misgivings in those who observed it. Already in the last, and in the earlier part of the present, centuries we find highly sophisticated reflections, culminating in Wölfflin's great *Principles of Art History,* on the nature of this discipline, which seems to be neither truly history, nor truly criticism, but some hitherto unencountered combination of the two. It is useful to begin where most of those reflections begin, by studying the nature of history itself.

Not everything has a history, even when it has a chronology, and even when its chronology can be explained. The geological development of the earth's crust occurred over a considerable period of time, and in accordance with complex scientific laws. Nevertheless we should, I think, rightly hesitate to describe this development as 'historical'. 'History' denotes the acts, thoughts and institutions of rational beings, that is, of beings motivated by a conception of their purposes. I think that we should respect this usage, since it would be begging all the questions that concern us to assume that the development of human thought and action can be described and explained in the ways that we describe and explain the chronology of rocks and stones and trees. This idea of 'history' as a process special to, and indispensable to the understanding of, human things, is part of the intellectual air we breathe. We find it encapsulated in the Hegelian and Marxist doctrine that man alone has an historical essence. We find it equally in the common assumption that history (unlike chronology) has its important or decisive moments, from which there is 'no turning back'.

Only of a very special kind of development could such a thing be true.

We owe much of our concept of history to the Hegelians. The idea of art history itself, as an autonomous discipline with a subject-matter and an intellectual tradition of its own, would scarcely be conceivable without Hegel, and the German tradition of *Kulturgeschichte* that Hegel inspired. Without that tradition, art history would be as formless as it was in the age of Alberti or Vasari, and as formless as 'Women's Studies' is today.

However, as we know, the coulisses of Hegelian speculation harbour intellectual monsters. The greatest of these is the *Zeitgeist*. Prompted by the illusion that the mere fact that one event is contemporaneous with another is already an explanation of both (since, if they happen together, it is because the *Zeitgeist* requires it), art historians have come to think of their subject as but one branch of cultural history, incapable of being studied in the refined isolation to which they might otherwise have become accustomed. In architectural history the game of 'style' and 'period' is now played almost entirely according to the rules of *Kulturgeschichte*. Architectural historians try to classify, not styles, but times. 'Post-modernism' (the latest label) could never have been considered to be either a significant style, or a significant period, were it not for the Hegelian supposition that what is happening in architecture exhibits some deep connection with what is happening everywhere.

Sir Ernst Gombrich has said that recent 'history of historiography of culture can perhaps best be interpreted as a succession of attempts to salvage the Hegelian assumption without accepting Hegelian metaphysics'[1] — the assumption being that of the deep interconnectedness of all cultural phenomena. This assumption has never been better expressed than by Wölfflin in this remark: 'To *explain* a style cannot mean anything but to fit its expressive character into the general history of the period, to prove that its forms do not say anything in their language that is not also said by the other organs of the age.'[2] However, it seems to me that the removal of the Hegelian metaphysics might, in loosening the grip of the *Zeitgeist,* have done a service to art history. For it has allowed us to think, what art historians need to think, that the discipline of art history is not just a part of *Kulturgeschichte*. In which case, it lies open for us to suggest that it has the kind of autonomy constitutive of a genuine independent subject.

The attempt to understand this autonomy takes us into the heart of an intractable philosophical problem, that of the nature of historical understanding. Is historical understanding a special case of scientific explanation — explanation by cause and effect — or is it not? If not, what is it? The difficulty here is created by our prior stipulation that history is a *human* thing. Human institutions, however, are regularly described and understood in ways that seem to have no connection with scientific explanation.

In particular, there is a great and much commented difference between understanding human institutions from within and understanding them from without. Consider the customs and rituals that constitute the religious institutions of a tribe. To a member of the tribe these are perceived as necessities which bind his conduct, imperatives of action, with meanings which in all probability he cannot convey in words. To the anthropologist, looking on these things from outside, these institutions are instances of some genus, to be described and explained in accordance with laws that apply, not to this tribe alone, but universally. What to the participant is an act of propitiation, with an inalienably local significance, designed to retain the comfort of ancestral presences, is, to the anthropologist, a 'cohesive strategy', a 'reaffirmation of identity' — in short, an action with a universal social purpose that is concealed from the participant. And in some sense it is the existence of this social purpose that will, from the external point of view, explain the activities of the tribe. But it will explain them in a way that the members of the tribe could never recognize. To accept this explanation is already to suffer a loss of faith. It is to lose sight of the specific significance which lies at the heart of the ritual. The ritual could no longer be intentionally performed by the man aware of its explanation: in which case there would cease to be anything to explain.

The case is by no means peculiar. The history of religious decline is, roughly speaking, the history of the invasion of religious practice by its own explanation. Such examples show how difficult the understanding of human institutions is likely to be. For, in theory at least, one form of understanding might actually succeed in abolishing its object. It would be very odd to think that the same could be true of natural (i.e., non-human) things: for example, to think that the growth of geological understanding could bring about the non-existence of rocks. If a geologist can talk a rock into annihilation, this is a quality of his voice, not of his science.

The example shows something else of considerable interest. Very often those explanations of human institutions that seem most plausible from the external point of view are of the very special kind that has been called 'functional'. And it could be argued with some force that the difficulties presented by historical understanding are related to a wider problem in the philosophy of science — that of the nature of functional explanation. How can the function of something (which would seem to be one of its effects) actually be part of its cause? If I leave this problem on one side it is only in order to attend to a yet more urgent matter.[3]

I want tentatively to suggest that external explanations, of whatever depth and complexity, are not what the art historian is or should be looking for. He should be observing the works of art that he studies with the receptive spirit of the participant, for whom meaning comes first and explanation later. I shall try to illustrate my point by reflecting on the well-known Marxian theory of history.

According to this theory, which in its most plausible form involves an application of the kind of functional explanation familiar in biology and anthropology, we explain all historical forces as a species of development. (It is characteristic of this theory, as of the Hegelian theory from which it stems, that it considers history to be a kind of development. All declines are abnormalities which prepare the way for the next advance.) Its distinctive feature lies in the view that the thing which develops is *not* the whole of civilization but only a part of it, and that the development of this part explains the changes apparent in the rest. Development resides in the productive forces of society: these develop because human mastery over nature increases. At each level of development a structure of economic relations emerges in answer to the need of the productive forces, and this structure of 'production relations' constitutes the material 'base' to which all other social phenomena are in a sense subordinate. The other phenomena include the legal and political 'superstructure' which consolidates through institutions of legitimization the economic relations of the base. The superstructure in turn demands and is consoled by a ruling 'ideology' — the system of received ideas which, on the Hegelian model, generates the movement of history, and which, on the Marxian model, is generated by it.

The Marxian theory implies that the self-image of those who participate in history is the product of activities in which that self-image plays no significant (because no determining) part. The motive force of history by-passes the motivation of its agents. Here the external view of things is dominant. It is, I believe, inherent in this switch to the external point of view that the value of human activities should become more difficult to perceive. Values are explained as 'ideology', in the way that the virtues of 'self-help' and 'thrift' are explained away, as contributions to the upkeep of the bourgeois state. The question 'Why be thrifty?' may have been a significant one for Samuel Smiles. In Marx it receives no answer that does not attribute to the questioner a motive that he is constitutionally unable to accept. The same must happen, I believe, to all values when the external point of view is so systematically adopted.

If the Marxian view represented the ideal (if not the reality) of historical analysis, it would be difficult to see how we could reasonably attribute autonomy to *any* part of history. Not only would there be no genuine history of art: there could be no history of law, no political history, no history of music, or of fashion: all these would be mere pseudo-disciplines, arbitrary tabulations of facts interesting in themselves but bearing no relation to one another except through a theory that deprives them of intrinsic causality. All history becomes economic history. Economic history can be subtracted from history without remainder.

The discomfort caused by that view has two sources. First, it seems to abolish many subjects that we know not only to exist but also to contain within themselves the fruits of substantial intellectual discipline. Secondly it refers things with which we are intellectually at ease, to a hypothesis (both unproven, and in all probability unprovable) which implies that we do not really understand them.

From the scientific point of view the suggestion might have considerable force. By the fortunate workings of nature, we can often invent what turn out to be largely classificatory and *ad hoc* sciences (such as biology and chemistry) which give us a partial understanding of the things that they study, while awaiting the development of that genuine science (in this case physics) from which they can be derived. Art history might similarly be taken to stand to economic history much as biology stands to organic chemistry, and organic chemistry to physics.

From the human point of view, however, the suggestion is far too narrow. For it is based on the false assumption that, in the human realm, as in the realm of nature, explanation is always one kind of thing. Explanation is the production of an answer to the question 'why?'. Traditional Aristotelian philosophy distinguished four kinds of answer to that question. As a rule, modern philosophy distinguishes at least two. If I ask 'Why did he raise his arm?' I might be given an explanation in terms of antecedent events, and laws which connect those events with the action to be explained. Here the 'why?' has been taken as the 'why?' of cause. There is reason why a causal explanation should not mention facts unknown and unknowable to the agent. It might be framed, for example, entirely physiologically, in terms of the stimulation of nerves and the resultant operation of the muscles. And it is a well-known, though admittedly contestable, thesis of philosophy that this 'why?' of cause not only fails to capture our ordinary way of understanding people; it may also render our actions *unintelligible*. For it removes that reference to 'how things seem' without which no action can be recognized as ours.

Hence philosophers have sought for what I shall call, in deference to that tradition in modern thought which originated in the works of Wilhelm Dilthey, and which now goes by the broad and confusing title of hermeneutics, the 'why?' of meaning. Our actions mean things to ourselves and to others, and are understood in terms of those meanings. Thus another answer to the question 'Why did he raise his arm?' might be: 'To signify assent'. On the surface, at least, this explanation seems to have nothing in common with the mechanistic explanations referred to in the last paragraph. Let us at least concede that, when we understand someone through understanding the significance of his actions, this does not require us to delve very far into their causes: for otherwise we should never understand ourselves.

The hermeneutical 'why?' has many varieties. Two in particular deserve mention at this juncture: the 'why?' of intention, and the 'why?' of style. The difference between these is not always noticed, though it is of the greatest importance to the subject under discussion. When I answer the question 'Why did he do that?' by referring to some purpose intended, then, because the explanation refers not backwards to the past but forwards to the future, it is quite reasonable (though not incontrovertible) to suggest that the answer refers not to a cause but to a reason. 'Reasons' are thereby marked out as a special kind of answer to the question 'why?'. But it is not always noticed that there is another answer to the question 'why?' which refers, not to reasons, but to the greater or less degree of coherence, or 'significant relation', between the action explained and those which surround it. 'That was the appropriate thing'; 'It was his way'; 'It was a fitting response' — all such answers, which do not so much specify a particular purpose as bring an action into perceivable relation with others of its kind, I shall call answers to the 'why?' of style.

We can now make a suggestion about the idea of historical under-standing, namely, that it involves an extension to human institutions of the 'why?' of meaning. It is in this way that an historian operates, for example, when he studies political and military achievements: the questions asked of, and the order found in, his subject are part of a 'revelation of intention' which is not unlike the process of understanding another human being. To imagine an external science of such things is almost impossible. It is, as Leibniz once put it, 'as if a historian should try to explain the conquest of some important place by a great prince, by saying that it occurred because the small particles of gunpowder, set free by the contact of the spark, escaped with a velocity capable of pushing a hard and heavy body against the walls of the place, while the little particles which composed the bronze of the cannon were so firmly interlaced that this velocity did not force them apart.'[4] It seems that we understand even modern Soviet history better if we ask ourselves about the enduring aims, methods and style of Russian conquests, than if we delve into the physical or economic factors that might be suggested to explain them.

Consider, too, the history of law. There is an important sense in which our idealized Marxian economic historian would have to overlook, in accounting for the development of law, the actual reasoning of judges (which will be just the rationalization by certain members of the ruling class of changes brought about by that class's need to consolidate its economic dominion). Actual legal history, however, is the history of a process of thought. The historian may indeed examine the ways in which legal thought has been disturbed or motivated by economic needs, but this will not be his primary concern. His concern is to 'tell the story' of a legal tradition, by understanding the words and reasons which define it.[5]

The example helps us to understand at once that, *if* we construe historical understanding on the hermeneutical model, then we begin to see that history might, after all, admit division into autonomous or quasi-autonomous parts. Consider the pattern of a person's thought, feeling and action from birth to death. Surely it is quite reasonable to think that these all stem from some underlying process of physical development. It is also reasonable to think that, when seeking order among them, we do not use the classifications that we would use in exploring this physical development. We trace patterns of influence and illumination, using a 'why?' of purpose, or of style. We can describe a pattern in the development of someone's scientific thought, without mentioning the different but in all probability related patterns exhibited by his emotional life, his taste in flowers, or his understanding of the opposite sex.

There is no doubt that such a conception of autonomy can be transferred, along with the internal viewpoint of which it is an offshoot, to the study of history. We are forced, indeed, by our sense of the role of consciousness in historical change, to see things from within. Consider the history of science: it is the history of arguments, experiments, conclusions, 'conjectures and refutations'. It looks absurd when reduced to its 'material' base (although there have been 'theories of scientific production' on Marxian lines which have attempted this reduction.[6]) The best way to understand scientific history is to examine the way in which, for example, Newton's *thought* is an improvement over Descartes's *thought*. It will not help to examine the complex and varied economic circumstances which produced first Descartes, then Newton.

But science is a special case. There are Marxian and neo-Marxian theories of historical development which (for reasons that I cannot elaborate here) consign the development of science expressly to the explanatory base, rather than to the superstructure that is to be explained. What distinguishes science from the humane disciplines (including the disciplines that concern us), is that in science there is a pattern of *discovery*. It was one of the early achievements of modern art history to reject the scientific and progressivist model of the evolution of art. It was recognized that, in this area, there is no single invariant movement, since there is nothing *towards* which art moves (in the way science moves towards truth). It was a fallacy to think the opposite, due partly to an over-emphasis on the role of representation in painting, and partly to a faulty theory of representation itself.[7]

Despite this lack of determinate direction, however, there may be answers to the 'why?' of art history which make no reference to phenomena outside the enterprise of art. When we ask the question 'why?' of some particular stylistic development, we are not usually enquiring after an external cause, nor after an intention. We are asking, for example: how is it that *this* can have *that* as its natural consequence? What has changed, and in what way? How might one describe the change so that the one can be seen as a continuation of the other? Is this a development of something already expressed, or a new aesthetic departure? And so on. These are the significant questions, since to answer them is to perceive the historical order that is internal to art. The order that art history looks for is diachronic: an order of 'before' and 'after'. But it is not, or at least not necessarily, an order of scientific explanation.

But a qualification needs to be introduced. I have referred to a host of somewhat vagrant 'why?' questions, and it may be asked why I should think that there is any genuine discipline that should result from attending to them. Might not the result be chaos? I think that it is this consideration, more than any, that has lain behind the search for 'method' in those subjects which, because they claim an autonomy in despite of science, have been described as 'humane'.

Consider architectural history. Here intellectual difficulties are more clearly visible, as is proved by the fact that they are more frequently answered absurdly. It has long been recognized that the minimum requirement of any discipline is some power of abstraction. The difference between the history of architecture and its chronology lies in this: in the first case there is assumed a capacity to find order in, and so abstract from, the particulars which are merely listed in the second. This abstraction has tended to proceed in one of two ways: according to style, and according to period. The first method introduces such classifications as 'mannerism', 'baroque', 'neo-classicism'; the second introduces 'mediaeval', 'Renaissance', 'post-industrial'; and so on. The master-thought of German idealism was that, with insight, the classifications generated by the first method will coincide with those generated by the second. And this will provide a test for a genuine, as opposed to an arbitrary, historical class. The class will be genuine since it will provide an internal explanation of the kind we require: to describe a building as 'baroque' will be to say *why* it looks as it does, and not just *that* it does. Here the 'why?' of style is used to define the conception of an historical period. Hence, if there is a method, a discipline, a practice, that can train the eye and the mind in such classifications, there will be a true subject of architectural history. Otherwise there may be chronology, there may be criticism, there may be anecdote, but there will be nothing that deserves the name of history.

However, it is precisely in this search for discipline that the danger of a loss of autonomy begins to creep in. The classifications of the architectural historian aim at, even if they do not always achieve, a certain generality. 'Mannerism' seems intellectually respectable to the extent that it identifies, first a common property of more than one artist, secondly a common property of more than one art. But the intellectual imperialism of *Kulturgeschichte* was such that it attempted to establish these conceptual beachheads in all territories at once. Having succeeded so triumphantly with its distinction between Renaissance and baroque in architecture, it attempted to demonstrate (or at least allowed itself to assume), that Mozart's music, for example, should be described as rococo (going so far as to influence at least the title, if not the style, of a famous piece by Tchaikovsky).

But now, having lost autonomy, architectural history looks around for a method that will justify the loss. It is then that it finds comfort in the external viewpoint of the economic historian, for whom the autonomy of the humane disciplines was never anything more than a ruse. It seems, then, that the need for discipline, and the need for autonomy, serve to constrain our subject in opposing directions.

We are now in a position to focus on our central question: does art have a history? Art certainly need not have a history everywhere. Perhaps the chronology of Persian carpets and Egyptian monuments is not really a kind of history. But our main concern must be, as ever, the art of our own, European, civilization, upon which more light has been cast by 'art history' than by almost any other discipline. To have a history art must have autonomy. I would like to argue that art does have the kind of autonomy to which I have referred. How to prove this I do not know, but I shall first take an example: that of the history of music.

It seems to me that there is a transition from the style of Bach, through Handel, J. C. Bach, Haydn and Mozart, to Beethoven. This transition is utterly intelligible to every music lover. It is part of music history to analyse it, and to lay bare its structure. We can, indeed, *hear* the historical relations between these composers — hear, for example, the Handelian elements in Mozart's arias, hear the stylistic negation of Bach's counterpoint in the chordal style of his son; and so on. The relations that are discussed by the historian of music are both internal to the art of music and at the same time pellucid to the listener. It is wrong to claim that there is an historical process that we understand better than we understand this one — for we understand this one more or less completely: so completely indeed that, when faced by some minor work of Telemann, Stamitz, or Spohr, we should have little difficulty either in dating it, or in showing its stylistic relation to the principal musical manifestations of its period. This crystal-clear segment of musical history would become obscure at once, were we to look outside it to the social and economic determinants which, on one view, constitute the true explanation of cultural phenomena. We should have to relate Bach's position as a Lutheran Kapellmeister in a bourgeois town, to Haydn's life at the Esterhazy court, and to Beethoven's attempts to live without patronage in a burgeoning modern city. We should have to be clear about the economic transitions from late seventeenth century mercantile capitalism in Germany, to post revolutionary industrialism in Austria; and so on. Let us cut the story short: we do not understand those things, and maybe we never will. We do understand the history of music. So the history of music has autonomy. If we start to play the game of the 'socio-economic context' we end up by misunderstanding music.

A similar example: the history of the classical styles in architecture. What can be better understood than that? We find the answer to a 'why?' asked of an Adam house in the ruins of Athens or Rome. But what of the social and economic relations between those contrasting times and places? A final example: the obvious stylistic development of the gothic from Arabic forms and of the Arabic from Indian and Greek: this is a fascinating and evident piece of architectural continuity, set against a near nonsense of social and economic variety.

Once we concede that art does have this autonomy, then the Marxian and all similar theories of history cease to apply to it. I shall assume that this autonomy exists, but before moving on to the significant question of the discipline which it may or may not support, I should like to draw a very important consequence, namely, that one and the same object might have more than one history. When we take the internal point of view of human institutions, our classifications, and the theories that we base on them, will depend upon our interests. If, as I should like to argue, the history of art is founded in aesthetic interest, then the history of art will not coincide with the history of engineering, or of politics, or of household religion, even when discussing objects which belong to all of those. The place of Brunelleschi's dome in the history of engineering is not the same as its place in the history of architecture, even though (unlike, say, the dome of Sancta Sophia, or Maillart's bridges) it has an important place in both. The place of Wagner's operas in political history is not the same as their place in the history of music; the place of the Russian icon is not the same in the history of painting and in the history of household religion; the place of the King James Bible or *Pilgrim's Progress* is not the same in the history of English literature and in the history of popular religion. And so on. Often when historians of art disagree about the significance of Poussin or Caravaggio it seems to me that it is from neglect of this fundamental observation. Not agreeing in their interests, they do not agree in what they see.

It is not sufficient to show that our interest in art confers autonomy. We must show that this autonomy can be the subject-matter of an historical discipline. A discipline requires that there be a true intellectual constraint upon our subject matter. The way you answer the question 'Why did this happen?' must constrain the way in which you answer the question 'Why did that happen?' Is there such a constraint? If not, then for all its autonomy, art history will remain no more than a series of intuitive ruminations. This brings me to the thesis with which I wish to conclude: aesthetic judgement is indispensable to the history of art, since it provides the discipline without which the subject does not exist.

We must first distinguish among human institutions between the purposeful and the purposeless. The two kinds of institution have different kinds of histories. In the case of purposeful institutions our 'why?' questions will be directed towards the discovery of motive, intention, and success. In the case of purposeless institutions there will be neither motive nor its fulfilment, but only the more diffuse kind of human order that goes by the name of style. Here understanding is not the understanding of a particular end or of the particular means to it; it consists in grasping a total human significance. (Thus the history of war moves in an orderly way, in accordance with the progressive sophistication of means, and the consequent simplification of ends, among our conquerors, while the history of that most purposeless of all human things, peace, remains unfathomable.)

Some works of art are purposeful — buildings, icons, funeral odes. But the discipline of art history has arisen from the attempt to understand the internal development of something classified as purposeless. The history of architecture, for example, is the history not of engineering but of stones, in their expressive aspect. You may say that it is parochial in us to found art history in this classification. At other places and at other times the objects that we know as art were made and esteemed for definite purposes, whether sacred or profane. Nevertheless this parochialism is unavoidable: it is through relating past objects to present interests that we impose upon them the historical order that they exhibit. One must not think that because we now see art as purposeless, we also see it as without value. Peace, love and friendship are purposeless, precisely because they contain their value within themselves. The same is true of art.

But what is the aesthetic judgement which constrains and orders the art historian's questions? A full answer is here impossible, but I shall mention some salient features that aesthetic judgement seems to possess. First, aesthetic judgement abstracts from the purposes of an object so as to view it not as a means to an end, but as an end in itself (as we see a person when moved by love). Secondly, aesthetic judgement involves experience. It is not made by proxy, but is disciplined by the reference to what is seen or heard in its object. (Hence an X-ray photograph of a painting may revise our opinion of its date, but it has bearing on its significance as a work of art only in so far as our *way of seeing* the painting is changed by a revised opinion of its date.) Thirdly, aesthetic judgement is animated by that particular application of the question 'why?' which is appropriate to stylistic understanding: the 'why?' which, having abstracted from purpose, questions the significance that remains. Finally, aesthetic judgement issues in judgements of value: it is concerned with the worth of certain experiences.

A full account of those features and of their interconnection is here impossible, but let me illustrate through a few examples the indispensability of the discipline of aesthetic judgement to the practice of art history. Consider the importance of the expressive relations between works of art. To fail to perceive these is to see not history but chronology. Suppose that someone fails to see the relation between Lippi's idealized madonnas, and Botticelli's secularized allegories of womanhood. The peculiar kind of security attached to the female physiognomy by Lippi is used by Botticelli against nature, so as to create the mythical experience of unassuaged temptation. This is a real historical relation (which presupposes, but is not reducible to, chronology). Not to see it is to miss the historical bond between those painters. But without aesthetic perception the relation cannot be seen.

A more complex case: it used to be thought that Constable's finished paintings constitute his principal *oeuvre;* looking at these we might consider Constable to be at the end of a tradition, with a pastoral and at the same time social flavour which sets him in relation to his eighteenth-century English forebears. His sketches, by contrast, used to be seen as *incomplete:* as gestures towards the finished product. As a result of a revolution in taste, such sketches as the 'Seascape Study with Rain Clouds' (Royal Academy, London) or the landscape sketches in the Victoria and Albert Museum, London, have come to be seen, not as incompleted gestures towards some other thing, but as works of art complete in themselves. Hence Constable is perceived as the great originator of nineteenth-century landscape painting, and as the true forerunner of impressionism. The aesthetic perception changes the whole history of the subject. This is because the historical order perceived in painting is an aesthetic order, and the creation of a discipline of taste.

Another example, so well known that it needs little discussion, is provided by the rediscovery of the primitive. At a certain point in the last century the knee of Giotto's great Madonna came to be seen, not as a step on the way to Masaccio, but as the culmination of pre-existing aesthetic endeavours. As a result of this aesthetic perception, the history of Florentine painting changed. Berenson tried to provide a theory to rationalize the change: but with or without the theory, there is no gainsaying that Giotto cannot be seen now as a forerunner of Masaccio, and that the aesthetic ambitions of the Giotteschi have to be re-described accordingly.

If we admit the centrality of aesthetic judgement in art history, then we must incorporate aesthetic judgement into the methods of that subject. This must surely lead us to acknowledge the aptness of the famous 'comparative method' of Wölfflin, which invites us to *perceive* historical relations, by seeing objects side by side. In the end, it seems to me, this must be the fundamental move in the construction of serious art history. For it limits the subject matter of art history to those chronological relations that can be subsumed under aesthetic classifications.

We should note also the two-way nature of the historical explanation of art. Scientific explanation proceeds always from past to future: in the present case, however, historical explanation can proceed equally from future to past. The aesthetic order may undergo a shift which changes the aspect of all that has preceded it: and the aesthetic object is constituted by its aspect. Michelangelo is as great an influence on Donatello as Donatello on Michelangelo. Perugino has become Raphael's predecessor, Ledoux the precursor of Le Corbusier, and there is no greater influence on Turner than the impressionist school of which he was wholly ignorant. This should not surprise us. The same thing occurs in our own lives, as we order and re-order our memories in accordance with the later perceptions that redeem them from the abyss of time.

This dependence on aesthetic judgement should make us beware of methods which attempt to be critically 'neutral' or 'value free'. There can be neutral methods of dating, but as I have argued, chronology and history are not the same thing. Consider the following art-historical questions: is there a Canadian school of painting? If so, does the Group of Seven constitute its central example? If that too is so, is Emily Carr to be regarded as central to the history of Canadian painting? Those are not insignificant questions. For of course there is no doubt that Emily Carr was influenced both by the *fauve* manner which she acquired in Europe, and also by a deep-seated attachment to her countryside and to the Indian people whose art had flourished there. Yet to give her an historical place you cannot avoid the lengthy and uncertain task of aesthetic comparison. You must see her paintings, now in their Canadian, and now in their European, context. No 'method' will substitute for that exercise of taste, or for the culture which is required by it.

14 The Architecture of Leninism

What is architecture, and what should an architect know? With characteristic clarity and circumspection, Alberti wrote that 'the art of building consists in the design and in the structure'. 'The whole force and rule of the design' he continued, 'consists in a right and exact adapting and joining together the lines and angles which compose and form the face of the building. It is the property and business of design to appoint to the edifice and all its parts their proper places, determinate number, just proportion and beautiful order; so that the whole form of the structure be proportionable.' Ideas of what is 'right', 'proper', 'just', 'appropriate', 'proportionable', and above all, the idea of order, determine from the beginning the direction of his thought. I have quoted from the first page of his treatise. On the next page he writes of the function of walls and apertures, the intricacies of roof construction, the effects of climate, sun and rain. He passes unhesitatingly from the abstractions of the philosopher to the realities of the working engineer. And yet the ideas of what is 'right', 'appropriate' and 'proportionable' never cease to dominate his argument. The architecture which he described and recommended through those conceptions has proved to be one of the most useful, satisfying and adaptable that the world has ever known. It would seem natural to suggest, therefore, that the architect should follow at least the spirit of Alberti's recommendations. He should study what is right, just and proportionable, and build in the light of his conclusions.

But how does one begin that study, and how does one apply it to the practice of construction? Architecture involves many aims and many standards of success. Why should one follow Alberti in putting aesthetic standards first? Alberti's terms seem peculiarly quaint when applied to contemporary buildings. Consider the Euston Tower, Warwick University, or the Lion Yard car park in Cambridge. These are assertive buildings. They do not ask to be accepted in terms of any norm or standard that is not internal to their purposes. To speak here of what is 'right' or 'appropriate', as though the criteria of 'correctness' could be specified universally, without reference to the particular function of the particular building, is to misrepresent not only the buildings but also the intention of the architects, the attitude of the public, and the age in which both architects and public live. To speak in Alberti's terms is to presuppose the constraints intrinsic to a common culture. We can make the 'appropriate' into our principal architectural value only if the 'appropriate' governs our lives. But we cannot pretend to that serene conception of things. Therefore, in all honesty, we should set aside the dogmas of the Renaissance and see contemporary architecture for what it is: an expression of the 'spirit of the age', and a product of functional conceptions. We should allow modern architecture to justify itself in its own language, and through its own hard-won ideals.

In 1967 Sir Leslie Martin, the architect of the William Stone building in Peterhouse, and of Harvey Court in Caius, set up in Cambridge an institute the name of which clearly reflects an ideology of building. The institute was called the Centre for Land Use and Built Form, reminding us that the traditional studies carried on in schools of architecture must now be finally abandoned. Since its foundation the Centre has carried out research into the fields of architectural design and town planning, under the directorship of Lionel March. It is staffed by mathematicians, computer scientists, economists and engineers, and it aims to provide an understanding of the 'art of building' which will satisfy post-graduates in the field. Being now more certain of its own centrality, it has changed its name to the Martin Centre for Architectural and Urban Studies. It has produced a large number of 'working papers' devoted to problems in engineering and 'comprehensive urban re-development' (a favourite theme). From time to time its work is published, giving the common reader an opportunity to understand contemporary architecture in its own authentic language. In *The Architecture of Form* the most up to date achievements of the Cambridge School are lavishly presented.[1] Not all the contributors work in the Martin Centre: one is a member of the Department of Architecture, another belongs to the Computer Laboratory, some are attached to universities and town-planning departments in other parts of the country. But they all share common aims and aspirations, and it is due to the industry and conviction of Sir Leslie Martin's school that their work is here brought together.

The aim, to put it very simply, is to reduce architectural problems to mathematical problems. In the view of Lionel March, the editor of the volume, 'no distinction can be drawn between engineering and architecture'. Alberti would have agreed with him, arguing that no engineer can act intelligently without that cultivated sense of the appropriate, the proportionable, the just, which governs all human activity and turns the satisfaction of a need into the pursuit of aesthetic perfection. But the language of Sir Leslie Martin's Centre is not that of Alberti. It is the language of the computer scientist, working in what Americans call a 'systems laboratory', attempting to solve, through mathematical representation, problems in solid geometry, statistics and the theory of choice.

Their work, Lionel March tells us in his introduction, takes us a step along the 'constructivist path towards rational design in architecture'.

'Constructivism' is in fact the only contemporary architectural movement that is acknowledged by the writers in this volume. So committed are they to its doctrines that they seldom either rehearse or even allude to them. Instead they apply themselves to the task of constructing a 'rational' architecture in accordance with the aims and outlook of the early Soviet school.

Constructivism began, shortly after the Russian Revolution, as a kind of bullying anti-aestheticism, a plain man's philosophy of building. Its conceptions are typified by the slogans put out in 1920 by A. Rodchenko and U. Stepanova: 'Kill human thinking's last remaining attachment to art!!', and 'Down with art which only camouflages humanity's incompetence!!' Architecture must adopt the collectivist ideology; its sole justification lies in the efficiency with which it answers to the collective need. Aesthetic considerations are not just secondary to the constructivist's aim; they are inimical to it. The sole task of the architect is to construct buildings suitable to the new social order and to destroy everything that stands in its way. It is not surprising that constructivism became, for a short while, the official credo of the Soviet architect. It began to support itself with scientific and pseudo-scientific rhetoric, asserting that architecture is just another application of that mode of 'dialectical' reasoning which is exemplified in philosophy, physics, mathematics, and indeed, in the process of history itself. In 1928 L. Komarova and N. Krasil'nikov wrote as follows: 'In projecting a building design the architect has to find the most correct, i.e., the most economic, arrangement of its individual parts.... Our aim is... to give a scientific-objective assessment of all the possible variants available to the projector....' The 'correct' arrangement of parts in a building is the most 'economic'. Alberti's attempt to derive a notion of correctness which transcends any economic considerations, indeed which provides the framework within which economic success can be evaluated, has now been finally rejected. Lionel March, quoting from Komarova and Krasil'nikov's article, explicitly reaffirms its philosophy as that of the Centre for Land Use and Built Form. He reminds the reader that Leslie Martin was himself one of the first supporters of the constructivist movement in England. Moreover, after the war, as London's Chief Architect and Planner, Martin was able to put his constructivist ideology into practice; and with the founding of the Cambridge Centre he gave Architectural Leninism its institutional basis. As understood by Martin and his followers, the constructivist ideology is tantamount to 'aesthetic consequentialism', i.e., to the view that appropriateness in architecture arises as a result of solving problems which are not themselves aesthetic problems.

It cannot be denied that there are problems in architectural practice which admit of a mathematical solution. For example, an architect may be required to place rectangular rooms, each of certain minimum dimensions, within a given rectangular ground-plan. He might wish to know which arrangement provides the greatest number of rooms. That is a familiar problem in combinatorial analysis. The peculiarity of *architectural* problems, however, is that they involve several factors and disparate aims. It may not be possible to fulfil all of an architect's requirements. While he may wish for the greatest number of rooms, he may also require rapid communication, a minimum number of corridors, and no cul-de-sacs. Further mathematical techniques can be called upon to combine the problems in pursuit of an 'optimal building plan', to use the language of the Martin school.

In general, the techniques for arriving at 'optimal solutions' require the quantification of relevant factors: it must be possible to specify *degrees* of fulfilment for each of the architect's aims. Consequently, the contemporary 'constructivist' designer can cater for an interest only if its object is quantifiable. Furthermore, he must try to limit the variables involved in his problem. If he were really to take into account every function of a building and attempt to find an 'optimal' plan which fulfils them, the resulting problem, considered as mathematics, would prove wholly intractable to the methods presented in this book. Until some limit is set on the factors to be considered, the 'solution' is no nearer for the mathematician than it is for the ordinary practical man. In particular, we find that the contributors to the present volume begin their investigations from a strikingly limited description of the available 'built forms'. Given a basic 'repertoire' of forms they proceed to set up arbitrary problems of optimization, for example: which arrangement lets in the most light while allowing the smallest loss of heat? The limitation of forms is based on the urgent desire to provide a clear mathematical problem which is also a problem in architecture. However, it is not only possible, but in fact extremely likely, that a true 'optimal' solution will require a departure from the premises here adopted, and an imaginative leap beyond the category of assembled concrete boxes. It is true that there exists a rich, though as yet very incomplete, mathematical theory of forms. But the techniques employed by the writers in this volume are too elementary and circumscribed to generate mathematical understanding, so that their architectural application cannot yield serious practical results. The mathematics is throughout entirely preparatory, consisting of standard axioms and definitions, expressing the sense that this or that theory *might* be relevant, but carrying nothing through to the point of proof.

It soon becomes clear that there is no guarantee that human intuition is not a more appropriate and more reliable guide to 'optimal' solutions than the results of existing computer analysis. Indeed, in one paper, P. Tabor compares various existing techniques for deriving an 'optimal' solution to the problem of communication between rooms. He finds that they are all inferior to the technique of intuitive assessment, called, in the author's language, 'eyeballing'. And the book ends on an agreeable note from Dean Hawkes, who recognizes that until we have adopted certain intuitive 'stereotypes', architectural problems are in fact quite incomprehensible. Within the limits set by a stereotype an architect can visualize his objectives more precisely; outside those limits he stumbles in the dark, and the torch of mathematics only serves to dazzle him.

Common sense might have made that conclusion more apparent from the beginning; but common sense is not a quality that is much in evidence among those addicted to the outlook of aesthetic consequentialism. Those maxims which govern the behaviour of the normal practical man appear not at the beginning but at the end of their arguments and gain no authority from the intervening mess of symbols. Hawkes, for example, after tabulating the results of experiments concerning noise and speech, air and temperature, and so on, with tables, graphs, and formulae, is able to draw the following conclusion: 'It becomes clear that acoustical design in office buildings is a matter of ensuring that noise levels within them do not inconvenience desired communication while ensuring, with or without the help of partitions or screens, that privacy can be found when it is required.' A theory which enables such a conclusion to 'become clear' is scarcely likely to contribute very much to the fund of architectural competence. It is evident that mathematical procedures are being used in a way that is divorced from any serious conceptual understanding, and the result is as irrelevant architecturally as it is mathematically trite.

An important question is raised, nonetheless, by such attempts to give a mathematics of architecture. Could this ever be a serious enterprise? In answering that question we must look more deeply into the motives of the contemporary consequentialist school. Something of the flavour of its idealism can be gleaned from a paper published in 1966 by Christopher Alexander and entitled, with characteristic Corbusian bombast, 'The City as a Mechanism for Sustaining Human Contact'. Here is a typical extract:

> Let us assume that there are two children per household in the areas where children live (the model figure for suburban households), and that these children are evenly distributed in age from 0 to 18. Roughly speaking, a given pre-school child who is x years old, will play with children who are $x-1$ or $x+1$ years old. Statistical analysis shows that in order to have a reasonable amount of contact, and in order for each child

to have a 95 per cent chance of reaching five such potential playmates, each child must be in reach of twenty-seven households.

If we assume that pre-school children are not able, or allowed, to go more than about 100 yards in search of playmates, this means that each house must be within 100 yards of twenty-seven other houses.[2]

Statistical analysis has shown that in order to achieve a 'reasonable' amount of contact with his neighbours a child must be within reach of twenty-seven houses. Did Huckleberry Finn have a reasonable amount of contact with his neighbours? If so, what possessed Mark Twain to ignore those twenty-seven houses, so vital to his hero's development? Many novelists have written about childhood in this irresponsible way. Fortunately the matter has been taken out of their hands. We can now 'quantify' the basis of a child's satisfactions; our administrative decisions can therefore reflect a more 'rational' assessment of the human situation.

Lionel March is not quite convinced. Alexander's argument is all right so far as it goes. But it ignores the element of uncertainty. Its numerical intuitions should be expressed in probabilistic terms; it is only the norm of human choice that is captured by Alexander's quantifications. So there can be no rational solution to Alexander's problem until it is framed in the language of probabilistic inference. March lays out certain commonplaces of probability theory in order to illustrate his meaning. He does not actually offer a 'solution' to the 'problem'; his point is to show that if there *were* a solution, it would have to be framed in probabilistic rather than 'deductive' terms. The numerical theory of human nature remains as charming for March as it is for Alexander. But the idea that there is such a thing as a 'reasonable' amount of contact, to be defined through 'statistical analysis', the mock exactitude of the decision that children need to be within reach of five potential playmates, the peculiar assumption that 100 yards is the limit to which children are able to stray from their homes: these conceptions are in fact entirely spurious. They are the upshot of an unserious fantasizing about human existence that is wholly inimical to true mathematical understanding.

The real difficulty comes out when we reflect on the premises of our architectural problem. How many factors, and of what kind, can we consider? Suppose that our 'optimal building plan' produces the fastest, safest and most economical route between the rooms of a hypothetical office-block. The ground plan of our building is designed to take the applicant who enters it as rapidly as possible to his final destination. It may be that the 'optimal solution', so calculated, defies our capacity to envisage it. The applicant is unable to retain a visual map of his progress, and wanders in bewilderment from one unwanted office to the next. If that is so, then the whole solution is nugatory. The existence of human beings is a source of immense irritation to those engaged in these researches. They are now faced with the Herculean task of quantifying the vagaries of our incompetence, of showing in numerical terms the extent to which their solutions can be visualized. It would be simpler to leave human beings out of consideration altogether. And that solution is in fact quite respectable. Le Corbusier and his followers have provided an agreeable rhetoric in terms of which to discuss these things, a rhetoric which reduces the human being to manageable proportions, which construes him as a collection of more or less quantifiable 'needs'. For example, the human being has a need for air, light, open space, movement, everything, in fact, that is *not* architecture. All the architect has to do is to ensure a man's ready access to those simple and quantifiable commodities. The concept of a need is well suited to the justification of that *'machine à vivre'* which Le Corbusier has recommended to us. It has an admirable hygienic quality, and suggests a straightforward biological idea of human fulfilment. The satisfaction of a need is a matter of degree: it can therefore be effectively quantified. The difficulty in arriving at a truly human architecture becomes a purely mathematical one.

Now Lionel March is aware that human beings have values as well as needs. So we must also find a way of incorporating values into our description of the architectural process. Values, March says, are really facts, facts about human preferences. So we can incorporate them into our description of the 'design problem' after all. Preferences are susceptible to a 'partial ordering' in mathematical terms. We can therefore balance them against other factors, such as biological needs, economic requirements, and environmental control. The theory of preference is now available to take us another step along the road towards 'a more rational approach to urban design problems'. Those are the words of Patricia Apps, whose contribution is noteworthy for one thing: she is prepared (in a footnote) to offer a definition of rationality. Rational behaviour, apparently, is behaviour in accordance with the axioms of 'preference' theory (i.e., the theory of 'revealed preference' which features in much modern micro-economics). The irrational being, who pursues satisfactions which cannot be quantified, or who is prepared to sacrifice 'utility' in the interests of some moral or aesthetic perfection, has only himself to blame if the architecture of the future displeases him. Did he not realize that he should follow the axioms of preference theory and learn to recognize, when he encounters it, 'the optimal building plan'?

It may be true that values are preferences. But not all preferences are values. Some of our preferences (for example, in food and wine) we regard as reflections of our own personality or constitution; these we are content to regard as *mere* preferences, and we consider ourselves under no obligation (although we may have a desire) to justify them when challenged. Values are more significant: not only do we feel called upon to support them with reasons when necessary, we also learn to see and understand the world in terms of them. A value, unlike a mere preference, expresses itself in language such as that used by Alberti: it pursues what is right, fitting, appropriate and just. It is the outcome of thought and education, and can be supported, overthrown or modified by reasoned argument. It does not manifest itself merely as an isolated preference in some factitious 'choice situation'. A value is characterized not by its strength, but by its depth, by the extent to which it brings order to experience. It is difficult to see how such a thing could be measured without denaturing it.

It becomes clear that there is something vital left out of the consequentialists' picture of architectural practice, something which again and again foils their researches and turns their 'rational' architecture into a caricature of true rational conduct. Some might say that there is no hope of establishing any useful relation between mathematics and architecture. But we should remember that the relation between mathematics and architecture has always been proposed as fundamental to the builder's understanding. Even the thinkers of the Renaissance considered that the relation between the two pursuits is deep and important. But for them the relation was an aesthetic one. And it is for that very reason that mathematics provided the Renaissance philosophers with a serious concept through which to envisage architectural problems. It is precisely the lack of any serious concept that is most remarkable in the writings of the contemporary Cambridge school.

What does it mean to say that the relation between mathematics and architecture is an aesthetic relation? I think we can make sense of the suggestion in the following way: from both mathematics and architecture we obtain a sense of *fittingness*. In contemplating the relations of numbers and the relations of architectural parts, we derive a similar satisfaction and a similar sense of the intrinsic order of things. The analogy between mathematical and architectural harmony enables us to use the former to understand, envisage and manipulate the latter. Furthermore our sense of what is fitting reflects a deeper demand for order. We can see architectural forms as 'fitting' because architecture reflects the desires and responses characteristic of our rational nature. Architecture helps us to see the world as familiar, as reflecting demands which have their origin in us. And something similar is true, according to Alberti, of our experience of mathematics. The harmony that we see in mathematics is a harmony that we find in ourselves.

It may be that we cannot accept that theory in quite the form which once made it so popular. But we cannot deny, all the same, that we see buildings according to the wider conceptions of our moral nature. We see them, for example, as expressive, forbidding, polite, brutal or welcoming. It is by virtue of this process of 'seeing as' that architecture becomes an intelligible object of aesthetic interest. Now Alberti recommended the builder to study what is 'just' and 'appropriate', and it may be thought that such a recommendation is in fact entirely empty. For what is just and appropriate and who is to decide? And how can one study such a thing? To refer to the analogy with mathematics is not to lay down an absolute standard, valid for all times and for all human purposes. It is, rather, to express only one among the varied concepts through which aesthetic organization has been tried.

We should remember that the study of what is right and appropriate does not lead to *theoretical* knowledge. There is no fixed and necessary body of rules which one must learn as one learns the axioms of a natural science. The study of the appropriate is a form of practical knowledge; it involves education rather than learning. In aesthetic education one acquires the capacity to notice things, to make comparisons, to see architectural forms as meaningful and respond to them as the manifestation of ideas. One comes to see buildings as familiar, and that process of education has the same structure, the same discipline and the same rewards regardless of whether the rules of composition involved in it and the particular comparisons made in it can be laid down as universal laws.

It is a natural consequence of this educative process that it should give to the builder, and to his client, the ability to envisage the effects of architectural forms: the builder is able not just to describe his projected building but actually to imagine the experience of it. Which is why I say that the endpoint of visual education is a form of practical knowledge. The architect acquires a sense of *what it would be like* to live and work in the completed building. In educating his perception he has educated his choice. Now the phrase 'what it would be like' points to a question which mathematics cannot solve. It is a question not about the quantity but about the quality of something, the quality of an experience. The question is answered when the architect can visualize the full effect of his completed building; it is neither pre-empted nor seriously affected by the functional questions which bother the proponents of aesthetic consequentialism. Architects who begin from that conception of the appropriate which Alberti recommended to us did not find the question difficult to answer. Their conceptions are, initially at any rate, aesthetic, and the principal aim of the aesthetic impulse is to render intelligible what is strange. It was an aesthetic impulse that led to the development of a language of architecture, with its own particular visual vernacular. I am not referring only to the

Gothic and Classical styles, but also to the everyday preoccupations of the jobbing builder. This vernacular language speaks to a man in recognizable visual accents, and gives him a sense of oneness with his surroundings. And because the sense is common to both architect and client, the work of the one can provide a comprehensible background to the activity of the other. The architect at his drawing-board can work with a prior conception of the quality of his client's experience.

I have suggested that the attempt to remove aesthetic considerations from architectural practice is not only difficult but in fact self-defeating. There is no coherent activity which corresponds to the aims of the consequentialist school. Their recommendation of a 'rational' approach to building is in fact a recommendation of its opposite. Aesthetic judgement is not merely an optional addition to the architect's psychology. It is an essential expression of his rational nature. To imagine a world purged of all aesthetic preoccupations is to imagine a world with neither concepts nor eyes. It is through aesthetic understanding that the eye is trained, and it is through the training of the eye that the architect is able to envisage the effect of his building. Without the process of education to which I have referred, there is no way in which an architect can seriously know what he is doing when he begins to build.

The consequentialist's attempt to *reduce* architecture to mathematics involves, then, a failure to understand the art of building in its true totality. It involves a fragmentation of architectural thought, and stands in the way of any serious solution to the problems with which it pretends to deal. Yet it is capable of practical application: the results can be seen everywhere, and they are disastrous. A tyrannical censorship is exercised over every aspect of building that does not have its numerical computation. And that process of suppression is carried out in the name of a theory that is in fact wholly irrational. The consequentialist architect, working without aesthetic limitations, is unable to define his project independently of a narrow range of functions. His anxiety to answer to the given 'need' turns every architectural problem into a unique one, requiring its own individual solution. But to the extent that the architect thinks in this way so does he lose the capacity to envisage his completed building. His problem resolves into a mathematical one; but as mathematics it is insoluble. He must therefore act blindly, without the guidance either of mathematical or of aesthetic conceptions.

15 Aesthetic Education and Design

In a letter, the great English architect, Sir Edwin Lutyens, wrote thus of the classical Orders:

> They have to be so well digested that there is nothing but essence left . . .
> the perfection of the Order is far nearer nature than anything produced
> on impulse and accident-wise. Every line and curve the result of force
> against impulse through the centuries.[1]

Lutyens's words are, I believe, well-chosen, and they suggest a three-fold distinction: essence, nature and force, opposed to accident, artifice and impulse. In this chapter I wish to explain the idea of aesthetic education which that threefold distinction embodies. It is an idea that is persuasive both as theory, and, when expressed in the classical tradition of design, as practice.

The distinction between essence and accident is fraught with philosophical difficulties, and its application in the field of aesthetics is especially precarious. Hegelians and Marxians draw a distinction between 'essence' and 'appearance', in a manner that has been highly influential in the discussion of social and psychological reality. For the Marxian economist 'price' denotes an appearance, the essence of which is 'value' or 'embodied labour'. Thus price is some kind of systematic mirage, generated by the social conditions that engender a market economy, but in no sense part of the underlying economic forces. I mention that theory, because it illustrates what happens when the distinction between essence and accident is confused with that between reality and appearance. It is widely argued that in Marxian economics, the important thing, price, never gets explained, precisely because it is 'explained away' as mere appearance. In fact, there is no greater error in the study of human things than to believe that the search for what is essential must lead us to what is hidden. The error has also created considerable confusion in the study of architecture, appearing, for example, in Le Corbusier's attempts to reduce building to frame-construction, or to the 'five essential points' of design. The frame is no more the essence of a building than the human skeleton is the essence of the human person, or labour the essence of price. A building, like a person, is a varied and significant appearance; a frame may be the means to sustain that appearance, but, apart from that accidental role, it is without architectural meaning. If it has a meaning, it is because it has been made part of the appearance — as in some of the 'high tech' architecture of Piano and Rogers (although, in the case of the Centre Pompidou at least, the frame which appears is little more than the appearance of a frame). In short, when talking of the 'essence' of design, we are not talking of something lying behind appearances, but of the appearances themselves.

A related fallacy lies in the assumption that every essence is a 'bare essence'. To find what is essential in architecture, therefore, you must 'strip away' encumbrances. Conversely, the more you clutter your forms with detail and ornament, the further you are from 'pure' architecture, and the nearer you are to 'crime'. That idea — associated, to some extent, with the 'stripped' classicism of Perret, and also with Adolf Loos and the Bauhaus — has been extremely influential.[2] It is a persistent philosophical error to hold that the distinction between essence and accident is identical with, or inextricably bound up with, that between substance and property, so that you reach the essence of something by 'stripping away' its qualities. There is hardly a philosopher now who would fall victim to such a confusion: it is established that the distinctions between essence and accident, reality and appearance, substance and quality, are not one distinction but three. But it is a first impulse of philosophical reflection to confuse them, and the confusion is prevalent in the naive speculations which issue from the pens of architectural critics and practitioners.

Not everything that has an essence has a bare essence. In the human world, essences tend to be cluttered. For the human world is a system of appearances, where what is essential is the flowering of the surface, in language, custom, manners, conversation, in life itself. The phenomenologists have rightly distinguished the *Lebenswelt* of human experience, from the 'hidden' world — the 'discovered' world — of scientific investigation. Human life accommodates the world to our activity, and our activity to the world. We describe the world, respond to it, act upon it, but largely because it presents an appearance to *us*. Architecture, when successful, belongs to that *Lebenswelt* of thought and action; its essence, like the essence of almost every human thing, lies in its elaboration. Oscar Wilde remarked that only a very shallow person does not judge by appearances. It is also only a shallow person who looks for 'simplicity' in architecture, as though it were the criterion of truth.

Modern philosophy has revived a controversy which began in the seventeenth century, and which received detailed discussion in Locke's *Essay Concerning Human Understanding*. It is a familiar empiricist claim that essences are relative to classifications. We can say that bachelors are 'essentially' unmarried, but only because this is the status conferred upon them by their classification. But no object, construed in itself, has an essence. Locke disagreed, and argued that objects may have 'real essences', which make them what they are, however we describe them. Locke added that real essences are unknowable; recent philosophers, reviving his idea, have not generally agreed with this conclusion. Instead, they have argued that the search for real essences constitutes one of the fundamental exercises of scientific explanation, and provides the basis for many of our classifications, in particular for those which aim to identify 'natural kinds'.[3] But there is another, less absolute, idea of 'real' essence that has emerged in recent literature. According to this idea, an essence may be relative, not to a classification, but to the interests and purposes of people. If architecture has a 'real' essence, it will be of this (relative) variety. For whatever architecture is, it is not a natural kind.

When someone chooses a knife it is usually with the purpose of cutting. This purpose is so important and recurrent a feature of human experience that we have a classification — 'knife' — which embodies it. Some properties of a knife will be directly connected with its purpose: hardness, strength, sharpness. Others will not be so connected: ornamentation, colour, sheen. We could therefore say that the first properties belong to essence, the second to accident.

If we could view buildings as we view knives, as similar, but of course vastly more complicated, artifacts predicated upon human purposes, then this would give us grounds for a like distinction. The essential in architecture would be that which contributes to function, the accidental that which does not. That thought inspired the modern functionalist theories, and the (no longer very fashionable) criticism of ornament. Whether or not ornament is a 'crime', at least there is a mistaken conception of human purposes, it was thought, involved in taking it as central.

Unfortunately, it proves impossible to state a function, or a ruling function, for architecture — at least not without radically simplifying and falsifying the relation of buildings to people. Of course, particular buildings have particular functions: but their ability to satisfy these functions, while it may explain their existence, does not describe their essence. Function may be the least important, and in any event the least permanent, feature of a building. What was once a factory becomes a museum or an apartment block; a church becomes an assembly hall, or a market; and so on. Buildings of the past — at least those that persuade us to preserve them — have lent themselves to functional transformations, and have developed under the influence of changes which were never foreseen by their architects. (Think of the functional changes which Sancta Sophia has undergone). If design is to be a rational activity, therefore, it ought to aim to produce objects whose purposes are indeterminate, and yet which lend themselves to the determinate purposes which we might find for them. The classical Orders, whatever their other merits, permitted just such a fertility and variety of function. They were useful precisely because they focused the education of an architect on what is, at first sight, the most useless part of a building.

A building must have *a* use: the problem is in specifying *the* use. *The* use of a building is always something which the building itself creates. The use is therefore so little separable from the context which the building provides, that it cannot serve as a criterion whereby to distinguish the essential from the accidental. There has been a tendency in modern 'design theory' to regard function as the premise of design, aesthetic quality as its consequence. In truth it is function which is consequential; aesthetic quality is the major premise from which function derives.

In order to illustrate that remark, I shall consider another, and in some ways simpler, exercise of design — the art (or craft) of the tailor. Plate 1 shows an engraving from the *Essays by Sir Wm. Cornwallyes*, published in 1632, representing two scholars at work in a library. Notice how far this is from the functionalist idea of a library: these forms would have suited a house, a cloister, a theatre, even a chicken farm. Which is another way of saying that they suit a library. Notice, too, the harmony that exists here, between the studious posture of the scholars, the lie of their dress, and the (crudely understood) forms of the surrounding architecture. Witness, for example, the relation between the round arches, the comfortable hats which they frame, and the bent studious heads contained in them; between the clear mouldings of the arches and columns, the stiff folds of the cloth, and the precisely orderly postures of the human figures. One is tempted to speak here of a single character, finding expression in three ways: in architecture, in clothes, and in posture. And we should not ask ourselves which of these comes first, which, as it were, is the *true* index of the character. Our postures are as much the products as the producers of the clothes and buildings we inhabit. Anne Hollander, in her perceptive book, *Seeing Through Clothes*, writes thus: 'Rubens' nudes, famous for their fatness, are actually not so much fat as multifaceted. They ripple with unaccountable fleshy hummocks exactly like the mobile surface of the clothes they have removed.'[4] The human body, when represented in painting, is seen as the last surface in a process of unveiling, which bears the imprint of the layers which must be removed from it. Although there is a limit to what we may do with our bodies, we seek to abolish that limit, to make our bodies infinitely plastic. In art, poetic licence enables us to extend to our own physical nature the process whereby we create our immediate surroundings. Clothes are less important to us now than drawing-rooms and studies, but the principle is universal. In what is near to us, we look for style, order, display, hoping not only to reveal ourselves to others, but also to realize ourselves for our own contemplation. The extreme point — the reconstruction in appearance of the human body — is one that we cannot achieve. But we constantly strain towards it, acting from a Kantian sense that this empirical world which hampers us cannot really contain us.

It is not surprising to find, therefore, that the 'function' of clothes is as elusive as that of architecture. First reflection might suggest that the function of clothing is two-fold: to protect modesty, and to provide warmth. But it has been clear for a long time that the first of those functions is not so much fulfilled as created by clothing. As Carlyle put it, 'Shame, dire shame, arose there mysteriously under Clothes', adding that 'clothes gave us individuality, distinctions, social polity'.[5] And as for the second function, how small a part it plays can be seen in any museum of costume. It would be impossible to guess, from a knowledge of climate alone, the very few points of similarity between the dresses of seventeenth-century England and those of today. We know of course that there is such a thing as 'utility' clothing, which came into being in the forties, when fashionable women found themselves in a war. This 'utility' clothing belonged, however, to the aesthetic of the war effort; it aimed to encapsulate the idea of a nation at war in forms which would also captivate the heart of the beholder, and lend social confidence to the working girl. When 'utility' is taken seriously, as an alternative to aesthetic conceptions of design, the result is peculiarly unstable — as in the utility clothing conceived (and at once abandoned) during the Russian revolution or the Maoist uniforms which are imposed by force, and which form part of what is perhaps more accurately seen as a collectivist aesthetic.

Often theorists experiment with the idea of clothes as a species of 'sign' or 'label', with the function of conveying information about the wearer. Some (for example Barthes, and Alison Lurie, in an otherwise extremely sensible book) even associate this species of 'sign' with a 'grammatical' structure, so that symbolism in clothes is assimilated to reference in language.[6] Without pausing too long over those ideas, it is worth saying something generally about the poverty of the suggestion, that clothes are to be understood as signs. The problem is to give an interpretation of the 'signs' which does not make the signs themselves into an ingredient in their meaning. A sign which 'means itself' violates the first requirement of language, which is that a symbol stand proxy for its object. Signs point beyond themselves, to a world 'referred'. There are of course definite signs in the world of clothing: uniforms, for example, which are like over-size badges, showing the office of the wearer. But it is precisely their character as clothes which prevents us from thinking of them as badges. Uniforms do not merely indicate office; they also identify the wearer with his office. They tailor his appearance to his function; his individuality becomes absorbed into the authority of a social role. The man becomes his dress, and the dress itself forms part of the office which he holds. Thus we find that a uniform cannot usually be changed or abandoned without radical alteration to the office which it serves. (Witness the rejection of the dog-collar by the trendy priest; of the wig and gown by the modern American lawyer; of the military uniform by the 'freedom fighter'.)

Uniforms are a special case. When we examine clothes that are used to indicate social role, rather than office, matters become more complex. In the two Ackermann prints of university dress (**2** and **3**), as recommended and adopted by Regency Oxford, we find again a sort of visual label — 'I am a gentleman commoner', says the one, 'And I a doctor in divinity' adds the other. But labels are devices governed by convention. Any mark can be made into a label, provided only that a convention specifies its referent. Convention is sufficient to discharge a semantic function. In these costumes we find a burgeoning of form and detail which goes far beyond convention, pointing not only to the narrow social role, but also to a style of life and a quality of experience. The scholar's costume plays a part in the larger process of constituting (rather than indicating) a social function. Convention is of course operative; but it is a convention absorbed into custom and style, so that all elements of visual arbitrariness are removed from it. The costume adds a dignity, seriousness, and distinction to the social role, and transforms it into something only partly resembling the day-to-day activities of a modern academic.

Let us now turn to a more commonplace use of clothes: clothes designed not to differentiate their wearers from the crowd, but on the contrary to assimilate them. A sociologist might say that Peruvian Indians regard their ponchos as instruments for affirming a social identity; that is why they take their dyes, patterns, and materials from a common repertoire (**4**). The perceived similarity of the ponchos is no different from the perceived similarity of the bodies, postures and mental outlooks that are wrapped up in them: the ancient, patient community, that has turned its back on the world. Of course, if the Peruvians had merely wanted to indicate social conformity, they could have chosen pin-striped suits or bathing costumes. In choosing to wear the poncho the Peruvian is not comparing a pre-existing idea of his identity with some new symbolic expression of it, and seeing that it fits. To do that, is to have lost the instinctive sense of social unity, and to try vainly to recapture it by dressing up. In the normal case the Peruvian acquires his social identity by unreflectingly wanting to dress and to appear like *this*. He fits himself into his clothes just as he fits the clothes to his body.

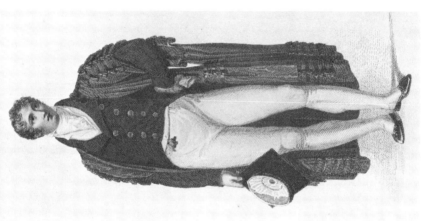

3

2

4

1

1 From *Essayes by Sir Wm Cornwalleyes*, 1632

2 and 3 From R. Ackermann's *History of
Oxford*: Gentleman Commoner, 1814;
Doctor in Divinity, 1813

4 Peruvian Indians

6

5 and 6 McKim, Mead and White: Pennsylvania
Railroad Station

7 Lutyens: Viceroy's House, New Delhi (*Country Life*)

5

7

8 Lower Manhattan

9 New York skyline

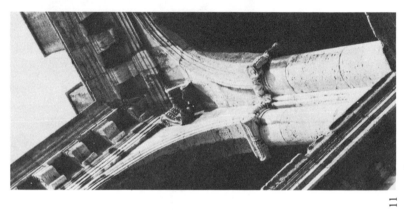

10

11

12

San Marco, Rome: 10 and 11, inner courtyard;   12 main courtyard

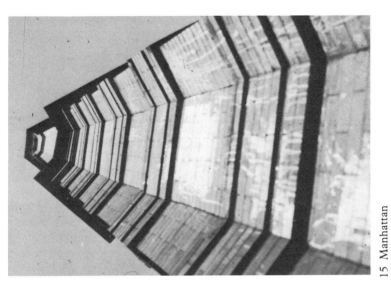

15 Manhattan

14 Ricardo Bofill: Palacio d'Abraxas, Marne-la-Vallee, near Paris

13 City Corp Building, New York

18 Sansovino: Logietta, Venice

16 The Corinthian Order, from Sir William Chambers, *Architecture*, (1825)

17 The Palace at Split, Yugoslavia

19 Sir John Soane: the Bank of England, 1828

20 The Bank of England

23 Radcliffe Camera and All Souls College, Oxford

21 From the Smolny, Leningrad

26

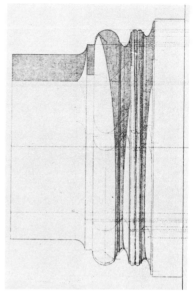

27

26 and 27 Shadows of the Ionic Capital and Base

24

25

24 and 25 Lower Manhattan

28 London Victoriana

29 'Joke classicism'

30 W. Curtis Green: Chiswick power station

31 Sinan: the Suleimaniye, Istanbul

2 Antoine Le Pautre: design for a palace, 1652

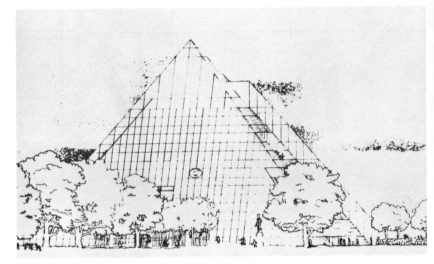

33 J. & F. Dixon Associates: design for Northampton Town Hall

34 Etienne-Louis Taravel: design for a hospital in the rue Jacob, Paris

35 Nicholas Hawksmoor: St Mary Woolnoth, London

Although there is a normal human nature, it is not a datum which precedes the construction of the human world. Each of us is to a large measure self-created through his own activity, and through no activity more than those which have, like clothing, the transformation of appearance as their aim. We do not choose our clothes as means to an end (as 'disguises'); rather we create the ends of our conduct through adjusting our dress. (The punk styles can be seen as a fervent declaration of that maxim.) The process is not arbitrary or 'subjective': it is guided by a pressure towards the normal, by an attempt to define a 'common human nature' which can form the background to our individual aims. The permanent in human nature consists in this striving for permanence, in this attempt to transform appearances so that they may contain — what would otherwise not exist as an objective entity — the self, and the common human nature in which the self participates.

How then do we, and how should we, guide our choice of costume? Only by studying appearances, and by searching in them for the marks of a relation to ourselves. This is the process of aesthetic education. It is very hard to say, in the abstract, what that process involves. But it is useful to begin from an example which illustrates its higher forms. Here is a passage from *The Young Englishwoman* of 1871, quoted by James Laver.[7] As an example of the educated eye, it could scarcely be bettered:

In dull November one seems instinctively to turn to brighter hues and richer materials in dress, as though to compensate for the chilling sights of fog and rain. There are some splendid tints in the new reddish browns, maroons, and violets of this autumn's *étoffes nouvelles;* and when dark shades are chosen, such as very deep blue, bronze, green and chestnut, the costume is relieved with pipings of some bright tint. Sky blue with dark marine blue, orange with brown, mauve with purple, maize or crimson with black, are favourite and tasteful combinations. I do not give this as a general fashion: it is suitable only for very elegant costumes, to be worn in the drawing-room or *en équipage* — for a *walking* costume it would not be in good taste. To walk the streets or, for that matter, country roads, a lady's costume should be of that sober description which, however rich the material or elegant the cut, is not meant to strike the eye or attract attention. A self-coloured costume, or a *costume ombré,* is the most elegant for walking, while a little more *fantaisie* may be allowed for those who are to appear *en voiture* only, or indoors. It is by such *nuances* that a lady reveals her good taste, and the present fashions will aid her to keep up that *convenance des choses* any infringement of which is considered such an offence in our *beau monde.*

English tartan and waterproof materials are much used in Paris just now for *costumes de fatigue.* The tartan has its own fringe and border for the trimming. Next, in point of elegance, comes the *costume complet* of drap de dame, or cachemire double, trimmed with flutings, biais, and braid work...

The writer goes on to describe some of the dresses that have captivated the Parisian *beau monde,* in language of extraordinary richness and evocative power. Here is a description of morning wear:

A dress of rich maroon faille silk is trimmed with pipings of pale orange. There are two flounces upon the skirt; they are arranged in double box pleats, with a plain space between each pleat, and are piped with orange silk. The tunic, richly trimmed with black lace, is turned up with two large revers of pale orange silk, fastened down with black lace bows. The bodice, buttoned up to the top with orange silk buttons, has wide sleeves, open from the elbow, trimmed with a deep lace border and bows of orange coloured ribbon and black lace. A similar bow is placed at the bend of the waist behind. A tight-fitting casaque of the same maroon silk has wide scalloped-out basques, all the fullness of which is thrown to the back in full, rich folds. The scallops are piped with orange silk, and a deep black lace flounce is placed just under the edge.

And here is an account of what a lady might wear in the evening:

An evening dress of the fashionable bluish-grey tint, *vapeur d'azur,* silk, has a very elaborate trimming, which I will, however, endeavour to describe. First, there is round the bottom of the dress, but not quite touching the edge, a deep lace flounce; then, as the tunic skirt comes down as far as the heading of this flounce at the back, the under skirt is trimmed in front only with a spiked flounce, arranged in godet pleats, so that one spike falls between each godet or hollow pleat; this flounce is edged with a satin biais, a shade deeper than the dress. The tunic is of crêpe de Chine, of the same colour as the silk; it is trimmed, at the back only, with a crape quilling, deep lace flounce, biais of satin, and lace heading; in the front there is no crape quilling, and the lace flounce and satin biais are not so deep; the tunic is twice looped up at the sides, with ornaments of silk passementerie and tassels. The low bodice is cut Princess fashion, with a deep basque, which falls plain in front, and is caught up behind and fastened at the waist with a passementerie ornament, while at the sides it forms long points; the trimming consists of a double lace border, divided by a biais of satin. Two full flounces of deep white lace, similar to that on the under skirt, fall *en cascade* from under the retroussis of the basque at the back. The bodice is trimmed round the top with lace, and with a biais of satin, and with passementerie ornaments upon the shoulders. The *tout ensemble* of this toilette is light and vapoury. A few roses in the hair and upon the corsage form a nice relief to the grey tint of the silk and crêpe.

The passage is, of course, exceptional. It would be difficult to find a modern fashion-writer with quite such command of his material, or of its social significance. *Vogue* and *Harper's* have virtually renounced the written word, in favour of unspeaking photographs. (It is a peculiar fallacy that a photograph is a better guide to appearances than words, a fallacy which comes from confounding appearances with glimpses.[8]) Sometimes we are given rough injunctions: 'Prepare to do away with crisp whites this winter: the new colours are flesh pink, café crême, oyster. The materials are as soft and smooth as the skin itself: the shapes cling to the lines of the body... wisps of feathers on fluffy angora and the ultimate — cashmere.' But such uneducated language condemns the uneducated perception that compels it. No reason has been given for the choice commanded, nor is anything said that conveys the atmosphere or social resonance of the style. We are not shown how the clothes are made, or how they move; we are given no idea of their relation to the body — except that they 'cling' to its lines. There is also no indication of what it feels like to wear them. What does one then become, in one's own perception, or in the eyes of others? This deficiency cannot be attributed to the reliance on photographs. *Ritz* magazine, which has only sparse illustrations in black and white, and which relies on a written text for its fashion column, manages no better; 'wonderful black and white linens and long chalk-striped blazers and skirts'. There is, so far as I have discovered, only one bizarre exception to this verbal impoverishment: the leather page of *Bike* magazine. However, its exuberant celebration of leather as a feature of the *Lebenswelt* is better left unquoted.

If we return to the extracts from *The Young Englishwoman*, we find three features which vividly display the effects of aesthetic education. First, the writer is able to attach words to, and make distinctions among, 'simple' or undefinable visual properties, such as colours: dove-grey, maize, and so on. This painterly sense of the experience of colour is important, but less so, from our point of view, than the second of the writer's virtues, which is her (I assume it is her) enhanced ability to observe and describe, not shape only, but shape conceived as the outcome and expression of human action, as 'thrown back', 'fastened down', 'scalloped out', 'caught up', 'arranged', 'edged', 'looped up', and 'divided'. These terms are not used merely for ornament's sake. The writer sees not geometry, nor even geometry in motion, but something altogether richer in expressive significance, which is the present record of human labour, the visible imprint of the shaping hand. (It is to be supposed that her readers understood her words partly as instructions, for the use of themselves or their dressmaker.)

More important still is the writer's ability to step naturally and effortlessly from the description of shapes and colours to the description of an ethos, even a moral character, to which they give public reality. When describing the walking dress she is most attentive to the social significance of details, and shows that, for her, good taste is not a matter simply of harmonious shape and colour, but also of a deeper harmony, between the wearer of the clothes and the social ambience in which she moves. Of course, that ambience is an impermanent thing, like the *vapeur d'azur* which evokes the writer's easy poetry. But it is not, for all that, a private thing, and the effort of its construction absorbs not the endeavours of one person only, but the social inspiration of a class and time.

With those observations in hand, we may now return to architecture. I have tentatively suggested that objects such as clothes and buildings have multifarious uses which they not only serve but also form; they play an essential part in our constitution as social beings. Hence aesthetic considerations must be paramount in the design of both. Appearance is the universal condition of the social world; aesthetic considerations concern the attempt to fit ourselves visually to our surroundings. It is only on the assumption of such a fit that we can act with full understanding in our day-to-day predicaments.

I shall begin by considering one of the most monumental of classical buildings: the Pennsylvania Railroad Station by McKim, Mead and White (**5** and **6**). This was demolished twenty years ago, on the erroneous ground that it was no longer functional. It is important to see how well it served as a railway station. The sedate arches invited the pedestrian, the great hall calmed him and coaxed him on unhurriedly; in every particular the building maintained a human vigilance over the activities which it sheltered. It is a significant virtue in this kind of classicism, that it is able to create emphasis, and to make easy visual distinctions among parts. Thus, by the device of a colossal order, it can reassure the observer that he is in the presence of a principal part of the building, rather than a coulisse or antechamber. It can use colonnades to direct the eye onward and upward; it can give detailing, even at ground level, which will indicate to the observer the relative importance of the place in which he finds himself. You do not have to be a student of the classical Orders to observe this — it is enough to have eyes, feet and feelings. The act of communication here is that of the costume rather than that of the badge: symbolism does not stand for, but creates, its 'meaning'. Modern airports are, for the most part, places of panic and dismay. This is largely because they are architecturally taciturn. They rely on labels to shepherd people from place to place: arrows, direction signs, arresting explanations, everything, in short, but architecture. Unlike the classical railway station, they have no visual language with which to guide the traveller, and with which to maintain a reassuring human presence around his agitation.

The Pennsylvania Railroad Station was, of course, an academic building, based on Roman archetypes (largely the Baths of Caracalla). It shows imagination and flair, but does not bear the marks of the highest aesthetic endeavour. While it follows classical models, the building is not truly informed by classical discipline. It is not so much an exercise of the Orders as a copy of them. When Lutyens wrote of the essence of architecture he was referring to the discipline which enables one, not just to copy what is old, but also to create something new, in the spirit of a tradition from which one departs. His own style at New Delhi illustrates his meaning (7). The classical Orders were here transformed. The Viceroy's House seems to renew the discipline which structures it, springing up in every particular fresh and alive. This is what Lutyens meant by 'force', as opposed to the partly imitative 'impulse' of the Pennsylvania Railroad Station.

The example of Lutyens is of one of the highest architectural achievements of the century, and it would be wrong for architects to try to rival it in all their creations, or to apply its conceptions in the quotidian context in which they work. Architecture, like clothing, is essentially a vernacular art; it aims at grandeur and beauty only rarely, and with the consent of fortune. The main task of aesthetic education is the search for appropriate forms and details, adaptable solutions to recurring problems, an idiom which will foster commonplace harmony and an easy, as it were, conversational, relation between buildings and people. How, in such an enterprise, may we distinguish 'force' from 'impulse', 'nature' from 'artifice'?

A distinction which in part corresponds to what Lutyens had in mind is that between detail and ornament. 'Detail' refers to those parts of a building which so enter into the composition as to prevent their detachment. Ornament, by contrast, is detachable. I do not mean physically, but rather aesthetically detachable. To perceive something as an ornament is to perceive it as *added* to a form which is intelligible (if at all) independently. An example from the New York skyline (9) illustrates what I mean: you see an absence of architectural conclusion, a sudden arbitrariness. The builder, not knowing how to break off, adds a whole new chapter of unrelated parts, which fail to stand in any relation to their neighbours, other than that of proximity. By contrast one may study another vignette from Lower Manhattan (8): a part of the world which vividly illustrates the ability of the classical 'language' to serve the most radical changes of function, this building having changed from factory to

212 The Aesthetic Understanding

offices, to private apartments, and destined, I hope, to be a theatre or a church. Here the surface decoration is an essential element in the design, serving to lift it lightly from floor to floor and so to justify the great tin panoply of cornicing, brimming with shadows, which is worn on top like a gangster's hat.

It is a well known result of philosophical aesthetics that there are no rules of beauty. In all matters of taste, guidance is least forthcoming when it is most required. What is detail in one context will be mere ornament in another. The handy adages of the modern movement, which purported to give a *procedure* for discovering what is 'merely ornamental', can therefore be cast aside. Of course, there are certain 'rules' which can be given an air of plausibility, by focusing on a narrow range of examples. It is initially plausible, for example, to suggest that coating a building with glazed tiles is simply decking it out with ornament, adding a surface to a 'form' that is intelligible independently. But the visual reply presented by Islamic architecture at once refutes the rule. In the mosque at Isfahan, for example, every line and curve takes its meaning from the incrustation. Here the serenity of the dome, its shallow breathing flexibility, its quality of a smiling sky, can be attributed neither to the 'form' nor to the decoration alone, but only to the form as lightened by the decoration, and the decoration as disciplined by the form. In his celebrated description of St Mark's, Ruskin praised the building as an example of pure incrustation, as all light, colour, surface, a kind of elaborate jewel, whose religious meaning is expressed in its preciousness, and whose preciousness is translated completely into visual effect.[9] In fact Ruskin admired precisely that quality of the building which is most profoundly oriental, most completely separated from the 'plastic' tradition that German art-historians have taught us to admire in classical art. Nevertheless, it is no mere ornament that drew Ruskin's attention, since nothing of the architecture of St Mark's would remain if this incrustation were removed from it.

It should be apparent, then, that the distinction between detail and ornament could never be reduced to a set of rules. Nevertheless, we cannot conclude simply that rules are irrelevant. For rules may generate a sense of the aesthetically normal, against which to measure and resolve the peculiar problems posed by any particular design. It is true that in the realms of high art — the realm occupied by such masterpieces as St Mark's and the mosque at Isfahan — rules of beauty are the flimsiest of fictions. But at the lower level, where the aspirations of the architect ought principally to be nourished, they have a genuine utility. The accumulation of past errors may generate a sense of what not to do, say, in turning a corner, in finishing a chimney stack, in setting a window, and the force of sufficient warnings may sometimes be resolved in a positive command. Aesthetic education attempts to produce such commands, by providing the contexts and comparisons that will remove their appearance of arbitrariness.

Some indication of what I mean may be extracted from the familiar study of corners. The classical language has always been esteemed as a source of variety. It enables an architect to set up a great number of concurrent but harmonious movements. In the colonnade from San Marco, Rome (**10** and **11**), may be observed a fine array of details which combine harmoniously and rhythmically into an ensemble. But the design is incapable of turning a corner: the two adjacent consoles in the arches crash into each other, while the ionic capitals go through an abrupt ninety-degree turn which leaves a point of immense visual weakness precisely where the effect of strength is needed. The result is to be compared with the neighbouring courtyard (**12**), where the use of the Order is beautifully controlled, producing an effortless accumulation of strength at the corner and an overall sense of repose.

The importance of detail is here apparent. It is only when a building has significant parts that this kind of orderly composition is possible. I have argued elsewhere that the 'sense of detail' must therefore be given absolute priority in aesthetic education.[10] Unfortunately there is very little in a modern architect's education that can be said to address itself to this requirement. The standard work on architectural parts — the 15-volume *Architects' Working Details*, by D.A.C.A. Boyne and Lance Wright (1953) — contains almost no instructions in the use of detail. It is concerned entirely with 'working parts', all attached to highly specific functions. Virtually nothing is said about the visual intelligibility of these parts, or how the multifarious question and answer of the classical idiom might be recreated, while using modern materials and modern scales. This deficiency is palpable at the corners of modern buildings (**13**). That place where complex lines of force should meet, generating strength in stasis and vitality in repose, is reduced to a vanishing line. Incidentally, the illustration — the City Corp Building in New York — points to another moral. This complete absence of detailing causes the building miraculously to disappear. The City Corp Building melts into the sky, from which it borrows its febrile character. Nothing remains to hold the eye, which drifts into space. One sees here a kind of effervescence of structure, an aesthetic impermanence precisely in what is most physically permanent. And there is, too, a kind of beauty in this.

Corners are, of course, a notorious problem, and the adoption of a classical 'vocabulary' will not be sufficient to solve the problem. Witness the militant, undisciplined corners of the Palacio d'Abraxas by the neo-classicist Ricardo Bofill (**14**). Here a classical affectation has merely added insult to injury, compounding the oppression, and generating a sense of unresolved and irresoluble lines of force. The effect contrasts with that of the cheerful Manhattan vernacular (**15**), in which the true classical tradition is revitalized to cope with the evident difficulties of industrial design. This delightful fugue of mouldings and false cornices shows both the variety to be extracted from classical principles, and also the surprising unity which they impose, even when allowed to run riot.

But what are those principles, and what conception of aesthetic education do they imply? I shall begin with two cautions against what I believe to be prevailing fallacies. First, the fallacy of 'organicism'. This admits the overriding necessity for a sense of detail; it also argues (rightly, I believe) that when we see something as beautiful, we see its parts in organic and inseparable relation. From these premises it proceeds to the fallacious conclusion that details must be entirely determined by the total aesthetic conception which they serve. Hence details must be generated afresh for each work of architecture, from a single organically unified inspiration. There is of course an *ideal* of architecture associated with that conclusion, an ideal that is exemplified both within the classical tradition (by Bramante's Tempietto in Rome, for example, and by Sinan's Suleymaniye), and outside it (for example, by much of the domestic architecture of Frank Lloyd Wright). Wright was able to conceive seemingly infinitely many forms for his domestic houses, and to work each conception down into the minutest detail, so that the mouldings of a window frame, or the tilework of a gable, would seem to imply, by a kind of inexorable logic, the entire structure within which they are situated. But, admirable though this is, it is not, and ought not to be, the normal case. The truth about aesthetic experience — that, when under its spell, we see an organic relationship among parts — does not imply that details must be peculiar to the buildings that contain them. If the implication held for architecture, it would hold for music too, so that we should have to criticize the music of Mozart, simply because all of its harmonic details are drawn from a standard repertoire of tonal progressions. In fact, the implication is not only fallacious, but also dangerous. Most architects are ordinary people, most of their public likewise. These two facts fatally constrain the emotional space within which the architect must move. Until he has a repertoire of forms intelligible both to himself and to his public, he is unlikely to be able even to intend the organic perfection of the highest forms of art, let alone to achieve it.

The second fallacy is more serious, although I shall here content myself with the briefest possible summary.[11] This is the fallacy of 'aesthetic consequentialism', the fallacy of regarding right appearance as a consequence of something else — of functional suitability, of a spatial conception, or of some other idea whose significance is primarily intellectual. The fallacy takes many forms, and is greatly exacerbated in its effects by the preoccupation with sites and plans that has been such an important feature of architecture since the Beaux-Arts school of urbanism. Moreover modern design lays great, and unwarranted, stress upon horizontal cross-sections.[12] The technique of isonometric drawing has fostered the illusion that the verticals will look after themselves; as a result, the outer shell of a building is increasingly made to seem like the consequence, rather than the subject, of design. The façade, which is of the essence of the building, becomes an accident of design. The fallacy of aesthetic consequentialism thereby effectively abolishes every considera-tion that permits a building to stand in relation to its surroundings.

In contrast to those fallacies, the education of the Orders focuses attention on essential features of design: on detail, appearance, vertical order, and the relations intrinsic to a façade. Let us consider briefly the Corinthian Order, as this was studied by architects during the eighteenth century (**16**). The illustration comes from Chambers' *Architecture*, and is based on the Order of the temple of Jupiter Stator in Rome, as this had been used by Vignola for the interior of the Pantheon. A naive view of the Corinthian capital is that it is simply one among many possible ornaments to a column, and, like all ornaments, capable of elimination without excessive damage to the composition in which it features. According to this view, the essence of the Order lies in geometrical ratios, and its discipline can be recaptured by any similar system of proportion — for example, that of the modulor, used by Le Corbusier in 'L'unité de l'habitation' at Marseilles. This view of the matter is in fact wholly at variance with the spirit of classical composition. Systems of proportion of the kind used by Le Corbusier lack the essential feature of classical design, which is that the parts related by the measurements are separately intelligible as details. The proportions of classical buildings are perceivable because of the visual emphasis provided by the details. In retaining the mathematics of classical proportion, while rejecting significant detail, Le Corbusier retained what is accidental, while jettisoning all that is essential in the classical conception. The Corinthian capital, while it is undeniably ornamental, is no mere ornament. It is both the symbol and the guide to the geometry which it crowns. The flowering of the stone in the capital requires the proportions of the column, and at the same time permits us to perceive those proportions as appropriate. The order is a system not of geometry but of answerability: part answers part, length answers length, moulding answers moulding, throughout the vertical extent of the arrangement. The foliage receives the thrust of the column and cushions it against the abacus. The mouldings effectively divide the sections, and cast shadows which create a varying counterpoint to the fixed geometry. Everything is calculated to give maximum repose — the serene stillness of geometry — together with maximum vitality — the play of light and shade, the impression of the carving hand, life revealed within the stone. (See **17**, from the Palace at Split.) Hence the capital contributes to the solution of the great and lasting problem of design: how to reconcile an overall appearance of rock-like stability with a surface that perceptibly yields to our transactions. It is no accident that sculpture looks so unthreatened and 'at home' within the embrace of a Corinthian Order. In the example from Sansovino's Loggietta in Venice(**18**), the quiet smile of the angel seems to illuminate the whole surface of the composition. The fragment is suffused with warmth, and the stone of the capital, despite the erosion of its foliage, is as much alive as the form of the angel and the furnishings of the architrave. To study such a detail is to become aware of the inexpressible power of the Orders, their ability to *incorporate* both light and shade, and to endow stone with the temper and the rhythm of human life.

In the Corinthian capital we have an example of a repeatable architectural detail, made apposite not because it is the consequence of some functional or spatial ideal, nor because it is an 'organic' part of some total conception, but simply because it brings piecemeal discipline to appearances. My description was brief, but it enables us to derive three 'principles', which have the same kind of persuasive force as the principles which were earlier derived from the study of dress.

The first, and most obvious, is that the discipline of architecture is a discipline of appearances: it is directed entirely to the eye. The mathematical relations are significant only because detail is dedicated to the task of making forms and surfaces perceivable. The classical discipline can therefore be used, even in the absence of an explicit Order. It can persist as implication, emphasizing and articulating the divisions between masses, surfaces and planes. The Orders abound in devices aimed at variety and articulation. These have proved far more useful to practising architects than any (abstractly conceived) system of proportion, and their influence can be observed everywhere in the architecture of the modern city. Consider, for example, the blank niche, or window-setting, which permits a builder to give vertical emphasis to the widest expanse, by gathering shadows(**19**, the wall of Sir John Soane's Bank; since made more forbidding, **20**), or by collecting rain and snow (**21**). In this simple device, we find an infinitely various system of effects, whose highest reaches involve a phenomenal concentration of architectural meaning. **22** shows the LCC transformer station in Islington (built 1902-7 by Vincent Harris), which, incidentally, now houses shops and restaurants. Here a detail imitated from the demolished Newgate Prison is used to gather the architectural impulse into two points of supreme vertical thrust, so transforming an excessively long brick wall into a genuine urban façade. I give the example because it illustrates the immense fertility of the classical tradition as a basis for vernacular design. It so instils the appearance of a building with visual implications that the architect is never at a loss for a telling detail with which to relieve monotony, to emphasize a movement, or to adapt his shapes to the visual requirements of the passer-by. The case should be contrasted with the unperceivable order of the Unité de l'Habitation, and the visually arbitrary detailing that results from it.

The second principle concerns light and shade. Detail captures significance because it gathers vertical precipitation, usually in the form of shadows, though sometimes, as in the illustration of the Radcliffe Camera looming behind the screen of All Souls, in the form of rain, sleet or snow (**23**). (It is instructive to study the bases of the three-quarter columns of the Camera, in order to perceive a new and surprising way in which the Corinthian Order retains the lineaments of vitality, even in unpropitious moments.)

The aesthetic error of the City Corp Building — which causes it to dissolve into air at the touch of sunlight — lies in its inability to resist the force of light. No contrasts of light and shade force back the equalizing influence of the sky. Such contrasts are essential to the life of a façade, and give purpose and charm to mouldings, as the two illustrations from lower Manhattan make clear (**24** and **25**). The shadows here play an ineliminable part in the architectural effect. Without them it would be impossible to perceive the dialectic of vertical and horizontal, or to appreciate the etched-out quality of the façade. Light needs shade, as good needs evil, in order to be known. Leonardo wrote: 'Shadow is the display *(pronuntiatione)* by bodies of their form; and the forms of bodies would give no impression of their quality without it.'[13] It is not form alone that is significant in a building, but the interplay of form and shadow. This is the major reason for thinking that mouldings cannot be dismissed as ornaments — not, at least, when used in accordance with the classical discipline. A moulding is a genuine detail, as much part of architectural form as the keystone of an arch. Moreover, shadow aligns a building behind it. The façades of lower Manhattan stand in the street without violence to their neighbours, the complex shadows alleviating all threat from otherwise monstrous forms.

Shadows fall vertically, and the emphasis on shadow is part of an overall emphasis on the vertical, which is one of the fundamental features of the classical discipline. It was normal practice, therefore, among architectural students versed in the Orders to learn how to draw the shadows cast by the parts of an Order. Plates **26** and **27** come from a standard American textbook used at the turn of the century, and show the immense finesse which was expected not merely in the understanding of detail, but also in the appreciation of volatile appearances. Even these drawings, however, serve only as preludes to the accomplished display of shadows in the illustration from Chambers (**16**).

The last principle is at once the most difficult and the most important of the three. It is to be observed that the Order is only one vertical section of a building, which can be explained completely, without reference to the whole, despite its powerful implications for the whole. The Order is a complete vertical element; the art of building can be taught almost entirely through the study of such elements, but never from the study of horizontal sections or ground plans. The Order is a visible posture which imitates and answers to the human frame. By learning the Orders you learn vertical discipline, tempered by horizontal licence. The Order can be extended sideways, into colonnades, courtyards, or façades; into straight lines or curves; into squares, streets or crescents. This flexibility is common to all styles that share the vertical emphasis: the Gothic, the Romanesque, and all the other variants of classical discipline from which our urban agreeableness ultimately derives. Its discipline gives humanity to a façade, and harmony to the ensemble which contains it.

The three principles to which I have referred must clearly be distinguished from their embodiment in this or that canon of architectural proportion. They do not themselves entail any particular system of measurement, but stand as it were behind the major systems of classical architecture, providing the unifying idea of aesthetic achievement which motivates them all. It is often said that, in holding on to the classical details, while ignoring or distorting the systems of proportions which they had been used to articulate, the nineteenth-century vernacular styles elevated accident over essence, and lost the true sense of the classical order. I do not believe that this criticism is well-founded, or that the undetailed systems of proportion introduced by neo-classicists and modernists have anything serious to offer as a rival basis for vernacular construction. Of course, the classical details can be used in arrangements that are grossly disproportionate, very often with results that are all the more nonsensical on account of the classical reference. (See **28**, an example of London Victoriana, and **29**, an example of the current 'joke classicism'.) But equally they may be present in buildings which derive their proportionality not from any classical module, but from a natural deference to the eye's requirements, a deference which the classical details encourage. Thus in the Chiswick Power Station by W. Curtis Green (**30**) we see a fine arrangement of arches and cornicing, whose proportionality owes nothing to the classical systems, but everything to the classical details from which it is composed. Nor must we take the term 'classical' too narrowly here. I mean to refer to a whole practice, of imprinting materials part by part with the record of human labour, of establishing correspondences and expectations based on vertical emphasis, of cultivating detail, shadow and visual intricacy. By this account, such architectural masterpieces as the Suleimaniye (**31**) equally deserve to be called 'classical', as much as those buildings which exemplify the central application of the term. This extension of usage is not arbitrary: on the contrary, it is designed to capture an aesthetic essence which anyone with eyes can be persuaded to esteem, as the true ideal of architecture, in all the many uses which architecture may serve.

I cannot prove, of course, that the three principles that I have expressed point to the essence of design. Nevertheless, I hope to have created a presumption in their favour. Something needs to be said in conclusion, as to how the classical conception may be translated into the present tense, and so made available to a generation that has suffered the most complete, and in my view most ill-considered, break in architectural tradition that has ever afflicted the history of building. It is useful to return to *The Young Englishwoman*, whose words first reminded us of the far-reaching effects of aesthetic education. I drew attention to the following features of the writer's experience: the ability to observe and describe the simplest, and therefore the most elusive, of visual qualities; the ability to perceive not just form, but process — to see form as the memorial of human action; finally, the ability to make those connections with the moral life without which all this would be mere aestheticism. In the case of clothes, such features are fairly obviously connected with aesthetic understanding. They express an ability to see an appearance in its full significance, as a part of the *Lebenswelt* in which we move and act. We must find an education for the architect that will inculcate comparable virtues. In the light of our three principles of 'classical' design, we might suggest the following: the architect's education must confer a perception of detail, an understanding of light and shade, an ability to see forms in terms of the labour that produced them; finally, an ability to relate all this to the human world in which we act and suffer.

The first ingredient in such an education is drawing — not the drawing of the drawing board, but that older discipline which teaches us to see buildings in their essential nature, as they appear. Plates **32** and **33** show two architectural drawings. The first, published in 1652, is for a palace, by Antoine Le Pautre. The second, by J. and F. Dixon Associates, recently won first prize in a competition for Northampton Town Hall. The first belongs to a well-known series of architectural fantasies, which were never intended for construction; nevertheless, it shows an attention to appearance, to detail, to posture, and to drawing technique; it attempts to represent the final form of the building in all its aspects, as an object of experience rather than a schematic design. You learn quickly what it would be like to pass by or enter such a building, how your steps would be welcomed or guided by it, and how you would be entertained by its light and shade. In the case of the lamentable Northampton Town Hall, all such vital information is withheld. It is impossible to say where the light falls, how the building touches the ground, or what it would be like to enter it. Even the trees cast no shadows, and are of a species that has yet to find its place in the great chain of being. It is difficult not to think of this featureless pyramid as issuing from visual incompetence, from an inability to perceive so great that all significant detail must be removed from the product, leaving a geometrical abstraction as an apology for architectural design. We find a turning away from detail towards pure geometry, from shadow towards reflected light, from the imprint that is left by human labour towards harsh synthetic abstractions. An even more pointed contrast can be drawn with the engraving by Taraval (**34**) from a design by Boullée (whose fantasy projects may well have been an 'inspiration' to Dixon Associates in their design for Northampton Town Hall). The design, for a hospital on the Rue Jacob, shows that when asked to design an actual building for human use, even the fantasist can find resources in the classical tradition which will guide his judgement. Here the discipline of an over-mastering Doric Order, enclosing the steps, the pilasters and the abrupt tympanum, accompanies an intense interest in light, shade and detail. As a result, the human figures in the foreground are wholly believable, in their unhurried relation to the composition which includes them. Compare the ant-like creatures which flee before the Northampton pyramid as though before an unexploded bomb.

It is by drawing appearances that an architect learns to perceive them. But drawing is not enough. The vertical emphasis must be restored: it is this that Lutyens was referring to in distinguishing force from impulse. We need to appreciate the true — which is to say, apparent — lines of force in a building, and the places where vectors meet, mingle, and resolve. There is no need to repeat what I have said concerning the Orders, and the use of moulding and shadow which they imply. But it is undeniable that, without some such expansion towards a 'vocabulary' of detail, it will never be possible to regard the vertical line as a dramatic exposition of essential forces, such as we may witness in Lutyens's own composition at New Delhi (the Viceroy's House, **7**), or, yet more impressively, in the side wall of Hawksmoor's church of St Mary Woolnoth (**35**[14]).

A third desideratum should also be mentioned, in response to what I have called the organicist fallacy. To learn something is to learn *how to go on,* from the familiar to the unfamiliar. Learning requires the mastery of procedure, of what is essentially repeatable, and yet complete enough to give an intimation of the whole. This is the root idea of the Order: you understand the component, and then proceed to apply your understanding to ever larger and more complex ensembles. Without such a procedural conception of aesthetic education, architecture could never be the applied, vernacular art that we require it to be.

Those are first steps. They do not suffice to take us to the end, which is the incorporation of buildings into the world of appearance. Architecture surrounds us, encroaches on us, and protects us. It is impossible to envisage a separation between our ways of living and the architectural forms within which they are accomplished. Although we do not seek self-expression in architecture, neither do we expect it to retreat from us into a hidden world of mere machinery. In being reduced to function, it becomes accident, and opposed to nature. Human nature is, I have argued, in one sense not a permanent datum. The main effort of culture is to create both human nature and the world which nurtures it. In another sense, however, there is a permanent in human nature, which is the striving towards a shared normality. In one of his more perceptive essays, Heidegger writes: 'Only if we are capable of dwelling, only then can we build.'[15] We must amend Heidegger's utterance. Only when we can build, only then are we capable of dwelling. For building is one inescapable part of the process of making ourselves at home in the world; and it is for this reason that aesthetic education is of the essence. Such education requires that we understand, not the plan, but the façade of a building; not the two-dimensional layout, but the interplay of verticals and planes; not geometry, but light and shade, angles and lines; not shape and form alone, but the visible imprint of the shaping hand. It requires us to carry visual implications from part to part; to fit a building to the ground and to arrest it in the air; to impose on it an order that is flexible enough to unite its details and rigid enough to give unity to the whole. It requires us to master the problems of design piecemeal, not by the fantasy creation of whole buildings, but by the real application of a mastered procedure. It is this education — embodied in the classical tradition — which represents the essence, force and nature of design.

16 Beckett and the Cartesian Soul

I wish to explore certain themes in Samuel Beckett's prose works — notably in the trilogy of novels called *Molloy, Malone Dies,* and *The Unnamable* — and to bring those themes into relation with the philosophical ideas which explain them. My purpose is not only philosophical but also critical; I wish to show how philosophical theories concerning the nature of the self underlie, and to some extent account for, the ingenious atmosphere of Beckett's prose. I believe Beckett to be a writer of genius, whose vision is entirely integrated into his style. I also believe that his vision is founded in a kind of moral and metaphysical illusion, and that this illusion has been a powerful and enduring influence in post-romantic literature. If it seems surprising at this juncture to imply that Beckett is a 'post-romantic', I hope that it will be less surprising later.

Anyone approaching the trilogy for the first time is likely to be struck by three features of its subject-matter: first, the characters enter into no comfortable relation with one another, and indeed, for the most part, no relation at all; secondly, they are aware of their fictional nature, and often substitute for themselves other fictions of their own devising, and while clinging with spasmodic obstinacy to the life that their author accords to them, usually relinquish it, in the end, with a gesture of equally spasmodic, and equally meaningless, consent; thirdly, that each of them is preoccupied with the question of his own existence, constantly seeks to say something that will prove it, or at least describe it, and then helplessly concedes that the attempt is impossible. Towards the end of the trilogy the Unnamable, reflecting on Worm — one of the fictions within fictions for whose existence he has momentarily felt some faint spasm of responsibility — argues as follows:

> Is there a single word of mine in all I say? No, I have no voice, in this matter I have none. That's one of the reasons, why I confused myself with Worm. But I have no reasons either, no reason, I'm like Worm, without voice or reason. I'm Worm, no, if I were Worm I wouldn't know it, I wouldn't say it. I wouldn't say anything. I'd be Worm. But I don't say anything, these voices are not mine, nor these thoughts, but the voices and thoughts of the devils who beset me. Who make me say that I can't be Worm, the inexpugnable. Who make me say that I am he perhaps, as they are. Who make me say that since I can't be he I must be

he. That since I couldn't be Mahood, as I might have been, I must be Worm, as I cannot be ... (p. 350)[1]

In such passages the three features come together in a figure of speech that Beckett has called 'the narrator narrated': the separation between the text and its subject matter has been, if not abolished, at least diminished, so that the text can be read as a kind of commentary on itself. Now there is a sense in which this separation is *always* diminished in fiction, since the fictional subject is the creation of the text that describes him. Nevertheless, it is the purpose of fiction, and in particular of dramatic fiction, to create a kind of 'aboutness': fiction involves the *creation* of imaginary characters, and bears a relation to those characters analogous to the relation that holds between any narrative and its subject-matter. One does not have to be a structuralist, or even a post-structuralist, to recognize that in Beckett, as in *Finnegans Wake*, this postulation of a created world distinct from the instrument of creation is not so straightforwardly a part of the fictional enterprise as it is, say, in Dickens. The subject-matter of the text is no longer wholly distinct from its narration. Thus it ceases to matter — or ceases to matter in the same way — that the narrative should be contradictory, that it should negate every concrete detail that it offers, that it should, even in passages of the greatest intensity, offer no definition to the objects of feeling. Consider the following passage from *Molloy:*

It was on a road remarkably bare, I mean without hedges or ditches or any kind of edge, in the country, for cows were chewing in enormous fields, lying and standing, in the evening silence. Perhaps I'm inventing a little, perhaps embellishing, but on the whole that's the way it was. They chew, swallow, then after a short pause effortlessly bring up the next mouthful. The neck muscle stirs and the jaws begin to grind again. But perhaps I'm remembering things. (pp. 8-9)

Here the prose moves under the apparent pressure of a great emotion, straining after words as though trying to match them against a recalcitrant reality. What we are given, however, is not so much an object of dramatic feeling as a huge, still, isolated image, detached from the narrative, and ending with the typical Beckett device of a cliché ('perhaps I'm imagining things') stunningly altered with its literal meaning laid bare: 'perhaps I'm remembering things'; the implication being, perhaps I'm not. It is as though the narrative has been dissolved, released from the control of any dramatic meaning, and the reader condemned to search for the emotion with which to match the image in the text. But the effect is then at once negated by the cliché, which dismisses the reader's efforts as futile and ridiculous. Consider too Molloy's devastating self-description:

'Chameleon in spite of himself, there you have Molloy, viewed from a certain angle', a description from which there is absolutely nothing to be learned, despite its symbolic and syntactical claim to give the plain and simple truth about an important matter. Many critics have discussed this character of Beckett's prose, that it moves by providing intense details which it then proceeds to negate. In what follows I hope to show why Beckett should have constant recourse to such a style.

It is important to note that even a bare self-contradiction may say something. If asked to describe what happened to me on the way to Oxford, I might say: 'I saw a woman brutally murdered on the train; but of course there was no such woman'. Clearly there is a sense in which I have said nothing; another sense, however, in which I have said much, about myself and the objects of my thoughts. Although the door that I opened was closed at once, it remained open long enough for you to glimpse a meaning. I might equally have said 'I saw a child sleeping, but there was no such child', and, while logically this sentence is on a par with the preceding one, it is, from the literary point of view, entirely different. In this way a literary language may evolve which, while it creates no fictional world independent of itself, conveys, nevertheless, quite precise states of mind. Beckett's language is partly like that. I say 'partly' because there are differences of degree here. The presence of a contradiction does not vitiate a fiction, as readers of *Our Mutual Friend* will know. And that is important, since it refutes the suggestion that fiction involves the construction of a Leibnizian 'possible world'. Nevertheless, a fictional world *cannot* be created by assertions, *all* of which are no sooner uttered than withdrawn. I do not think that it helps to ruminate, in post-structuralist manner, on the logical status of the text thereby created. Nevertheless, such a text will produce the irresistible impression that it is *itself* part of its own subject-matter. It draws attention to the process, as well as to the product, of fiction.

Any attempt to explain the literary mannerisms that I have just described must, I believe, reach to the heart of Beckett's meaning. The 'narrator narrated' is not merely a sophisticated trope; it is constitutive of Beckett's style, and of the vision which that style expresses. To explain it is to capture the 'I' who haunts the text, peevishly 'remembering things' for the benefit of a creator with whom he is less than satisfied. It is necessary, then, to turn our attention to the content of Beckett's narrative.

It has been denied, but it is I think true, that the trilogy concerns itself in the first instance with certain *characters*. Molloy, Moran, The Unnamable are definite agents, or at least impatients; moreover they resemble human beings in ways which we should be careful not to overlook. There are also subsidiary characters — Moran's son, and the many elusive and unknowable creatures who appear with messages of great importance and then disappear over emotionally charged horizons: e.g., Gaber in *Molloy*, and the woman who briefly enters Malone's 'cell'. However, the existential status of the principal characters is almost continuously in doubt. Molloy and Moran at first seem to be distinct: the second, after all, is looking for the first. But, by the end of his narrative, Moran seems effectively to have negated all that distinguished him from Molloy, and is looking round in a circle of existential despair for some proof of his individuality. Moreover, he has obscure and inexpressible antecedent knowledge of Molloy — even has his own name for him ('Mollose') and for his mother. His sadistic, viperish character is present from time to time in Molloy, whose studious isolation gradually invades Moran. Malone ('since that is what I am called now', p. 223), like Moran, expressly assimilates Molloy to Murphy, Mercier (of *Mercier and Camier*), Watt and Yerk (a character from an unwritten story), and regards them all as 'attempts' to define something that remains undefined, and perhaps indefinable. Finally the Unnamable himself, although he seems partly to be distinguished from Malone at the beginning — since it is Malone who is passing before him at intervals, or, if not Malone, Molloy wearing Malone's hat — gradually appropriates to himself Malone's vestiges of self-identity, and, by the word-play on 'me alone', manages at last to imply, not perhaps that he is identical with Malone, but at least that he and Malone are indiscernible, largely because nothing very definite can be said of either. He argues:

All these Murphys, Molloys and Malones do not fool me. They have made me waste my time, suffer for nothing, speak of them when, in order to stop speaking, I should have spoken of me and me alone . . . I thought I was right in enlisting these sufferers of my pains. I was wrong. They never suffered my pains, their pains are nothing, compared to mine, a mere tittle of mine, the tittle I thought I could put from me, in order to witness it. (p. 305)

All the principal characters (if characters they can be called) suffer a like fate. They are gradually stripped of their assets, attributes and possessions, and reduced to a state of solipsism. Their names too are uncertain; applied, invented and transformed at will — although the will is not necessarily theirs. Names are received like irrebuttable but arbitrary imperatives: Molloy discovers his by accident; he gives his mother her name with the same autocratic finality with which he is given his own: 'I called her Mag, because for me, without my knowing why, the letter g abolished the syllable Ma, and as it were spat on it, better than any other letter would have done' (p. 17). One might say that all of the principals are obsessed with the arbitrariness of names and descriptions. But this arbitrariness extends, as the example indicates, to their relations to each other. Sexual relations are grotesque, accidental, with only arbitrary tendernesses, and usually occur between crippled old people, e.g., between Molloy and the woman whom he decides to call Ruth, having tried the name Edith, and whom he at first thinks of as his grandmother. He meets her on a rubbish dump and is never wholly sure that she is a woman. (See also the story 'First Love' in *Four Novellas*.) Love is discarded and negated, or, when it appears, it is as though by accident, as when Malone suddenly surprises himself with the mention of it in the following passage:

> And if I tell of me and of that other who is my little one, it is always for want of love, well I'll be buggered. I wasn't expecting that, want of a homuncule... [a self-centred digression, and then:] yes, a little creature, I shall try and make a little creature, to hold in my arms, a little creature in my image, no matter what I say. And seeing what a poor thing I have made, or how like myself, I shall eat it. Then be alone a long time, unhappy, not knowing what my prayer should be, or to whom. (p. 226)

This absence of relation calls forth, as the passage indicates, an emotion of pity — an emotion significantly illustrated in the attitude of the Unnamable to Worm, the character whom he just succeeds in failing to create at the end of having been himself inadequately narrated. Pity extends further, however, pervading all would-be relations; it is identical, in the end, with the awareness that relations are impossible. Thus pity reaches out equally to objects, as when Malone refers to the

> foul feeling of pity that I have often felt in the presence of things, especially little portable things in wood or stone; and which made me wish to have them about me and keep them always, so that I stooped and picked them up and put them in my pocket, often with tears, for I wept up to a great age, never having really evolved in the fields of affection and passion in spite of experience. (p. 248)

This correlation between pity and non-relation is reflected in the impossibility of genuine ownership. The narrator can own nothing, because he can give nothing, besides the pitying recognition that he has nothing to give. Thus when Malone attempts to define his possessions he can think of nothing better than this:

> ... only those things are mine the whereabouts of which I know well enough to lay hold of them, if necessary, that is the definition I have adopted, to define my possessions. (p. 250)

The result is that, losing his stick, he thereby loses his possessions (p. 256). The Unnamable stands in no active relation to objects whatsoever; as he puts it, 'the days of sticks are over' (p. 303). The very possibility of owning things has been removed, and the result is, to put it succinctly, nothing:

> But all is forgotten and I have done nothing, unless what I am doing now is something, and nothing could give me greater satisfaction. (p. 310)

Note again the literalized cliché. Several critics have commented on this device in Beckett, at least two — Ricks and Cavell[2] — associating it with ideas of death, believing that the tragi-comedy seemingly contained within the Beckettian style is to be understood as an 'intimation of mortality'. While I think that the interpretation is one-sided, it is right in two respects: the cliché is essential to Beckett's method of negating, and the meaning of his texts is to be found *within* the negative style. Here is a fairly sustained passage from p. 364, clichés being marked with a star:

> Perhaps there is only one of them, one would do the trick (★) just as well, but he might get mixed up with his victim, that would be abominable, downright masturbation (★). We're getting on (★). Nothing much then in the way of sights for sore eyes (★). But who can be sure who has not been there, has not lived there, they call that living (★), for them the spark is present, ready to burst into flame, all it needs is preaching on, to become a living torch (★), screams included . . .

The first cliché negates the tone of enquiry established by the preceding phrase; it also ambiguates the subject of the sentence ('one' could be referring to the Unnamable himself); it refers to a trick, i.e. to a specific idea of carnal intercourse (with a 'victim'), by calling it 'masturbation', so suggesting the absence of intercourse. The next refers to 'we', when the prevailing thought has been that there is no 'we', and also suggests progress in the midst of inertia. This suggestion of progress is immediately negated by the next sentence; and so it proceeds. Compare 'There at least is a first affirmation, I mean negation, on which to build' (p. 347). (Ricks says that Beckett is expert at 'falling in slow motion', although clearly there is more to it, and perhaps also less to it, than that.)

Cliché is a form of literary habit; it is ready-made and mechanical. Unless diverted from its standard application it must reduce and falsify that to which it is applied, by abolishing its individual nature. In a sense, therefore, cliché is the ultimate universal, the ultimate negation of the particular. It involves an escape from solitude, and from the suffering of solitude, into a comforting association with the commonplace and the normal — with the condition that the existentialists have described as 'otherness'. But art, according to a theory of Beckett's to which I shall shortly return, is the rediscovery of solitude, and the road back into the individual self (or rather, into what is misdescribed — since every description is a misdescription — as the self). It therefore cannot tolerate the cliché, and the spurious relations with the world which the cliché encapsulates. So, by using cliché to negate, and never to affirm, Beckett makes it work against itself, forcing it to deny the world of habit, description and relation, and placing in its stead a quintessential loneliness which would be the true subject matter of his works if it were possible for works like his to *have* (rather than to deny) a subject.

Furthermore, since cliché arises from shared experience, and shared response, it is always *active* in its implications. That is, it suggests standard reactions, ways of proceeding, usually a cheerful acceptance of common annoyances and a rugged morality for daily use. To use cliché by way of negation is therefore always to negate both action and the possibility of social relations. (Cf. the 'we're getting on', which occurs in the above quotation, and which serves as a kind of refrain to the trilogy, and to other works too, notably *Endgame*.)

The result of this constant paring away, not just of all relationships, but also of the very language of relationship, is to leave the 'I' at the centre of the stage. However this 'I' too is a cliché, and must be negated:

> Do they believe I believe it is I who am speaking? That's theirs too. To make me believe I have an ego all my own and can speak of it, as they of theirs. Another trap to snap me up among the living. It's how to fall into it that they can't have explained to me sufficiently . . . (p. 348)

And earlier:

> But enough of this cursed first person, it is really too red a herring. I'll get out of my depth if I'm not careful . . . (p. 345)

Note how cleverly Beckett uses the cliché of getting out of one's depth to negate his own denial of the 'I': into whose depth, as it were, is he trying to sink? Again, he remarks that 'any old pronoun will do, provided one sees through it', so using the ambiguity of 'one' to negate all pronouns together. In *All Strange Away* Beckett invents a new grammatical case to contrast with the first person as its final opposite:

> Light off and let him be, on the stool, talking to himself, in the last person, murmuring, no sound, Now where is he, no, Now he is here . . .

Interesting also is the mouth in *Not I*, which reaches moments of hysterical climax at which it forces itself to resist the first person case. At these moments the observing figure makes a movement. This movement,

Beckett says, in his notes to the play

> consists in simple sideways raising of arms from sides, and their falling
> back, in a gesture of helpless compassion. It lessens with each
> recurrence till scarcely perceptible at third. There is just enough pause
> to contain it as MOUTH recovers from vehement refusal to relinquish
> third person.

This refusal of the first person is effected also by the constant re-naming
of characters, and the narrator's positing of himself as identical with the
characters he creates, or not, according to whim. The fiction thereby
becomes intertwined with the self of the narrator, and the self becomes a
fictional artifact. It is this self-obsessed self-abnegation that is expressed in
the 'narrator narrated'.

It is significant, however, that where, as in some of the later pieces,
Beckett experiments with a subjectless style, many of his characteristic
effects disappear. In *Texts for Nothing* the 'I' is still present; in 'For to End
Yet Again' and 'Still', in *For to End Yet Again,* as in *Imagination Dead
Imagine,* there is no subject. The last-named work tries to develop a style
without personal pronouns at all. As a result, it seems, the comedy
suddenly disappears, and a real bleakness comes in place of it. The effect
must therefore have depended upon the *self*-irony of the narrator.
Whatever his confusion of identity, his mutability, it was indispensable
that he should have been there as an 'I', taking, so to speak, the periphery
of the stage. The reader needs the narrator, even when merely narrated; he
needs the point of view from which these negations are to be observed.
Without the narrator the text lacks meaning altogether.

The 'I', then, is vital to the style, and creeps back, even in the face of
Beckett's attempt to eliminate it. It is present even in the act of questioning
its own existence, and is — in the end — identical with that 'last person' to
whom Beckett refers in *All Strange Away,* and again, in one of the most
recent works, *Compagnie:*

> And why where? Why in another dark or in the same? And who asks,
> who asks? And replies: he, whoever he is, who imagines it all. In the
> same dark as his creature, or in another. So as to keep company. [*Pour se
> tenir compagnie* — the 'se' being ambiguous between singular and
> plural]... Nowhere to find, nowhere to look. The unthinkable
> ultimate. The unnamable. The altogether last person. I...[3]

In this kind of minimalism one can see the point of Beckett's own remark,
that there is an art which prefers 'the expression that there is nothing to
express, nothing with which to express, no power to express, no desire to
express, together with the obligation to express'.[4] But there is, I think,

more to it than that, more to it than meets the 'I'. I wish now to say something about certain philosophical doctrines that Beckett himself endorses here and there in his monograph on Proust, and which can be extracted relatively easily from the passages that I have quoted.

The first, it almost goes without saying, is the Cartesian theory of mind. It may or may not be significant that Beckett began his literary career with a thesis (never completed) on Descartes, and that he has had a life-long obsession with Descartes. It would be too easy to summarize my comments on the narrator-narrated with a reference to the Cartesian doubt, or to take Beckett as an illustration of the famous remark of Lichtenberg's, that Descartes should have said, not 'I think', but 'It thinks'.[5] Nevertheless, two thoughts seem extremely important to Beckett's literary atmosphere. The first is that, if there is anything of value in the individual existence, it is to be found in the first person case. The second is that this first person is in fact the last person, the thing that is revealed when all else has been pared away: the true 'I' (Not-I) is hidden behind every property and everything that it might claim as its 'own', even behind the 'I' itself. Which raises the question, why should we wish to give quite so much attention to it? To borrow a pertinent remark of Wittgenstein's: would not a nothing do as well as a something about which nothing can be said?[6] The answer is, not quite, or at least not yet.

Beckett's monograph on Proust is significant partly because it shows how two further important ideas are connected in imagination, if not in logic, to the Cartesian idea of the self: the first is that the moral life of the individual is to be understood through a contrast between habit and suffering; the second is a kind of nominalism, which holds that the individual can never be understood as he is in himself, that all descriptions falsify, that the true individuality of a thing is always a mystery and revealed only by miracles — the miracles being precisely the Proustian moments when the individual capacity for suffering breaks through the veil of habit and shows the intense inner solitude to which we are all condemned. It is instructive to explore these two ideas.

First, then, the contrast between habit and suffering. Habit, according to Beckett, is a duty, fulfilled in boredom. It is the repetition which makes the individual action into a member of a class, and so, by generalizing, destroys the relation to ourselves. Habit is comforting, because it hinders objects, actions and people from presenting to us the problem of who or what we are. There is no escape from habit except in suffering;[7] for if we break through habit we come face to face with our loneliness, and with the duration, the seeming eternity, which that loneliness foretells. At the same time, unless we break through habit, we see neither ourselves nor others.

Secondly, the nominalism. This is summarized by Beckett as follows:

When the object is perceived as particular and unique and not merely the member of a family, when it appears independent of any general notion and detached from the sanity of a cause, isolated and inexplicable in the light of ignorance, then and only then may it be a source of enchantment. Unfortunately, Habit has laid its veto on this form of perception, its action being precisely to hide the essence — the Idea — of the object in the haze of conception-preconception.[8]

The purpose here is not to present a general metaphysical vision, but to point to contrasted modes of perception. The quotation shows how much the nominalistic vision — which urges us to see everything in its individuality — is of a piece with the condemnation of habit. The observer who can free himself from habit also has access to the truth: 'the notion of what he should see has not had time to interfere its prism between the eye and its object...'[9]

Now the connection between this kind of nominalism and Cartesian ideas of the self is not hard to find. The thought goes something like this: all description is both arbitrary and, through its very generality, false: it assimilates objects one to another and so eliminates the individuality from each. We are given predicates, but no subjects. And all individuals that we identify in the world seem arbitrary — points of intersection where competing descriptions coincide. Only one entity within our perspective seems to escape the falsehood and arbitrariness of description — the self, which we know not by description, but directly, by acquaintance, and with a kind of self-guaranteeing awareness that assures us both of the existence, and even of the essence, of this individual thing. Hence, by compelling movements of thought and imagination, we find that the nominalist for whom the individual is everything, ends up with the self as his only model of that individual, since it is the only thing within our perspective which is known *as* an individual — detached, as Beckett puts it, from the sanity of a cause. However, by that very fact, there is nothing to be said about what is known: all attempts to transcribe in words the content of our first person acquaintance must fail — they classify the self, and so miss its individuality. (A related doctrine: they give us what Russell calls 'knowledge by description', in the place of a 'knowledge by acquaintance', which they cannot in fact replace.) Hence the first person can be known only as the last person, that pure existence (the 'individual essence' of the Scotists) which survives when all description, even the 'I' itself, has been pared away.

It is worth pausing to comment on what philosophers have thought to be the logical illusion underlying that idea of the self. Shortly I shall return to it, and to the theme of habit, in order to examine the more important moral illusion which it dignifies. Perhaps the best historical attack on the

Cartesian illusion was made by Kant, who argued roughly thus: I have privileged awareness of my states of mind, and this is an 'original' or 'transcendental' act of understanding. Descartes and the rationalists had sought to deduce from this privileged knowledge a specific theory of its object. They had thought that, because of the immediacy of self-awareness, the self must be a genuine object of consciousness: only this could explain the transparency, so to speak, of self-knowledge. In the act of self-awareness I am presented with the 'I' which is aware.

Such reasoning is erroneous, since it moves from the purely *formal* unity of self-consciousness (the unity which weaves all the objects of awareness into the tapestry of 'mine') to the substantial unity affirmed in the doctrine of the soul (the unity of a 'me' to whom all experience belongs). The purely formal unity of consciousness tells me nothing about the kind of thing which bears it. It does not tell me that I am a substance, as opposed to an 'accident' or property. And if I cannot deduce that I am a substance, so much the less can I deduce — as Cartesians generally try to deduce — that I am individual, indestructible or immortal. The unity of consciousness does not even assure me that there is something knowable to which the term 'I' applies. The peculiar features of self-consciousness are simply features of a 'point of view' on the world. The 'I' as so described is not part of the world but a perspective upon it (a way things seem). It is no more possible for me to make the 'I' the object of consciousness than it is to observe the limits of my own visual field. 'I' is the expression of my perspective, but denotes no item within it. Hence the absurdity of Beckett's comedies, which vest all significance in this entity which eludes its own grasp.

Beckett is of course aware that the 'I' is not only indescribable, but also in some such way metaphysically precarious. On one reading, the trilogy might be taken as a kind of extended satire on the human disposition to believe in the existence of the 'I', to assume that it is the true repository of value, and the fount of life. With a charming pun, the Unnamable sums up centuries of human frailty: 'But can that be called a life which vanishes when the subject is changed? I don't see why not' (p. 356). Naturally, 'I' can never see why not, since, while the 'I' persists the subject has not changed — or if it has, this is a fact which cannot be perceived from 'my' point of view. On another reading, however, the persistent nominalism of Beckett's vision shows a covert sympathy for the Cartesian idea. The emotional pressure of the prose pushes us towards the view of the self as the true individual, the infinitely valuable thing which we can know as subject, but never as object, and yet which dissolves in the act of knowing it. Nor is Beckett alone in sharing Kant's suspicion of the Cartesian self, while clinging to the idea of the indescribable individual, who perceives a world to which he does not and cannot belong. The Kantian arguments have been accepted by many philosophers, from Schopenhauer to Husserl and Heidegger, who have nevertheless retained the belief in the 'transcendental ego' as the only thing that ultimately matters, or minds. Kant himself was tempted by that new contradiction.

It is to Schopenhauer, however, that we should turn in order to illustrate the moral illusion which Beckett, in common with many writers of his generation, manages so generously and touchingly to dignify. This further illusion exists in a related (but niggardly) form in Sartre. Because our only knowledge of an *individual* is of the self, there can be no real relation to any individual outside the self: all attempted relations are merely arbitrary, in the manner of descriptions, or else modes of habit which obliterate the terms that they relate. Hence art — which is the attempt, or rather the obligation, to express that intimation of individual existence which is our sole metaphysical certitude and guarantee, the attempt, as Beckett elsewhere puts it, to eff the ineffable — must be 'the apotheosis of solitude'.[10] Beckett attacks, or represents Proust as attacking, both love and friendship, as forms of lying, since 'friendship, according to Proust, is the negation of that irremediable solitude to which every human being is condemned'.[11] 'For the artist,' Beckett adds, 'who does not deal in surfaces, the rejection of friendship is not only reasonable, but a necessity'.[12] Such thoughts underlie the subsequent negation of personal love and affection in the trilogy. They also lead to a peculiar, and, I believe, highly significant view, both of tragedy and of ordinary human morality. Tragedy becomes the true guarantee and expression of individual existence, and morality a mere subsumption of the individual under the arbitrary habits and nomenclatures of a code which, because it claims to be universal, can be the property, and the truth, of no individual self. Beckett's own attitude to the ideas of right and wrong is consonant with his nominalism. As Molloy puts it:

> And if you are wrong, and you are wrong, I mean when you record circumstances better left unspoken, and leave unspoken others, rightly if you like, but how shall I say, for no good reason, yes, rightly, but for no good reason as for example that new moon ... (p. 41)

But once again the significant utterance comes in *Proust:*

> Here, as always, Proust is completely detached from all moral considerations. There is no right and wrong in Proust nor in his world ... Tragedy is not concerned with human justice. Tragedy is the statement of an expiation, but not the miserable expiation of a codified breach of a local arrangement, organized by the knaves for the fools.

> The tragic figure represents the expiation of original sin, of the original
> and eternal sin of him and all his 'socii malorum', the sin of having been
> born. (pp. 66-7)

Beckett goes on to quote two lines from Calderón's *La Vida es Sueño*,
which say something similar in Spanish: '*Pues el delito mayor/Del hombre
es haber nacido . . .*' In fact, however, he is borrowing more directly from
Schopenhauer, who was enamoured of Calderón's verses, and who
explained them thus: 'The true sense of tragedy is the deeper insight, that
it is not his own individual sins that the hero atones for, but original sin,
i.e., the crime of existence itself [*die Schuld des Daseins selbst*] . . .'[13] It is this
Schopenhauerian view of tragedy — as the purgation of original sin, of the
'crime of existence itself' — which is adopted by Beckett in the monograph
on Proust, and which recurs, as a kind of moral refrain, through the many
reflections on human suffering in the trilogy.

If we return to the trilogy, however, we find that the possibilities of
tragedy are denied, by the very process of elimination which is supposed to
confront us with 'original sin'. The sense of solitude in Molloy, for
example, comes through comedy, and although critics sometimes speak,
borrowing a term that Beckett himself applied to *Waiting for Godot*, of
'tragicomedy', the elements of tragedy are dissolved. Beckett uses, and can
use, only comic devices to isolate his heroes in their 'pure undifferentiated
being' — i.e. in the state where their only sin is original. Molloy expresses
himself thus, by way of negating an offer of friendship:

> Let me tell you this, when social workers offer you, free gratis and for
> nothing, something to hinder you from swooning, which with them is
> an obsession, it is useless to recoil, they will pursue you to the ends of
> the earth, the vomitory in their hands. The Salvation Army is no better.
> Against the charitable gesture there is no defence, that I know of . . .
> (p. 24)

And the intimate condition of the impersonal subject who is thus isolated
from all contact with his kind (n.b. the double meaning of 'kind', and
Beckett's 'your fellow men, if you have any'), is infected by the same sense
of the ludicrous that first placed him in his state of isolation. For that
reason it becomes odd to regard the state of the Unnamable, isolated in his
'pure being', as one of tragedy, or as containing even a 'tittle' of tragedy.
No individual survives the process of paring away that reveals the 'last
person'; no suffering remains in that transcendental isolation, since there
is neither desire nor action, neither will nor its abnegation, only a pure but
heartless perspective on a world about which one has ceased to care. The
moral illusion consists in a belief in the 'purity', the 'sanctity' of the self,
together with a simultaneous, but in fact incompatible, desire to retain all

human dignities, and not merely the empty memory of dignities that have been pared away. To contrast the pretensions of the Cartesian self with its actuality — its infinite ambition with its metaphysical nothingness — is the substance of comedy. To think of it in tragic terms is, however, to share in its deep delusion, to believe not only that it has existence, but also that its existence could rise to the dignity of a crime.

Nevertheless there is an undeniable poignancy in the pure, or rather pared away, being of the Beckettian subject. It lies, not in its inner nature (since, even if there were such a nature, it could never be displayed), but rather in the glimpses of objects which lie outside of it, and by contrast with which it gains its cavernous ineffability. That is the source of the intensest emotion in Beckett's prose: witness the feeling contained in the description of cows which I quoted at the beginning of this chapter. The intensity of the description, being unsustained by any dramatic cogency in what is described, reflects back into the unknowable observer, whose identity resides wholly in the contrast between himself and what he observes. At the same time, the episodes and details which so define the metaphysical 'solitude' of the self must inevitably appear ludicrous, through the perceived impossibility that they should be anything more than accidents, attached to an 'essence' which can neither pursue, nor possess, nor reject them. The poignancy too is an offshoot of the nominalistic vision. Since 'words fail', and since to describe is to falsify, all experience lies forever beyond our reach. Our only hope of being true to our inner nature is to follow the path of negation: to deny what habit tempts us to affirm, to reject what common morality requires us to pursue, to cease to be troubled by anything except the *Schuld des Daseins*.

Thus we can summarize the philosophical background to Beckett's atmosphere in a set of closely connected doctrines: the individual is essentially the *self* (the 'for-itself' of Hegel and Sartre); he cannot be described as such except in the 'last person' — i.e. by paring away all descriptions and leaving him defined only by negation; he is in this sense a fiction (a perspective on the world, and not an item in it, as Kant (almost) put it). At the same time his existence is a crime that must be expiated through tragedy, in which his individuality — which is comic when subjected to the rash discipline of description and relation — is overcome, and he returns to the womb of being: I then, at last, as he is extinguished into the not-I. (That final thought is Schopenhauer's.)

There is another idea which belongs, in imagination, if not in logic, to that congeries, and I should like to end by focusing on it, so as to reveal a further moral significance in the metaphysical theories that I have mentioned. This is the idea of mud, or slime. According to the nominalist position sketched above, the individual exists essentially by contrast with all that is not individual — with the undifferentiated, the uncomposed, the undisclosed. Since all descriptions are arbitrary, all relations unreal and all habits erroneous, the world upon which they are imposed by the forlorn individual in his self-contradictory attempt to postulate another existent in relation to himself (even a relation of identity) is forever recalcitrant to them; it answers to no description, no relation, no habit; it systematically eludes our attempts to know it; it exists, for us, merely as a pervasive negation of the *true* individuality that we discover only in ourselves. It exists as mud or slime — the *visqueux* which Sartre celebrates in *Being and Nothingness* as the metaphysical otherness against which we struggle and in which we drown. It is this mud that forms the ambience of Beckett's novels, and which is explicitly acknowledged as such in *How it is.*

The idea of slime is a well-tried symbol in the post-romantic perception of the world. The self-consciously 'modern' individual, who finds value in himself, but only corruption and falsehood in social relations, regards all reference to others, and all description of his own condition that is not of his own devising, as fraught with illusion. His state is such, he believes, that only in pure subjectivity can moral significance be found. He may not go so far as Kierkegaard, so as to believe that truth *is* subjectivity; nevertheless he will tend to believe that there is no point of refuge from the Miltonic chaos into which he has been thrown, other than the sanctuary which he carries within. The self, although indescribable, remains pure. It retains its purity, however, only by becoming a phantom: it flees before every charitable gesture, before every word, relation or value that is significant of the poisonous slime of 'outside'. At the same time it can never forget that its very existence undermines its purity. The individual is not the pure observer that he longs to be. He exists only because born into the world, from the very slime of 'otherness' that he vainly refuses. The self is irreversibly tainted and defiled by an 'original' encounter with slime. For it was from one of slime's disguises — that of the mother — that the self was born. The self is born from the slime of not-being, and first becomes an individual in that act of original sin. (To be a Freudian for a moment: Schopenhauer's sense of the tragic is an incestuous perception of parental intercourse, the guilt of the Oedipus child who wishes to mingle again with the slime from which he once emerged.)

I have deliberately described the symbol of slime in terms that show its relation to the philosophical underpinning of Beckett's trilogy. If we return now to the texts we shall see this post-romantic agony given constant enactment, and used to enforce the rhetorical identity between slime and not-self. The women in Beckett's trilogy are either old or in some way directly referred to the idea of motherhood (Ma-hood). Their names for the most part begin with the syllable 'ma', for which Molloy devises the letter 'g', the better to 'spit on it'. Even the most negative of all these intimations of tenderness — that of the woman who watches over the jar in which the limbless Unnamable lingers on — is called (with the usual deliberate imprecision) Marguerite or Madeleine. Her gestures of compassion and intimacy are limited, but vivid. And they contrast with the deliberate cruelty earlier evinced towards the Unnamable's 'family', who may be real or imaginary, but who are given the role of pure spectators of his circumambulations (he still, at this stage, retains a leg of sorts), and who die of sausage poisoning (he fantasizes), which fact in no way inconveniences him, since he can as well walk over their dead bodies as over the ground which is obstructed by them.

The 'Ma' is the cunt from which one emerges and to which one returns (or alternatively, from which one again emerges into non-existence). It is the necessary defilement inflicted upon the individual, the defilement of having been born, of having been attached (and perhaps sometimes re-attached) to another human being. This is the 'original sin' referred to, borrowing from Schopenhauer, as the origin (birth) of tragedy. Beckett's fictions confine their sexual encounters to women so old as to be without moisture, symbols of past sin who cannot tempt to present sin. What they threaten, they can never achieve, for their slime has dried. Like the Houyhnhms, they emit only dry and tangible effluvia; they are no longer the offensive Yahoos which, in love and child-birth, they once had been.

Thus the slime of the other, which defiles the Cartesian self is (speaking not philosophically but in terms of the real state of mind conveyed) the slime of the vagina. The existential anguish (from which Sartre tries to leap and from which Beckett petulantly recoils) is that of the adolescent male disgusted by that first re-encounter with the anonymous mouth from which he once emerged.

In scorning and deriding his sexual parts Molloy (pp. 35-6) quotes a line of Leopardi, which Beckett had already quoted in *Proust: 'non che la speme, il desiderio è spento'* He thereby associates his own sense of sexual incompetence with a poem which expresses, as well as anything in Beckett, all the philosophical themes that I have been trying to bring to the reader's attention. It is through studying this poem that we may perceive more clearly how close are the Cartesian images of the self, with their associated rejection of the morality of 'habit', to the sexual anguish embodied in the image of slime. The poem is *A sè stesso,* by Leopardi:

> *Or poserai per sempre*
> *stanco mio cor. Perì l'inganno estremo*
> *ch'eterno io mi credei. Perì. Ben sento,*
> *in noi di cari inganni,*
> *non che la speme, il desiderio è spento.*

Posa per sempre. Assai
palpitasti. Non val cosa nessuna
i moti tuoi, nè di sospiri e degna
la terra. Amaro e noia
la vita, altro mai nulla; e fango è il mondo.
T'acqueta omai. Dispera
l'ultima volta. Al gener nostro il fato
non donò che il morire. Omai disprezza
te, la natura, il brutto
poter, che, ascoso, a comun danno impera
e l'infinita vanità del tutto.

(Now you will rest for ever,
my tired heart. The last deception has perished
which I believed eternal. Perished. I feel it well,
how in us not only the hope of dear illusions,
but also the desire for them, is extinguished.
Rest for ever. Much
have you throbbed. Not one thing is worth
your motion, nor is the earth worthy
of sighs. Bitter and tedious
is life, never otherwise; and the world is slime.
Quieten now. Despair
for the final time. To human kind fate
offers only death. Now despise
nature, the brutish
power which, hidden, holds sway to common evil,
and the infinite vanity of everything.)[14]

Note first the title of the poem: 'to himself'; both directly reflexive, and also wholly impersonal (*sè*, not *me*). The subject is therefore the impersonal first person of Beckett's novels, who succeeds in giving himself a name (but only just) in *Molloy*, but who has become utterly nameless and affirms himself to be nameless by the time the trilogy has ended.

The impersonal *sè* becomes *me* in the second line (my heart), and even *io* in the third, but has retreated to *noi* by line four, and then becomes *tu*, as the poet addresses his spent impersonal heart. ('Any old pronoun will do, provided one sees through it'). Later the subject retreats further, becoming *gener nostro*, which is something even vaguer than the 'human kind' of my rough translation. Finally it is mere 'nature' who is addressed as *te*, and moreover the *te* is ambiguous, referring back to *disprezza* and forward to *la natura*. At the same time as addressing nature Leopardi also negates her, by describing her as a brutish power who holds empire over us, to our common damnation. This description negates all the romantics' illusions (*inganni* — also 'naiveties'), and sets up as the principal subject of emotion an inhuman thing (which is why he does not refer to 'human' kind, but only to *gener nostro*), a thing that is identified with fate and death: the latter being all that is offered to us. Thus the subject of the poem (the *sè* of the title), is offered only a systematic negation of being, a steady approach towards the last person.

The world itself is negated along with the subject who observes it. Thus it becomes *fango*, i.e. mud or slime, the undifferentiated primeval stuff whose only attributes are bitterness and tedium, the *fango originale* of Iago's negative confession in Boito's *Otello*. (Incidentally, the line *E fango è il mondo* provided the motto for the original Grove Press edition of *Proust*.) There is no attempt to attach the 'despair' of the poem to anything particular: on the contrary, its object is general, described only through negative attributes; with the sinking of the subject into desirelessness, comes the sinking of the world into undifferentiated chaos.

I believe that it is no accident that Leopardi's anguish is recalled by Molloy, and recalled, what is more, with an explicitly sexual meaning. Leopardi, like Beckett, pursues a phantom of the self, and, not finding it, or finding only that 'last person' from which props and pronouns have been cut away, sinks into infinite disillusion. He sees the world as slime, he too will become slime, his individuality absorbed at last by the chaos that surrounds him. In both writers the reduction of the subject to a pure but ineffable perspective emotionally requires that the object be reduced to undifferentiated mud. Leopardi's poem suggests, however, that it would be wrong to over-emphasize the sexual interpretation that I have offered. This association of ideas has equally been taken — and was continually taken in post-romantic literature — to be indicative of a premonition of death. Ricks and Cavell, to whom I earlier referred, might consider that it is the experience, or non-experience, of death that is being intimated in the double aspect of self-less selfhood and slime. That was certainly what Leopardi *took* his meaning to be. And it is interesting to find a more modern poet concurring:

> Not but they die, the teasers and the dreams,
> Not but they die,
>   and tell the careful flood
> To give them what they clamour for and why.
>
> You could not fancy where they rip to blood
> You could not fancy
>   nor that mud
> I have heard speak that will not cake or dry.

Our claims to act appear so small to these
Our claims to act
      colder lunacies
That cheat the love, the moment, the small fact.

Make no escape because they flash and die,
Make no escape
      build up your love,
Leave what you die for and be safe to die.[15]

If I had to say what was most striking — if not most ultimately impressive — in William Empson's poem 'The Teasers', I would refer to the carefully inflected pentameters, with the strong spondaic hand raised in admonition at the beginning of each verse. It is this rhythm, heavy with rhetorical implications, which gives to the verse its atmosphere of 'pastness', of monumental reflection on the transience of human things. A critic concerned to disinter Empson's feeling would, I think be further struck by the elegiac quality, and by the post-romantic persistence of illusion in the midst of disillusion. He would naturally associate this quality with death, and discern the true resonance of the 'mud' invoked in the second stanza in that idea.

It is, I think, undeniable that the same elegiac tone occurs in Beckett's writings, especially in the more recent lyrical pieces. Consider the following sentences, from *Ill seen ill said:*

Wooed from below the face consents at last. In the dim light reflected by the flag . . . How serene it seems this ancient mask. Worthy those worn by certain newly dead. True and light leaves to be desired. The lids occult the longed-for eyes. Time will tell them washen blue.[16]

Although thinly disguised as prose, this exemplifies precisely the same rhythmic movement as the Empson, and shares Empson's atmosphere. A complete account of Beckett's prose would try to explain the elegiac quality, and in doing so must surely take seriously the idea that it is *thanatos* and not *eros* which haunts Beckett's prose. In discussing the earlier works, however, I believe we are faced with a quite different mood, or at least, with a quite different emphasis. The sexual interpretation that I have suggested, even if it is only one part of the truth, seems to me to explain the tetchy refusal of human relations in Beckett, just as it explains the narcissistic grovelling of Sartre's *La Nausée:* in both cases we are concerned with a *nostalgie de la boue*, the *boue* made pungent through metaphysical cookery. But I cannot establish my interpretation, and I prefer to leave it as a suggestion; nor can I do more than mention its important corollary, which is that the sexual revulsion implied in the trilogy is a natural consequence of the erosion of normal social relations, and of the contempt for habit, custom, and social order which the monograph on Proust attempts to justify. But that theme belongs to another, perhaps greater, Irish writer: Yeats.

I am grateful to Victoria Rothschild, Christopher Ricks, and Mark Platts, for comments which stimulated both the writing and the rewriting of this chapter. I am particularly grateful to Christopher Ricks for drawing my attention to William Empson's 'The Teasers'.

Acknowledgements

The author and publishers wish to thank the editors of the publications in which some of the material in this book has previously appeared:

'Recent Aesthetics in England and America' was first published in French in *Critique*, 36 (1980), pp. 818-29; the text printed here is a revised version of the English reprint in the *Architectural Association Quarterly*, 13 (1981), pp. 51-4.

'Public Text and Common Reader' first appeared in *Comparative Criticism: a yearbook*, 4 (1982).

'The Aesthetics of Music' is adapted from an article which first appeared in the Royal Musical Association's *Research Chronicle*, 17 (1981), pp. 115-16.

'Absolute Music', 'Programme Music' and 'The Nature of Musical Expression' are all reprinted, with corrections and slight alterations, from Stanley Sadie (ed.), *New Grove Dictionary of Music* (London, 1981).

'Representation in Music' first appeared in *Philosophy*, 51 (1976), pp. 273-87, and is reprinted here in a slightly amended version.

A shorter version of 'Understanding Music' appeared in *Ratio*, 25, 2, (1983).

'Photography and Representation' is reprinted, with corrections, from *Critical Inquiry*, 7 (1981), pp. 577-603.

'Emotion and Culture' originally appeared as 'The Significance of Common Culture' in *Philosophy*, 54 (1979), pp. 51-70. An amended version was published later as 'Emotion, Practical Knowledge and Common Culture' in Amélie Rorty (ed.), *Explaining Emotions* (California, 1980), pp. 519-36. The second version is here substantially reprinted.

'Laughter' is reprinted from the *Aristotelian Society, supplementary volume*, 56 (1982), pp. 197-212.

'The Architecture of Leninism' is adapted from 'The Architecture of Stalinism', *Cambridge Review*, 99 (1976), pp. 36-41.

A shorter version of 'Aesthetic Education and Design' will be given as a Royal Society of Arts lecture, entitled 'Aesthetic Education and the Classical Tradition', to be published in the *Journal of the Royal Society of Arts*, 131 (1983).

'Beckett and the Cartesian Soul' is the text of one of the Chichele Lectures delivered at All Souls College, Oxford, in 1982. They were all printed in Peregrine Horden (ed.), *Philosophy and Fiction* (All Souls College, 1983).

Acknowledgement is made to Sir William Empson, Chatto & Windus Ltd, and Harcourt Brace Jovanovich Inc. for permission to quote 'The Teasers' from *Collected Poems*. Acknowledgement is also made to John Calder (Publishers) Ltd for short extracts from the works of Samuel Beckett, and Burke Publishing Co Ltd for the extracts quoted by James Laver in *Clothes*.

The illustrations are reproduced by kind permission of the Mansell Collection (2 and 3), *Country Life* (7), and the Conway Library, Courtauld Institute of Art (32 and 34). The author wishes to thank the photographers Bernard Brown, Rosemary Ind and Derek Parfitt for their help.

The music examples were transcribed by Richard Higgins.

Notes

1 Recent Aesthetics in England and America

1 G. E. Moore, 'Internal and External Relations', 1920; reprinted in *Philosophical Studies* (Cambridge and Atlantic Highlands, NJ, 1922).
2 'Reality and Sincerity', *Scrutiny*, XIX (1952-3); reprinted in F. R. Leavis (ed.), *Selections from Scrutiny* 2 vols., (Cambridge and New York, 1968), II.
3 I cannot undertake to show this here, but some reasons are suggested in 'Public Text and Common Reader', chapter 2 below, and in the articles to which it refers.

2 Public Text and Common Reader

1 For examples of this stance, see Geoffrey H. Hartman and W. Hillis Miller (eds.), *Deconstruction and Criticism* (New Haven, 1980).
2 E. D. Hirsch, Jr, *Validity in Interpretation* (New Haven, 1967; London 1973), pp. 5-6.
3 Hirsch, chapter 4, and especially pp. 131ff.
4 L. Wittgenstein, *Philosophical Investigations* (Oxford, 1953; 3rd edn New York, 1973), part I, sections 241-317.
5 'Spacing as writing is the becoming-absent and becoming-unconscious of the subject . . . The original absence of the subject of writing is also that of the thing, or referent.' *De la grammatologie*, (Paris, 1966), p. 100; (*Of Grammatology*, London and Baltimore, 1977).
6 Technical term of heraldry, for the figure which contains itself as a component, and therefore reproduces itself *ad infinitum*.
7 See G. Frege, 'On Sense and Reference', in *Translations from the Philosophical Writings*, edited and translated by P. T. Geach and M. Black (Oxford, 1952; 3rd edn New Jersey, 1980); also Donald Davidson, 'Truth and Meaning', *Synthese*, 7 (1969), pp. 304-23.
8 *Lectures and Conversations on Aesthetics, Psychology and Religious Belief*, ed. C. Barrett (Oxford, 1966; California, 1967).
9 See *Communications*, 2 'Le vraisemblable' (1968), especially the introduction by Tzvetan Todorov.
10 'Midday the just composes there from fires/the sea, the sea, always begun again'.
11 Principal among the modern exponents of rhetoric are Roman Jakobsen, especially in *Questions de poétique* (Paris, 1973), and Paul Ricoeur, *La Métaphore vive* (Paris, 1975). The account of metaphor on which I rely originates in Wittgenstein (*Philosophical Investigations*. part II, p. xi) and has been expounded, for example, in my *Art and Imagination* (London, 1974; New York, 1979), part I.

12   There are certain rather peculiar exceptions to this rule, such as John
     Donne's 'No man is an island', which is trivially true. Its point as a
     metaphor, however, can only be understood in terms of the contrasted
     falsehood, 'Some man is an island'. That is, the figure consists in the
     idea: man as island. Contrast the non-figurative 'No man is a three-
     ton lorry'.
13   See Donald Keene, *World Within Walls* (London, 1976; New York,
     1979), pp. 23-4.
14   R. Barthes, *S/Z* (Paris, 1970; New York, 1974), *passim*.
15   See especially, 'The Thought, a Logical Enquiry', in P. F. Strawson
     (ed.), *Philosophical Logic* (Oxford, 1967); and Michael Dummett's
     extremely influential discussion, *Frege: Philosophy of Language*
     (London, 1973; Cambridge, Mass., 1981).
16   Jonathan Culler, *Structuralist Poetics* (London and Ithaca, NY, 1975),
     chapters 6 and 11.
17   Charles Rosen, *The Classical Style* (London, 1968; New York, 1971).
18   G. W. Turner, *Stylistics* (London, 1973), p. 144.
19   For example, E. H. Gombrich, *Art and Illusion* (London, 1960;
     Princeton, 1961).
20   'Tradition and the Individual Talent', in *Selected Essays* (London and
     Boston, 1963).
21   See my 'Dante in Context' in *The Politics of Culture* (Manchester,
     1981).
22   See Wagner, letter from Venice to Mathilde Wesendonck, 1
     December 1858: 'The pathway to the complete pacification of the Will
     through love, and that no abstract love of mankind, but the love which
     actually blossoms from the evil of sexual desire'.
23   I have tried to show this for certain literary examples in 'The
     Impossibility of Semiotics', in *The Politics of Culture*. For the
     extension to music, see 'The Semiology of Music' in the same
     collection; and for architecture, my *Aesthetics of Architecture*
     (London, 1979; Princeton, 1980), chapter 7.
24   Nicolas Ruwet, 'Limites de l'analyse linguistique et poétique', 1966;
     reprinted in *Langage, musique, poésie* (Paris, 1972).
25   See the argument of my *Art and Imagination*, part II.

3   The Aesthetics of Music

1   E. Hanslick, *Vom musikalisch-Schönen* (Leipzig, 1854, revised 1891;
    The Beautiful in Music, New York, 1974).
2   Deryck Cooke, *The Language of Music* (Oxford and New York, 1959);
    J. J. Nattiez, *Vers une semiologie de la musique* (Paris, 1975). On Cooke,
    see 'The Nature of Musical Expression', reprinted here. On Nattiez,
    see 'The Semiology of Music', reprinted in *The Politics of Culture*.

4   Absolute Music

1   I. Stravinsky, *Poétique musicale sous forme de six leçons*, Charles Eliot
    Norton Lectures series 1939-40 (in French and English; Cambridge,
    Mass., and London, 1970). For Schenker, see chapter 6, note 11.

Some useful source material may be found in Peter le Huray and James Day (eds.), *Music and Aesthetics in the 18th and early 19th Centuries* (Cambridge, 1981).

5 Programme Music

1 F. Liszt, *Gesammelte Schriften* (Berlin, 1880-83), IV, pp. 297-342.
2 F. Niecks, *Programme Music in the last Four Centuries* (London, 1956; New York, 1969).
3 Liszt, IV, p. 69.
4 See further, 'Representation in Music', chapter 7 below.
5 A. Schering, *Beethoven und die Dichtung* (Berlin, 1936).
6 A. Palm, 'Mozarts Streichquartett d-moll, KV421, in der Interpretation Momignys', *MJb 1962-3*, p. 256.
7 See 'Understanding Music', chapter 8 below.

6 The Nature of Musical Expression

1 R. Descartes, *Compendium Musicae* (Utrecht, 1650; 1656).
2 G. Santayana, *The Sense of Beauty* (London and Norwood, Mass., 1896).
3 D. Diderot, *Le neveu de Rameau* (Paris, 1821; *Rameau's Nephew*, Harmondsworth and New York, 1976); J. J. Rousseau, *Essai sur l'origine des langues* (Geneva, 1754), *Dictionnaire de musique* (Paris, 1768).
4 J. Addison, 'The Pleasures of the Imagination', *The Spectator* (London, 21 June-3 July 1712); J. F. Lampe, *The Art of Musick* (London, 1740); A. Malcolm, *A Treatise of Musick* (London, 1752; 1956; New York, 1970).
5 G. W. F. Hegel, *Vorlesunge über die Ästhetik* (Berlin, 1835; *Aesthetics: Lectures on Fine Art*, 2 vols. Oxford and New York, 1975).
6 B. Croce, *Estetica, come scienza dell'espressione a linguistica generale* (Milan, 1902; *Aesthetic*, London, 1953; Boston, 1979).
7 R. G. Collingwood, *The Principles of Art* (Oxford, 1938; New York, 1958).
8 E. Gurney, *The Power of Sound* (London, 1880), p. 313.
9 V. Galilei, *Dialogo della musica antica e moderna* (Florence, 1581); A. Kircher, *De musurgia antiquo-moderna* (Rome, 1650); G. Zarlino, *Le istitutioni harmoniche* (Venice, 1558; 1965; 3rd edn 1573; 1966).
10 I. Stravinsky, *Poétique musicale.*
11 H. Schenker, *Neue musikalische Theorien und Phantasien, I: Harmonielehre,* (Vienna and Leipzig, 1906-35; *Harmony*, Chicago, 1974; London, 1980); D. Tovey, *Essays in Musical Analysis,* 6 vols. (Oxford and New York, 1935-9).
12 C. Rosen, *The Classical Style.*
13 E. T. A. Hoffmann, *Schriften zur Musik, Nachlese* (Berlin, 1827; 1963); W. A. Ellis (ed.), *Richard Wagner's Prose Works,* 8 vols. (London, 1892-9), especially III.
14 S. Kierkegaard, 'The Immediate Stages of the Erotic or the Musical Erotic', *Either/Or,* 2 vols. (Copenhagen, 1843; Princeton, 1971), I, pp. 34-110.

15 E. Hanslick, *Vom musikalisch-Schönen.*
16 A. Mahler, *Erinnerungen und Briefe* (Amsterdam, 1940; *Memories and Letters,* 2nd edn, London, 1968; Seattle, 1972).
17 D. Cooke, *The Language of Music.*
18 N. Goodman, *Languages of Art* (Indianapolis, 1968; London, 1969).
19 W. Crotch, *Substance of Several Courses of Lectures on Music Read in the University of Oxford and the Metropolis* (London, 1831); G. Frege, 'On Sense and Reference', *Translations from the Philosophical Writings.*
20 See further, 'Understanding Music', chapter 8 below.
21 S. K. Langer, *Philosophy in a New Key* (London and Cambridge, Mass., 1957).
22 G. Ryle, *The Concept of Mind* (London, 1949; 1960; New York, 1969).
23 L. B. Meyer, *Emotion and Meaning in Music* (London and Chicago, 1956).

7 Representation in Music

1 For further considerations bearing on the analysis of representation, see 'Photography and Representation', chapter 9 below.
2 The analysis of this last feature has preoccupied philosophers since Plato and Aristotle. For some of the (enormous) difficulties, see Chapter 2, 'Public Text and Common Reader', above.
3 Cooke, *The Language of Music.*
4 See, for example, R. Wollheim, *Art and its Objects* (New York, 1968; Cambridge, 1980); N. Goodman, *Languages of Art;* and in relation to the present subject: J. O. Urmson, 'Representation in Music' in *Philosophy and the Arts,* Royal Institute of Philosophy Lectures (London, 1973).
5 Cf. Frege's strictly comparable idea that only in the context of a sentence do words have *'Bedeutung',* and the holistic view of language that springs from that insight: see M. Dummett, *Frege.*
6 Many considerations relevant to the logical status of sounds are raised by P. F. Strawson, *Individuals* (London, 1959; New York, 1979), chapters 1 and 2.
7 On the question what might be meant by a 'strictly visual property' see the admirable discussion in H. P. Grice, 'Some Remarks about the Senses' in R. J. Butler (ed.), *Analytical Philosophy,* First Series (Oxford, 1966).
8 It is precisely such a model of musical understanding that is implicit in V. A. Howard's attempt to apply Goodman's theory of representation to music: see 'On Representational Music', *Noûs,* 1972.
9 For further remarks on 'understanding music' see my *Art and Imagination,* chapter 12, and 'Understanding Music', chapter 8 below.
10 'He who fears the point of my spear, will never go through the fire!'

8 Understanding Music

1 See chapter 7 above, 'Representation in Music'.
2 See chapter 6 above, 'The Nature of Musical Expression'.

3 In this chapter and in 'Photography and Representation', chapter 9 below, I assume familiarity with the concepts of intentionality, and intentional object. For some indication as to how analytical philosophy must treat these concepts, see my 'Intensional and Intentional Objects', *Proceedings of the Aristotelian Society* (1970-1), pp. 187-207. For further remarks on 'intentional understanding' and the *Lebenswelt*, see 'Emotion and Culture' below, chapter 11.

4 See my *Art and Imagination*, chapter 12; *The Aesthetics of Architecture*, chapter 4.

5 See, for example, D. N. Ferguson, *Music as Metaphor* (Minneapolis, 1960); Carl Stumpf, *Tonpsychologie*, 2 vols. (Leipzig, 1883), I; and the extremely suggestive, though indecisive, discussion in V. Zuckerkandl, *Sound and Symbol*, trans. W. R. Trask, 2 vols. (London, 1956; Princeton, 1973).

6 See A. Wellek, *Musikpsychologie und Musikästhetik* (Frankfurt, 1963), p. 299.

7 See C. C. Pratt, *The Meaning of Music* (London, 1933).

8 I. Kant, 'Concerning the Ultimate Foundations of the Differentiation of Regions in Space' (1768), in *Selected pre-Critical Writings*, trans. G. B. Kerferd and D. E. Walford (Manchester, 1968).

9 See further, Bas C. Van Fraasen, *An Introduction to the Philosophy of Space and Time* (New York, 1970), pp. 134-8.

10 The exceptions to this law, discussed in a lecture by Saul Kripke, are independently puzzling. For example, the case of a plant and its stem raises special questions about identity through time which are not, I think, raised by inorganic things.

11 Cf. Zuckerkandl, pp. 82-3.

12 *The Power of Sound.*

13 Thus I uphold a thesis argued for very differently by both Zuckerkandl and Ferguson. On the importance of 'direction' in the experience of music, see *The Power of Sound.* pp. 139-40. Gurney notes the complete absence of this feature from the experience of the colour spectrum. (I am grateful to Malcolm Budd for drawing my attention to this passage.)

14 The locus classicus (drawing on many of the arguments of earlier phenomenologists) is M. Merleau-Ponty, *The Phenomenology of Perception*, trans. Colin Smith (London and Atlantic Highlands, NJ, 1962). Of more immediate relevance to the above remarks are thoughts contained in Charles Taylor, 'The Validity of Transcendental Arguments', *PAS* (1978-9), p. 154. See also the discussion in Gareth Evans, *Varieties of Reference* (Oxford, 1982), p. 155ff.

15 Strawson, *Individuals*, chapter 2.

16 That is, for every instance of a tertiary quality, there are instances of secondary qualities on which it depends, such that, to remove the secondary qualities is to remove the tertiary qualities. But not vice versa.

17 On this point, and all the points in the preceding paragraph, see my *Art and Imagination*, part II.

18 Robin Holloway, *Debussy and Wagner* (London, 1979), p. 44.

19 For theories along these lines, see Ernst Maumann, *Untersuchungen*

zur Psychologie und Ästhetik der Rythmus (Leipzig, 1894); Ernst Kurth, *Musikpsychologie* (Berlin, 1931); W. V. Bingham, *Studies in Melody* (Baltimore, 1910).

20　See for example, T. Lipps, 'Das Wesen der musikalischen Konsonanz und Dissonanz', in Lipps, *Psychologische Studien* (Leipzig, 1905).

21　See *The World as Will and Representation*, trans. E. F. J. Payne, 2 vols. (Colorado, 1958), I, 2, section 52, and II, chapter 39.

22　For example, the theories, largely of eighteenth-century provenance, seemingly endorsed by Peter Kivy in *The Corded Shell* (Princeton, 1980).

9 Photography and Representation

1　See for example, the discussions in Allardyce Nicoll, *Film and Theatre* (London, 1936; New York, 1972).

2　See Franz Clemens Brentano, *Psychology from an Empirical Standpoint*, ed. Linda McAlister (London and New York, 1973); Roderick M. Chisholm, *Perceiving* (London and Ithaca, NY, 1957), chapter 11; and G. E. M. Anscombe, 'The Intentionality of Sensation', in R. J. Butler (ed.), *Analytical Philosophy*, Second Series (Oxford, 1965).

3　I think that in this area nonextensionality (intensionality) and intentionality should be sharply distinguished, so that the claim is not affected by any argument to the effect that causal relations are non-extensional.

4　I pass over the problem here of selecting and describing the appropriate intention.

5　For the material/intentional distinction, I rely on Anscombe.

6　The most famous arguments for this conclusion occur in Kant's *Critique of Pure Reason* (in particular in the 'Transcendental Deduction') and in Wittgenstein's *Philosophical Investigations*, part I.

7　The importance of 'common knowledge', its complexity as a phenomenon, and its natural co-existence with conventions has been recognized in the philosophy of language; see especially the interesting discussion in David K. Lewis, *Convention: a Philosophical Study* (Cambridge, Mass., 1969; Oxford, 1972).

8　I have discussed elsewhere what I mean by the 'embodiment' of thought in perception; see my *Art and Imagination*, chapters 7 and 8.

9　G. Frege, *Translations from the Philosophical Writings*, p. 79.

10　There is a problem here about 'identity of appearance' on which I touch again, pp. 116-17.

11　Nelson Goodman, the most important exponent of a semantic theory of art, manages to reconcile his approach with a view of photographs as representational; see his *Languages of Art*, p. 9n.

12　I draw here on the now familiar arguments given by Donald Davidson in 'Truth and Meaning,' which originate with Frege and which were given full mathematical elaboration in Alfred Tarski's theory of truth.

13　That is, provided the painting is independently *of* the Duke of Wellington.

14　See n. 8, above.

15　Hence the tradition in philosophy, which begins with Kant, according

to which representation constitutes a threat to the autonomy of art.
16 I am thinking of recent exercises in 'photographic' realism by such
 painters as Ken Danby and Alex Colville. More traditional styles of
 realism have also emerged in open opposition to both the clinical lines
 of the photographic school and the contentless images of abstract
 expressionism. Witness here the paintings of David Inshaw and
 Robert Lowe.
17 See for example, Stuart Hampshire, 'Logic and Appreciation' in
 William Elton (ed.), *Aesthetics and Language* (Oxford, 1954; New
 Jersey, 1970).
18 See Richard Wollheim's interesting discussion 'Style now' in Bernard
 William Smith (ed.), *Concerning Contemporary Art* (Oxford and New
 York, 1975).
19 This argument is hinted at in B. Croce, *Estetica*, 10th edn (Bari, 1958),
 p. 20.
20 See for example, Aaron Scharf, *Creative Photography* (London, 1975)
 and Rudolf Arnheim, *Film as Art* (California, 1957; London, 1958).
21 See especially Henry Peach Robinson, *The Elements of a Pictorial
 Photograph* (London, 1896).
22 Holmes, quoted in Beaumont Newhall, *History of Photography* (New
 York, 1964; London, 1972), p. 22.
23 'Meaning', *Philosophical Review*, LXVI (1957), pp. 377-88.
24 See my 'Representation in Music', above.
25 See Sergei Eisenstein, 'Word and Image', *The Film Sense* (London,
 1943; New York, 1969).
26 Discussed by V. I. Pudovkin, *Writings*, trans. I. Montagu (London,
 1954), p. 88.
27 The point is made at greater length, and more rigorously, in the
 chapter which follows.
28 See *The Standard Edition of the Complete Psychological Works of
 Sigmund Freud*, ed. James Strachey, 24 vols. (London, 1953-74; New
 York, 1976), IX, p. 153; XI, p. 50; XII, p. 224; XIII, pp. 187-8; XIV,
 pp. 375-7; XX, p. 64.

10 Fantasy, Imagination and the Screen

1 'Formulations Regarding the Two Principles in Mental Functioning'
 (1911), in *Collected Papers*, trans. Joan Rivière, 5 vols. (New York,
 1924-50), IV.
2 *Biographia Literaria*, chapter XIII.
3 But see above.
4 Cf. Spinoza's ideas about *'conatus'*, *Ethics* III, 7, and IV, *passim*.
5 Cf. Aristotle's account of virtue and vice in *Nicomachean Ethics*.
6 The contrast reflects the more metaphysical distinction offered by
 Kant, between imperatives that are self-imposed, since they proceed
 from the autonomy of the will, and imperatives that are
 'heteronomous', reflecting a constraint on the will.
7 On the photographic 'simulacrum', see 'Photography and Representation' above.
8 Described in George Painter, *In Quest of Proust*, 2 vols. (London,

1959; New York, 1978), I.
9 For further reflections on this theme, see 'Laughter', chapter 12 below.
10 Chapter 9, 'Photography and Representation'.

11 Emotion and Culture

1 I am greatly indebted, here and elsewhere, to unpublished work by John Casey on the theory of virtue.
2 It should be said that Hare has never agreed with those critics who have described him as a subjectivist, believing that a utilitarian decision procedure is implied by the very act of universalizing choice which, for him, lies at the heart of moral judgement. See especially *Moral Thinking* (Oxford, 1981).
3 The need for this 'non-accidental' relation is established, I think, by the examples presented by E. L. Gettier in 'Is Justified True Belief Knowledge?', *Analysis*, 23 (1962-3), pp. 121-3.
4 The opposition of 'dread' and 'innocence' is already suggested by Kierkegaard in *The Concept of Dread,* trans. W. Lowrie (Princeton, 1944).
5 See also John Casey, 'The Autonomy of Art' in G. Vesey (ed.), *Philosophy Looks at the Arts*, Royal Institute of Philosophy Lectures (London, 1973).
6 To make this distinction between universal and particular emotions fully clear is not easy. I have explored the matter at greater length in 'Attitudes, Beliefs and Reasons' in John Casey (ed.), *Morality and Moral Reasoning* (London, 1971).
7 See 'Truth' in M. Dummett, *Truth and Other Enigmas* (Cambridge, Mass., 1978; London, 1981).
8 I have made some suggestions in 'Reason and Happiness' in R. S. Peters (ed.), *Nature and Conduct,* Royal Institute of Philosophy Lectures (London, 1975).
9 See the discussion of these matters in H. Putnam, 'Is Semantics Possible?' and 'The Mental Life of Some Machines' in *Collected Papers*, 2 vols. (Oxford, 1975), II; also D. Wiggins, 'The Stream of Consciousness, etc.', *Philosophy* (1976), and *Sameness and Substance* (Oxford, 1980), chapter 3.
10 See A. J. Kenny, *Action, Emotion and Will* (London and Atlantic Highlands, NJ, 1963), p. 189; also 'Laughter', chapter 12 below.
11 Cf. P. F. Strawson, 'Freedom and Resentment' in *Freedom and Resentment and Other Essays* (London and New York, 1974).

12 Laughter

1 Michael Clark, 'Humour and Incongruity', *Philosophy*, 45 (1970).
2 D. H. Munro, *Argument of Laughter* (Melbourne and Cambridge, 1951).
3 *The World as Will and Representation,* 1, section 13.
4 See J. P. Sartre, *L'Imaginaire* (Paris, 1940), 2, III, in which the example of mimicry is discussed in detail.

5 *Action, Emotion and Will,* p. 189.
6 Clark, p. 24.
7 Cf. Mark Platts, *Ways of Meaning* (Boston, 1978; London, 1979), chapter 10.
8 Henri Bergson, *Le Rire* (Paris, 23rd edn, 1924; *Laughter*, Philadelphia, 1977; London, 1980).
9 I have tried in *Art and Imagination,* pp. 143ff.

13 Art History and Aesthetic Judgement

1 E. H. Gombrich, *In Search of Cultural History* (Oxford and New York, 1969), p. 26.
2 H. Wölfflin, *Renaissance and Baroque* (Munich, 1888; London, 1964), p. 58.
3 For an illuminating treatment of the problem, see G. A. Cohen, *Karl Marx's Theory of History* (Oxford and Princeton, 1978).
4 G. W. Leibniz, *Discourse on Metaphysics,* reprinted in *Leibniz, Selections,* ed. Philip Weiner (New York, 1951), section 19.
5 See for example, F. W. Maitland's unsurpassed *Constitutional History of England* (Cambridge, 1908).
6 See for example, L. Althusser, *Pour Marx* (Paris, 1965; *For Marx*, London, 1977; New York, 1979), chapter 3.
7 This fallacy was corrected, and in a sense over-corrected, by Gombrich. See his *Art and Illusion.*

14 The Architecture of Leninism

1 Lionel March (ed.), *The Architecture of Form* (Cambridge and New York, 1976). This review is included, despite its polemical character, in order to provide an introduction to the issues discussed in the next chapter, 'Aesthetic Education and Design'.
2 Transactions of the Bartlett Society, 4 (1966), pp. 93-136; reprinted in W. R. Ewald (ed.), *Environment for man, the next fifty years* (Bloomington, Indiana, 1967).

15 Aesthetic Education and Design

1 Letter to Sir Herbert Baker, quoted in Christopher Hussey, *Life of Sir Edwin Lutyens* (London and New York, 1950), pp. 134-5.
2 See especially the articles in Adolf Loos, *Sämmtliche Schriften,* I (Vienna, 1962).
3 See H. Putnam 'Is Semantics Possible?'; S. Kripke, *Naming and Necessity,* (Oxford, and Cambridge, Mass., 1980); D. Wiggins, *Sameness and Substance,* chapter 3.
4 *Seeing Through Clothes* (New York, 1978), p. 106.
5 *Sartor Resartus,* Book I, chapter 5, 'The World in Clothes'.
6 R. Barthes, *Système de la mode* (Paris, 1967); A. Lurie, *The Language of Clothes* (New York, 1981; London, 1982).
7 James Laver, *Clothes* (London, 1952), pp. 137-9.
8 See chapter 9 above, 'Photography and Representation'.

9   John Ruskin, *The Stones of Venice*, 3 vols. (London, 1851-3), II, chapter 4.
10   *The Aesthetics of Architecture*, chapter 9.
11   See 'The Architecture of Leninism' above.
12   For a discussion of this practice and its consequences, see my 'Architecture of the Horizontal' in *The Politics of Culture*.
13   *Notebooks*, Paris manuscript C.
14   I have commented on the meaning of this wall in *The Aesthetics of Architecture*, pp. 232-3.
15   'Building, Dwelling, Thinking', in *Poetry, Language, Truth*, trans. A. Hofstadter (New York, 1975), p. 160.

16 Beckett and the Cartesian Soul

1   All page references in the text are to the edition of the trilogy published in one volume by John Calder, 1959 (New York, 1965).
2   Christopher Ricks in unpublished work: Stanley Cavell, 'Ending the Waiting Game' in *Must we Mean what we Say?* (Cambridge and New York, 1976), pp. 115-62.
3   *Compagnie* (Paris, 1980), p. 31. The work has been translated by the author as *Company* (London and New York, 1980). The above translation is my own. The important ambiguity of the reflexive pronoun in Romance languages is illustrated in the poem by Leopardi discussed below.
4   'Three Dialogues with Georges Duthuit' in *Proust* (New York, 1957; London, 1969), p. 103.
5   Cf. J. P. Stern, *Lichtenberg: a Doctrine of Scattered Occasions* (London, 1963), p. 270.
6   *Philosophical Investigations*, part I, section 304.
7   *Proust*, p. 28.
8   pp. 22-3.
9   p. 27.
10   p. 26.
11   p. 63.
12   p. 64.
13   *The World as Will and Representation*, I, 2, no. 51.
14   My translation.
15   *Collected Poems* (London, 1955; New York, 1961), p. 67.
16   1982, the English version of *Mal vue, mal dit* (Paris, 1981).

Index of Names